I0760057

★FIGHTING★★★ FALCONS

Titles in the Series

Delivering Destruction: American Firepower and Amphibious Assault from Tarawa to Iwo Jima

Studies in Marine Corps History and Amphibious Warfare
William A. Taylor, *editor*

This series advances understanding of Marine Corps history and amphibious warfare by publishing original scholarship across a broad spectrum of innovative studies. The series analyzes an extensive array of vital aspects of the Marine Corps, amphibious warfare, and their collective role in global security, including battles, leaders, strategy, operations, tactics, doctrine, technology, personnel, organization, and culture. Incorporating both historical and contemporary perspectives, this series publishes important literature about the Marine Corps and significant works relevant to amphibious warfare that span the globe, feature diverse methodologies, and reach general audiences. As a result, the series provides a professional home, central venue, and premier destination for the best and newest research on Marine Corps history and amphibious warfare.

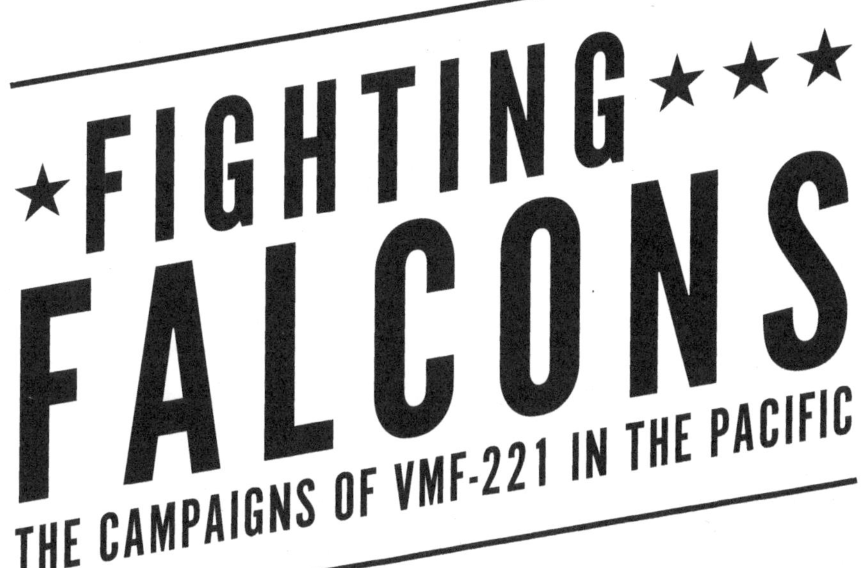

PETER F. OWEN

Naval Institute Press
Annapolis, Maryland

Naval Institute Press
291 Wood Road
Annapolis, MD 21402

ISBN: 978-1-68247-823-3 (hardcover)
ISBN: 978-1-68247-841-7 (eBook)

Library of Congress Cataloging-in-Publication Data is available.

♾ Print editions meet the requirements of ANSI/NISO z39.48-1992 (Permanence of Paper).
Printed in the United States of America.

34 33 32 31 30 29 28 27 26 9 8 7 6 5 4 3 2 1
First printing

Maps and figure created by Peter F. Owen.

★CONTENTS★

★ILLUSTRATIONS★

FIGURE

MAPS

TABLES

★FOREWORD★

Lt. Col. Peter Owen, USMC (Ret.), is a remarkable historian devoted to telling the story of the U.S. Marine Corps. *Fighting Falcons: The Campaigns of VMF-221 in the Pacific* provides the reader with insights into how Marine aviation was employed in World War II and the opportunities for its future employment.

As a Marine aviator with almost forty years of service, having commanded a Marine Fixed Wing Fighter Attack (VMFA) squadron, a VMFA group, and an aircraft wing with VMFA squadrons and now serving as the National Commander of the Marine Corps Aviation Association (MCAA), I can confidently say that Lieutenant Colonel Owen's new book will help readers understand the past employment of Marine fighter squadrons and assist Marine leaders with their future application.

Pete's dedication to writing on World War II Marine aviation became apparent to me through my roles as the National Commander at MCAA and as a board member of the U.S. Naval Institute (USNI). He is the author of "Marine Air's Dark Day at Midway," published in USNI's *Naval History* magazine, and was awarded first prize in the 2022 CNO Naval History Essay contest for his article "The Marine Corps' Air War over the Pacific."

He graduated from the U.S. Naval Academy with a major in history, and he brings operational credibility having served as a career Marine infantry officer in combat. His PhD dissertation was titled "U.S. Marine Corps Aviation in the Second World War: Its Effectiveness in Support of the Pacific Fleet." He is the author of the book *To the Limit of Endurance: A Battalion of Marines in the Great War.*

This book helps to answer an operational debate that has gone on in the Marine Corps since World War II regarding how Marine fighter squadrons should be employed. It explains why Marine fighter squadrons like VMF-221 were critical throughout the Pacific Fleet's successful campaign because of their unique ability to operate both ashore and at sea. VMF-221's distinctive three campaigns supporting the defense of an advance base at Midway, the unit's support of the larger naval campaign while operating ashore in the Solomon Islands, and finally its operations aboard *Bunker Hill,* a Navy aircraft carrier conducting strikes against mainland Japan, defending the fleet from aerial attacks, and supporting Marines assaulting Iwo Jima and Okinawa, demonstrated the agility to flex from shore-based operations to ones at sea.

You will enjoy reading about VMF-221's individual commanders, pilots, and maintenance Marines because Pete puts a very personal touch to their challenges and successes operating in the Pacific during World War II. Just as important, this book offers strategic lessons on how Marine air was used in World War II and explains why divisions continue today regarding how Marine fighter squadrons should be employed.

Robert Walsh
Lieutenant General, USMC (Ret.)
December 2024

★ ★ ★

Introduction

This book is an organizational history and a critical analysis of Marine Fighting Squadron 221 (VMF-221) in World War II. It is not a chronicle of dogfights, but a case study of the effectiveness of marine aviation in support of the U.S. Pacific Fleet, using VMF-221 as an example.

The doctrinal mission of marine aviation during World War II was to support landing forces, principally through close air support. Much more often, marine aviation protected the fleet and its bases and struck enemy vessels and ground targets to help the fleet achieve sea control. From 1942 to 1945, marine squadrons supported the fleet about five times as often as they supported landing forces ashore.[1]

In 2018 the Commandant of the U.S. Marine Corps, Gen. David Berger, reminded his marines, "During World War II, we as a Service, clearly understood that Marines operated in support of the Navy's sea control mission."[2] As the twenty-first-century Marine Corps seeks ways to revisit fleet integration, a deeper understanding of its historic effectiveness in this role may prove informative.

Because VMF-221 was organized in June 1941, it affords a window into the status of marine aviation when Japan attacked Pearl Harbor. The squadron's three campaigns provide case studies through which to examine marine aviation in fleet actions. At Midway in June 1942, the squadron defended the atoll from the Japanese attack. In 1943 the squadron participated in the long aerial battle of attrition in the Solomons that culminated in the isolation of Rabaul. In 1945 the squadron deployed aboard USS *Bunker Hill*, striking targets in Japan, providing close air support at Iwo Jima and Okinawa, and protecting the fleet from Japanese aircraft. The squadron flew all three of the Marine Corps' principal fighter aircraft: the F2A Buffalo, the F4F Wildcat, and the F4U Corsair. The squadron's experience is thus representative of some principal roles marine aviation performed in support of the Pacific Fleet. The three case studies reveal notable achievements, troubling shortcomings, and a clearer understanding of marine aviation's role in the Pacific War.

This work uses standard distances vice metric, except where descriptions of ordnance, such as 20-mm guns, are concerned. Miles are statute miles, not nautical miles, and speeds are expressed in statute miles per hour. Time is depicted in the military twenty-four-hour custom. All times are local to events. Place names are those used by the U.S. armed forces during World War II. For example, Taiwan is referred to as Formosa. An individual's rank is that held at the time of the event described. Often an individual will be referred to by different ranks within the same chapter; promotions often occurred with such rapidity that highlighting each one would have detracted from the narrative.

Japanese names are presented in the Western style, with surnames last. Japanese aircraft are identified by code names assigned by the U.S. armed forces, with the exception that the A6M2 Type 00 "Zeke" is referred to by the commonly used term, "Zero."[3] Japanese ranks and terms are expressed as their American equivalents.

Any errors of fact, analysis, and style are entirely the fault of the author.

I am indebted to many individuals for their generous assistance. First, and foremost, I am deeply grateful to my dissertation supervisor at the Royal Military College, Dr. Arthur Gullachsen, Captain, Canadian Army. His guidance, enthusiasm, and counsel focused my efforts and ensured that my motivation never flagged. This work benefited immensely from the encouragement and scrutiny of Padraic (Pat) Carlin, Dr. Bill Taylor, Mindy Conner, and the superb editorial team at the Naval Institute Press. Annette Amerman at the Naval History and Heritage Command shared insights into frequently overlooked sources and her perspective on early marine aviators. Dr. Fred Allison, a marine aviation historian, lent invaluable counsel on my framework for analysis. Aviation historians Rick Dunn and Barrett Tillman shared their unmatched perspective on some hazy historical issues. Jon Parshall, Midway and Imperial Japanese Navy expert, took time to check the map of the 4 June 1942 action. Guadalcanal historian Dave Holland helped interpret period photographs. Cdr. Stan Fisher at the U.S. Naval Academy provided enlightening insights into naval aviation maintenance. Dr. Chris Hemler confirmed important details about control of air support at Iwo Jima. Cdr. Peter Mersky shared a hard-to-find photograph from his collection. Justin Taylan at PacificWrecks.com provided illuminating insights into Japanese naval source records. Jacob Haywood at the National Archives in College Park, Maryland, provided crucial research assistance. At the Marine Corps University in Quantico, Virginia, Mr. John Lyles helped locate essential records, and Dr. Seth Givens took time to track down squadron muster rolls unavailable elsewhere. Two Marine fighter pilots, Col. Lance "Boil" Lewis and Col. Jayson "Cooch" Tiger, kept this ground-pounder from committing egregious aviation gaffes. Jim Burns shared biographic details and personal papers that illuminated much about his father, Col. Robert R. Burns. The family of Col. Edwin S. Roberts Jr., particularly Colonel Roberts' daughter-in-law, Judy Roberts, was especially generous with copies of the colonel's papers and diary. And I am deeply grateful to Lt. Gen. Robert S. "Whaler" Walsh, USMC (Ret.), National Commander, Marine Corps Aviation Association, for contributing the Foreword.

Most important, I am grateful to my wife, Elena, my love and my best friend, for her encouragement and support.

PART ONE

★ ★ ★

MIDWAY, 1942

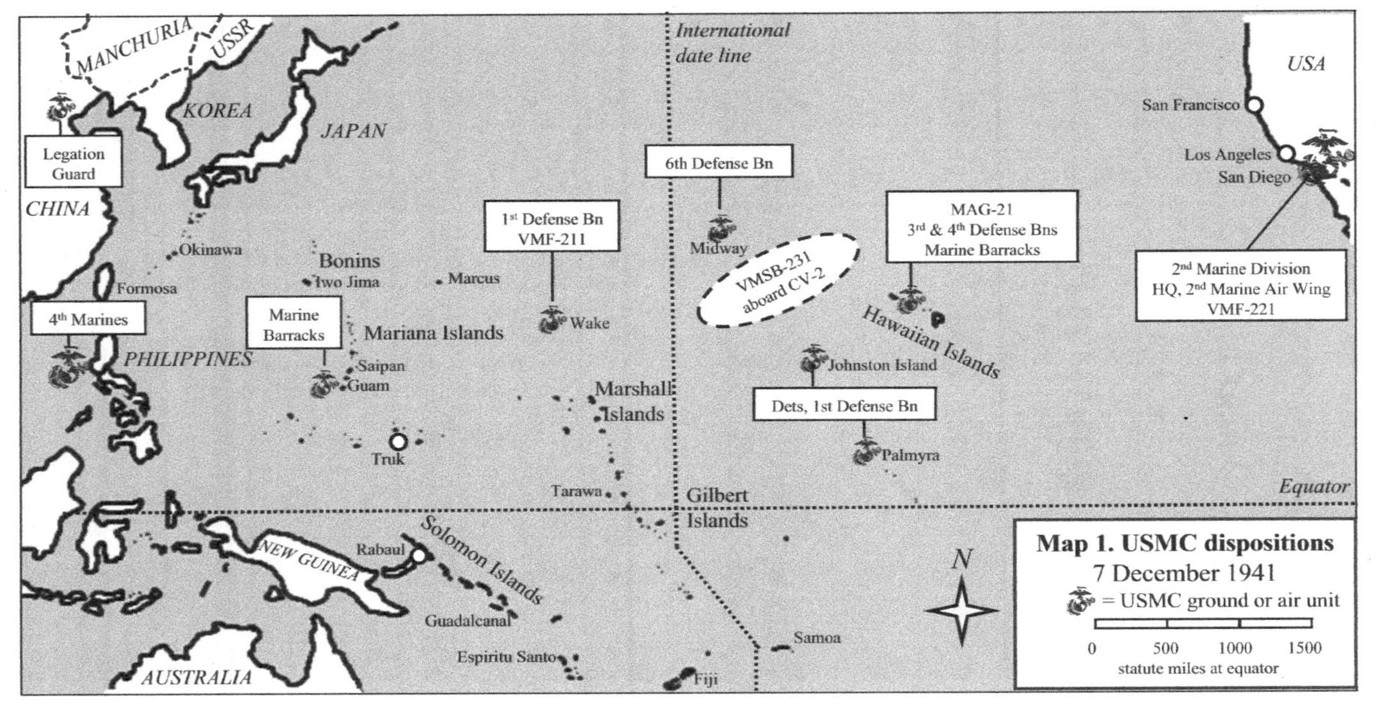

MAP 1. USMC dispositions, 7 December 1941

1

★ ★ ★

VMF-221 and Marine Aviation Prior to World War II

VMF-221, July–December 1941

The Marine Corps organized VMF-221 on 11 July 1941 as part of a larger naval expansion directed by President Franklin D. Roosevelt and authorized by Congress in 1940.[1] In mid-1939, marine aviation comprised just 1,408 of the Marine Corps' 19,432 marines.[2] These marines served in the two aircraft groups of the Fleet Marine Force: one at Quantico, Virginia, and the other at Naval Air Station, North Island near San Diego, California. Each group consisted of four squadrons: one observation, one fighting, one bombing, and one utility.[3]

When Germany's armed forces overran western Europe in May 1940, Roosevelt ordered the Pacific Fleet forward from San Diego to the naval base at Pearl Harbor to deter Japan from exploiting the crisis to move against British and Dutch possessions in the western Pacific.[4] The Pacific marine aircraft group, Marine Aircraft Group 21 (MAG-21), deployed with the fleet to Ewa Field on Oahu.[5]

Following the Pacific Fleet's deployment, the Naval Expansion Act of 14 June 1940 further expanded naval aviation to 4,500 aircraft. A month later, Congress more than tripled that authorization to 15,000 aircraft.[6] In

October, Roosevelt authorized Secretary of the Navy William F. Knox to call up the Marine Corps Reserve.[7]

Marine aviation expanded to 13 active squadrons and 204 aircraft. In July 1941, the Marine Corps transferred 7 officers and 51 enlisted marines from MAG-21 in Hawaii to form the new squadron at North Island. By 7 December 1941, the squadron had grown to 20 officers and 127 enlisted marines and operated 14 F2A-3 Buffalo fighter aircraft and a single North American Aviation SNJ-3 Texan scout trainer aircraft. The squadron included twenty-one pilots: all the officers were naval aviators, and one master technical sergeant was designated a naval aviation pilot. VMF-221 was one of four new squadrons and one of just four marine fighting squadrons in December 1941.[8]

Second Lt. Marion Carl, one of the squadron's original aviators, recalled the period from July to November as "an uncommonly pleasant assignment." Pilots trained in section tactics and air-to-air combat. The marines practiced carrier landings ashore and observed navy pilots launch and recover aboard the carrier USS *Saratoga* (CV 3) at sea, but did not qualify as carrier pilots themselves.[9]

As the Marine Corps wrestled with rapid expansion, commanders and aviators were rotated at an astonishing rate. Between July 1941 and June 1945, fifteen different officers would command VMF-221, for an average of merely three months each.[10] Maj. William G. Manley commanded VMF-221 for its first three months, until the Marine Corps ordered him to Europe to learn about developments in aerial warfare. Maj. Verne J. McCaul took command on 6 October. McCaul retained command until 19 April 1942, when he became the executive officer of the marine aircraft group on Midway.[11]

Because McCaul commanded the squadron for more than six months, he had a key role in developing VMF-221. He appears to have been a good commander and a disciplinarian. He was popular with his marines and looked out for their welfare. However, McCaul was apparently not a natural fighter pilot. During this period at North Island, an inexperienced second lieutenant defeated McCaul in air-to-air combat. According to Lieutenant Carl, McCaul "came back in and he was so mad at himself. I remember him taking his gloves off and throwing them on the deck and saying, 'I'll be a son of a bitch. There's only two ways to turn and I invariably pick the wrong way.'"[12]

The squadron's flight officer suffered no such handicap. In Carl's words, Capt. Harold W. Bauer enjoyed a reputation as the "reigning top dog." A standout athlete at the U.S. Naval Academy, Bauer had earned his wings in February 1936. He was an experienced, gifted, and aggressive fighter pilot and a demanding, no-nonsense leader.[13] Carl had run afoul of Bauer in VMF-1 at Quantico. A couple of weeks after Carl joined VMF-221, Bauer told Carl, "OK. It's you and I today." Carl strapped in tight and determined not to lose the duel. His twisting turns wore the skin off his tailbone. At one point, he found himself in a dangerous inverted spin at low altitude but recovered with a half snap-roll and battled on. Back on the ground again at North Island, Bauer conceded a draw. "He had a little more respect for me than he had had before," Carl recalled.[14]

On 30 November, the squadron received orders to embark on *Saratoga* a week later and sail to Hawaii to join MAG-21. The marines scrambled to prepare their aircraft and equipment. By Sunday morning, 7 December, they had staged their aircraft and equipment on the pier at North Island. As *Saratoga* completed mooring, her loudspeakers announced that the Japanese had attacked Pearl Harbor. The sailors and marines leaped into action, completing the twenty-four-hour embarkation in fourteen hours, and *Saratoga* and VMF-221 sailed for Pearl Harbor on 8 December.[15]

U.S. Naval Strategy and Doctrine in 1941

VMF-221 was sailing into a war that American planners had been preparing for throughout the interwar period. By 1934 the navy had settled on a step-by-step drive across the central Pacific that would culminate in a decisive fleet engagement with the Imperial Japanese Navy (IJN).[16] The Marine Corps' role would be to seize and defend advance bases that would enable the fleet to sustain and maintain its ships and base its aircraft.[17] According to the Navy's 1938 *Landing Operations Doctrine*, aviation's first task in amphibious operations was to gain and maintain air superiority through fighter protection and strikes against enemy airfields and air defenses. Throughout the assault, aviation would attack ground defenses; spot for naval gunfire and artillery; protect troops, ships, and aircraft from enemy air attack; and conduct reconnaissance.[18] By 1940, Marine Corps doctrine stated the primary mission of marine aviation was "for the support of the Fleet Marine Force in landing operations" with a secondary mission of providing replacement squadrons for the fleet's carriers.[19]

How naval doctrine conceived that navy and marine aviation would support the Fleet Marine Force in landing operations requires explanation. Throughout the 1930s, naval planners struggled to reconcile the limited range of land-based aircraft and the fleet's limited number of aircraft carriers.[20] The challenge of transporting marine aircraft to the objective and getting them ashore confounded planners. In 1937 the commanding officer of the marine aircraft group at Quantico underscored this problem in a letter to the commander of the U.S. fleet's Aircraft Battle Force: "It has been apparent for a long time to some of us that Marine Corps Aviation cannot perform its primary mission, that of furnishing air support in the capture of a hostile base, under most conditions, unless we are prepared to operate from carriers."[21] But until the United States commissioned more aircraft carriers, only navy squadrons would fly from them; marine squadrons could not join the battle until aviation could be established ashore.

Organization

Since its inception in 1912, marine aviation has been both a subordinate element of the Marine Corps and a component of naval aviation. Reconciling this division has often vexed the Department of the Navy as well as marine and navy commanders.

In 1941 the Department of the Navy's Bureau of Aeronautics administered most aspects of marine aviation. While the Commandant of the Marine Corps retained authority over personnel, the Bureau of Aeronautics made recommendations on assignments and training for aviators and mechanics and procured, managed, and maintained aircraft, equipment, and supplies.[22] The Chief of Naval Operations—not the Commandant of the Marine Corps—determined the number and type of marine squadrons.[23] In other words, the navy determined the type, quantity, and organization of marine aircraft, provided matériel, trained aviators and ground personnel, and had a substantial voice in who flew for the Marine Corps.

In the fleet, marine aviation served within the Fleet Marine Force. However, on the eve of war, the degree of control the Fleet Marine Force commander retained over marine squadrons was a bit murky. Fleet Marine Force units were assigned to the Atlantic and Pacific fleets. In July 1941, VMF-221 and the other squadrons of MAG-21 belonged to the Fleet Marine Force, but Vice Adm. William F. Halsey, Commander, Aircraft, Battle Force, Pacific Fleet, directed their tactical training and exercised operational control. Maintenance was divided between naval air stations and marine aircraft groups. At air stations such as North Island, marine squadrons depended on navy airbase detachments for overhaul of aircraft and engines. The headquarters and service squadrons at each marine aircraft group provided similar support at temporary fields. Maintenance of engines and airframes as well as services such as fuel, supply, and ammunition were centralized within the group's headquarters and service squadron.[24]

The squadron was the basic tactical and administrative unit of marine aviation. Marine squadrons had eighteen aircraft in 1941. Fighters operated in three divisions of two sections each. Each section consisted of three aircraft. As described in a lecture given by Maj. Frank D. Weir at Marine Corps Schools in 1941, a fighting squadron organized into three divisions could maintain a continuous air patrol or alert with one division aloft and two on the ground in rotation.[25]

The ground side of the squadron was organized into sections that specialized in different aspects of aircraft operations and service. The senior enlisted marine, a master technical sergeant, filled the billet of leading chief and oversaw aircraft maintenance. The squadron's first sergeant, junior in rank to the leading chief, oversaw personnel and administration. An engineering and check crew section performed the most technically difficult aircraft maintenance. Plane captains performed routine maintenance, fueled the aircraft, completed preflight inspections, and started the engines when an aircraft had to take off at short notice. An ordnance section maintained the machine guns and loaded ammunition and bombs. A radio shop maintained communications equipment. Other specialists packed parachutes and refilled oxygen systems. A surprisingly large number of marines, perhaps 10 percent of the ground crew, served as cooks and messmen.[26]

Aircraft

The Brewster F2A Buffalo was the U.S. Navy's first monoplane fighter. Because Brewster struggled with production, the Bureau of Aeronautics curtailed acquisition of the F2A in early 1941. As the navy reequipped squadrons with Grumman F4F Wildcats, it allocated the F2As to marine and training squadrons. When VMF-221 embarked on *Saratoga*, the squadron brought fourteen F2A-3s aboard. The F2A-3's top speed was 321 mph, and its rate of climb from sea level was 2,440 feet per minute.[27]

In October 1941, VMF-221 temporarily possessed a single F4F-3 Wildcat, and some pilots qualified in it before it was reassigned to a navy squadron. Pilots appreciated the F4F-3's stability as a gun platform. Unlike later variants, the F4F-3 did not have the folding wings that enabled carriers to use deck space more efficiently. The pilot had to retract the F4F-3's landing gear manually, a cumbersome and distracting feature.[28]

As aviation historian John B. Lundstrom pointed out, on paper the F2A-3 and the F4F-3 performed similarly. The F4F-3's top speed of 329 mph barely exceeded the F2A-3's 321 mph. The two aircraft climbed at virtually the same rate. Both carried four .50-caliber machine guns and two 100-pound bombs. The F4F-3's 450 rounds per gun gave it 34 seconds of firing time, while the F2A-3's 325 rounds per gun gave the pilot only 24 seconds. The F2A-3's cockpit surrounded the pilot with armored protection and a bullet-resistant windshield. The F2A-3's fuselage tank was self-sealing, and the wing tanks were equipped with a carbon dioxide purge system. These protective measures traded speed and maneuverability for ruggedness and survivability. The F4F-3 began the war without such defensive features, but they were incorporated later.[29]

According to Marion Carl, who flew both aircraft and became a test pilot after the war, the F4F edged out the F2A-3 in survivability and stability: "A lot of people put down the Buffalo. I don't think that the [F4F Wildcat] was any more maneuverable or any faster than the Buffalo, but it was a much more solid airplane and that's about the only thing that I could give it. The

F4F was the more solid airplane, and it would take a heck of a lot more punishment and it was a little bit more stable. The Buffalo was a little tricky to fly under certain circumstances."[30]

At the end of 1941, VMF-221 and USS *Lexington*'s (CV 2) squadron, VF-2, were the only fleet squadrons still flying the F2A-3. VF-2 would receive its F4Fs long before VMF-221 would. When Commander, Aircraft Battle Force allocated aircraft, the newest and best went aboard carriers.[31]

Marine and Navy Fighting Aviation Doctrine and Tactics, 1941

Two 1941 documents articulate how the Marine Corps and navy expected their fighting squadrons to operate.[32] One of the corps' aviation pioneers, Maj. William J. Wallace, lectured officers at Quantico on "Fighting Aviation." Wallace's lecture, informed by the ongoing Battle of Britain, provides exceptional insight into the Marine Corps' expectations for its fighting squadrons. An order issued by the commander of the navy's Aircraft Battle Force in March 1941, *USF-74, Current Tactical Orders and Doctrine U.S. Fleet Aircraft*, volume 1, *Carrier Aircraft*, detailed how the navy directed its carrier-based squadrons to fight. Since Commander, Aircraft Battle Force, Pacific Fleet directed the tactical training of marine squadrons, *USF-74* offers the closest evidence of a tactical directive to marine fighting squadrons.

Wallace told his students that "the mission of fighting aviation is to deny enemy aviation freedom of action, by destruction, threat of destruction or by attrition in air combat." He emphasized that "action is always offensive" because the object is to destroy hostile aircraft. Wallace explicitly stressed three principles: "surprise, maneuver, and hold offensive action," and implicitly added a fourth principle, mass.

Fighting aviation was now conducted en masse and coordinated by radio, not in individual sorties reminiscent of World War I. Though in 1941 marine aircraft groups were composites of fighting, bombing, scouting, and observation squadrons, marine aviators sought to imitate the Royal Air Force and consolidate fighting squadrons into fighting groups. Such groups would echelon in depth and altitude—by divisions within a squadron, and by squadrons within the group—extending fighter protection to the largest area possible.

A commander could assign fighting aviation one of two missions: general support (offensive) and special support (defensive). General support included attacking hostile aircraft and denying the enemy freedom of action. In general support, Wallace lectured, "the fighters are 'on the prowl,' looking for trouble, and usually finding it." Special support entailed protecting specific air, sea, or ground operations, such as escorting bombers.

Wallace preferred general support because it allowed greater freedom of action. Special support was preferable when the enemy held a substantial advantage in fighter strength. Fighters in special support, Wallace explained, "must wait for trouble to find them." Wallace concluded, "The rule, then, for the employment of fighter units should be—*general support wherever and whenever possible*" (emphasis in original).

In both missions, fighting aviation operated in some combination of three different methods that the Royal Air Force had employed in the defense of London. The air patrol consisted of a screen of two- or three-plane patrols to limit hostile scouting. Air patrols were considered wasteful; they consumed an eighteen-plane squadron to maintain a six-plane screen that was too weak to intercept a large bomber formation. The second method, air alert, concentrated six fighters together above a geographic point or a naval task force, awaiting intercept directions. Air alert consumed the same fighting strength as an air patrol: eighteen planes to maintain a six-plane alert. The preferred method, ground alert, reserved all eighteen fighters for interception but depended on an early warning system to detect attackers in time for the fighters to launch, climb above the attackers, and intercept them.

In a section devoted to naval and amphibious operations, Wallace discouraged strafing hostile vessels to suppress enemy air defenses. "In naval warfare, no less than in land warfare," he insisted, "the proper employment of fighters is in the air against the hostile aviation." If fighting aviation could not accomplish its purpose, "there [would] be no landing" and secondary missions such as ground attack would be "suicidal" for the fighters.

In a section regarding defense of advance bases, Wallace suggested a combination of air patrol, air alert, and ground alert. The earlier the warning, the more likely hostile aircraft would be detected, and the greater fraction of fighting strength the commander could assign to ground alert. In a key point,

Wallace pronounced, "Seldom will there be enough fighting units available to permit their employment as protective escorts for bombing missions directed at hostile naval objectives. The proper place for the defending fighters is at home, prepared to repel any aerial boarders that might happen along."

While acknowledging that the Marine Corps had employed fighters in a ground attack role in its small wars of the 1920s and 1930s, Wallace noted that such missions had never been flown in the presence of hostile aviation. Notwithstanding the priority the Marine Corps placed on supporting its landing force, Wallace discouraged using fighters against ground targets "except in *extreme emergency against highly important objectives*" (emphasis in original).

While dismissing the popular belief that fighting aviation required better pilots than other types of aviation, Wallace noted that fighter pilots did require more training, particularly in gunnery. Fighter pilots had to think quickly in the thin air at high altitude and withstand the physiological demands of maneuvers and rapid changes in altitude. Because it took a year to train fighter pilots, Wallace opposed squandering them on missions poorly suited to their aircraft and skills.

Wallace described how marine fighters would meet the enemy, but he did not specify what they would do once combat was joined. A chapter of *USF-74* titled "Tactical Instructions and Doctrine for Fighting Squadrons" filled that gap. Rather than attempting to prescribe tactical methods for every situation a fighting squadron might face, *USF-74* emphasized the importance of applying basic principles and teamwork:

> The tactical situations which may confront the fighting squadron are so numerous and varied that definite tactical rules of procedure cannot be set down to cover them. Drilled in fundamental principles of aerial combat, the pilots trained to think and act as a unit, a properly indoctrinated fighting squadron should meet any tactical situation without any commands from the leader other than the signal for going into action.

USF-74 emphasized two principles of aerial engagement: superiority of fire power and superiority of position. Fighters should use speed, the sun, and clouds to achieve surprise. Pilots should constantly seek an altitude advantage to enable them to select when and how to engage. Fighters were discouraged from individual dogfights; concentrating the force in the initial attack and regrouping afterward enabled the squadron to fight as a team. Once the enemy was spotted, fighters should attack immediately. Initial attacks should target enemy leaders. Rather than holding fire until getting close to the enemy, *USF-74* advocated firing at the earliest possible moment. If the enemy formation maneuvered to maximize its defensive firepower, the attacking squadron should split its attack into three divisions so that at least one division could exploit the enemy aircraft's blind spots.

Defensive principles emphasized preventing surprise, retaining an altitude advantage, concentration, attacking enemy lead aircraft, and protecting friendly blind spots. A fighter who was attacked from above should turn toward the attacker, stay out of view under the attacker's nose, and force the attacker to roll inverted to maintain visual contact, thereby disrupting the attack. If friendly fighters were nearby, the defender should lead the attacker into their guns.

USF-74 advocated three six-plane divisions for air-to-air combat. When the division attacked, sections spread out, with the section in the best position initiating the attack. The remaining sections exploited the enemy's evasive maneuvers or followed the lead section in rapid succession. Aircraft attacked in column, one after another. Upon completing a diving run, the section used the speed of the dive to climb, regain altitude, and commence another attack. In an ideal attack, sections continued the sequence: dive, attack, recover, regroup, and reattack.

USF-74 repeatedly admonished fighter pilots to maintain unit cohesion as long as possible and regain it as soon as possible. When a fighter did attack a lone enemy fighter, he should use surprise, dive to a position on the enemy's tail, and fire at very close range. For pilots on the receiving end of such an attack *USF-74* prescribed heading directly beneath the attacker and climbing. After passing underneath the attacker, the friendly aircraft would scissor toward and away from the attacker until reaching the same altitude, and then maneuver to gain an advantage in altitude or position.

USF-74 provided fighter pilots with additional instructions for escort missions, protecting service vessels, attacking surface vessels, and antisubmarine patrols. It established a thorough doctrine that directed fighting squadrons how to fight. It helpfully balanced standardized procedures with flexibility. However, its instructions on fighter-versus-fighter combat appear to have assumed that friendly and enemy fighters would be evenly matched.

USF-74 did not delve into the technical aspects of aerial gunnery. In addition to learning to attack from directly astern of an adversary, navy and marine fighter pilots learned a difficult technique known as deflection gunnery. Deflection gunnery required the attacker to maneuver to the rear quarter or side of the target aircraft and then lead his gunfire so that the bullets intersected the target's path. How much to lead the target—the deflection part of gunnery—was a function of the attacker's speed, the target's speed, and the angle of attack. Setting up such a deflection shot required the attacking pilot to execute a precise combination of turns and rolls, which varied considerably depending on whether the attack began from the side, front, or rear; the speed differential between the aircraft; and the altitude difference. Mastering deflection gunnery required considerable practice. John Lundstrom has asserted that the U.S. Navy was the only Allied force whose aviators used deflection gunnery tactics in World War II; the only other air force that trained its fighter pilots in this tactic was the Imperial Japanese Navy—the principal adversary of U.S. Navy and Marine Corps aviators.[33]

Though extremely difficult to master, deflection gunnery afforded exceptional advantages. It enabled the attacker to begin an attack from almost any position relative to the target. Able to choose from a number of methods, the attacker could select an approach that would mask his fighter from defensive guns in the rear or side of the target. And since he would finish the attack by diving underneath the target, the pilot could use the additional speed gained in the dive to climb and set up another attack.[34]

Manning and Training Marine Aviators

To execute this doctrine, the naval services had to obtain aspiring pilots and train them to fly. Though the Navy Department had ramped up its recruiting and training before Pearl Harbor, it was struggling to meet the fleet's demand for aviators.

During World War II, nearly all marine aviators were regular or reserve officers. Between the world wars, the Marine Corps procured regular officers almost exclusively from the Naval Academy, the noncommissioned officer ranks, and ROTC units. Regular officers served as ground officers for several years before flight training. While the Marine Corps obtained reserve officers from several sources, including the Platoon Leaders Class that began in 1935, the corps acquired its reserve aviators exclusively through the marine aviation cadet program.[35] In this program, an applicant first enlisted as a private first class in the reserve. Instead of attending basic training at one of the corps' recruit depots, the enlistee reported to one of several naval air stations. During a fifteen-day period of active duty, he learned basic flying skills and soloed. The program's intent was to eliminate unsuitable candidates; those who passed were offered appointments as aviation cadets and ordered to Pensacola for flight training. After flight training, the reserve aviator remained on active duty as a second lieutenant for twelve months and then could apply for a regular commission or return to civilian life and occasional reserve training. In mid-1941 the Secretary of the Navy ended the separate marine aviation cadet program and appointed all aviation cadets into the Naval Reserve, commissioning marines at the end of intermediate flight training.[36]

A summary of VMF-221's aviators in December 1941 illustrates where the Marine Corps obtained its aviators and how much experience they had accumulated by the outbreak of war. Four (Major McCaul, Captain Bauer, Capt. John L. Smith, and 1st Lt. John F. Dobbin) had obtained regular commissions and served as ground officers before flight training. MTechSgt. Robert L. Dickey had begun flight school as a private. As an enlisted marine he was designated a "naval aviation pilot" instead of a "naval aviator." The other sixteen pilots had been aviation cadets. McCaul, Dickey, and Capt. Robert M. Haynes had been flying for more than a decade. Two other captains and all three first lieutenants had completed flight school at least five years earlier. Captain Smith and all but one second lieutenant had earned their wings between 1938 and 1940. Only one second lieutenant had been out of flight school less than a year. McCaul, Bauer, Dickey, Capt. James L. Neefus, and 1st Lt. Frederick R. Payne were qualified to land aboard carriers, and some others may have been as well.[37]

When McCaul took command in October 1941, all his pilots were graduates of a naval aviation pipeline that was still "an elimination training course to weed out the unfit," according to the Bureau of Navigation's official history, rather than a progressive training curriculum designed to meet fleet requirements. Training consisted of three phases: primary, intermediate, and operational. Primary training lasted about three months. Students flew at least eighty-five hours and took classes in navigation, communications, aircraft recognition, and gunnery. Intermediate flight training included up to 120 hours of flight.[38] Intermediate students mastered flying, navigating, and instrument landings. Intermediate students who were headed to fighters specialized in acrobatics, formation tactics, gunnery, combat tactics, bombing, navigation, and night flying. Ground school classes covered engineering and maintenance, navigation, communications, aviation weather, survival training, and squadron operations.[39] Marine and naval student aviator training was fully integrated during primary and intermediate training.[40]

Upon completion of intermediate training, aviation cadets were designated naval aviators and received wings and commissions. Marine lieutenants then reported to Fleet Marine Force squadrons for operational flight training in combat aircraft. *USF-74* directed four progressive phases for operational flight training. First, aviators flew familiarization flights in the squadron's assigned model of aircraft. These flights, essentially a review of intermediate training in the assigned aircraft, included acrobatics and combat maneuvers, and were flown day and night and under marginal weather conditions. In the second phase, the aviator practiced maintaining position in section formations while performing combat maneuvers. In the third phase, the aviator trained with the division and squadron in combat formations. In the final phase, the squadron trained as a team to attack enemy aircraft, attack ground targets, and to practice defensive tactics when attacked in the air.[41]

In the years leading up to World War II, marine squadrons would next join the ground element of the Fleet Marine Force in a landing exercise.[42] From Lieutenant Carl's account, it does not appear that VMF-221 trained to attack surface targets while at North Island. The squadron's focus was aerial combat, section tactics, and instrument flying.[43]

Manning and Training Marine Ground Crew

VMF-221 deployed from San Diego with 127 enlisted marines. Just under half were noncommissioned officers (NCOs). Almost one in five was a senior NCO detailed to aviation. In addition to Dickey, the naval aviation pilot, the squadron had three master technical sergeants, the highest of the Marine Corps' six pay grades in 1941. Nine technical sergeants and seven staff sergeants were also detailed to aviation duties.[44]

Twenty-seven of these enlisted marines were reservists. In a practice that might make marines today apoplectic, no drill instructors had indoctrinated these enlisted reservists and aviation cadets in close order drill, physical fitness, and rifle marksmanship. Reservists merely attended weekly training and two weeks of active duty each summer.[45] Inculcating these marines with the identity and high standards of the Marine Corps was left to the regular marines of VMF-221.

In the late 1930s, the Bureau of Aeronautics operated several twenty-six-week to thirty-five-week technical schools to train navy and marine ground crews. However, only a fraction of the aviation ground crews had attended them. Until 1941 most aviation maintenance training still took place on the job. A review of the squadron's muster rolls reveals that almost none of VMF-221's NCOs, who had all enlisted prior to 1941, had attended technical courses. At least three of the senior NCOs had attended a navy mechanics course at Great Lakes, Illinois and four had visited the Grumman Aircraft Factory on Long Island for training on the new F4F.[46]

The same act that authorized 15,000 naval aircraft spawned a swift ramp up in aviation technical schools. By the outbreak of war, navy schools could seat 8,720 students.[47] Twenty-two of the squadron's junior marines—eleven of them reservists—completed aviation mechanics courses in Jacksonville or Pensacola, two completed an aviation metalsmiths course, and two an aviation ordnance course. Aviation mechanics and metalsmiths maintained the aircraft from nose to tail—engines, instruments, hydraulic systems, and airframes. Aviation ordnance marines maintained and calibrated machine guns and ammunition, bombs and bomb racks, and gunsights and bombsights.[48]

Japanese Naval Aviation Aircraft, Tactics, and Training

During 1942, VMF-221 would encounter four types of Japanese aircraft: the Kawanishi H6K Type 97 flying boat ("Mavis"), the Nakajima B5N2 Type 97-3 carrier (torpedo) attack aircraft ("Kate"), the Aichi D3A Type 99 carrier (dive) bomber ("Val"), and the Mitsubishi A6M2 Model 21 Type 00 fighter ("Zeke" or "Zero"). The Zero was the IJN's aerial combat fighter.[49]

On 22 September 1941, the Pacific Fleet's Fleet Air Tactical Unit issued an intelligence bulletin on the Zero warning of its superior speed. A report from the American Volunteer Group in China estimated the Zero could climb at 3,500 feet per minute and reach 16,000 feet from sea level in just 6 minutes. The report also warned of the Zero's superior maneuverability.[50] After an extensive review of primary evidence, aviation historian Richard Dunn concluded the Zero's maximum speed was probably 345 mph at "war emergency" or "boost" power. It was certainly faster than the F2A-3 and F4F-3—probably at least 30 mph faster than the F4F-3 in combat conditions—and its superior rate of climb and maneuverability gave the Zero immense advantages.[51] The Zero traded armor for its high performance, though, and it lacked self-sealing gas tanks and so was more vulnerable to machine-gun fire.[52] The Zero carried 680 rounds for each of its 7.7-mm machine guns, but these lighter weapons often proved ineffective against rugged American aircraft. The Zero's powerful 20-mm cannons fired more destructive explosive shells, but with just 60 rounds per cannon, the 20-mm had only 8.67 seconds of firing time.[53]

To attack ships and ground targets, the IJN utilized the Kate carrier attack aircraft. The Kate could drop torpedoes at low levels or bombs from high altitude. The Kate had no armor and no self-sealing gas tank, and carried a single 7.7-mm machine gun with a field of fire limited to the left and right of the tail. Its maximum speed was just 225 mph, and it took over 8 minutes to climb to 10,000 feet, so an F2A-3 could easily overtake it.[54]

Despite its fixed landing gear, the Val dive-bomber was a hair faster than the Kate. It could climb to 10,000 feet in about 6.5 minutes. It had twin 7.7-mm machine guns up front as well as a rear machine gun similar to the Kate's.[55] As a dive-bomber, the Val was less vulnerable to fighters and antiaircraft fire than a Kate in a horizontal bombing or torpedo run.

The Mavis was a long-range reconnaissance flying boat and bomber. With an operational radius of 1,000 miles, the huge Mavis was an ideal scouting platform in the vast Pacific. At 190 mph, the Mavis was slow, but it was heavily armed with 7.7-mm bow, dorsal, and side machine guns and a 20-mm cannon in its tail. A fighter attacking a Mavis flying at sea level would be unable to approach from below and would face defensive weapons no matter the angle of approach.[56]

Like U.S. naval aviation, Japanese naval aviation emphasized massing air power. Unlike U.S. carrier task forces, the IJN could mass two hundred aircraft from two or three of its mobile strike force's carriers in a single wave. To control such large strikes, the Japanese maintained large formations. Three-plane sections formed vees, with the leader at the apex and the trailing aircraft 30–50 yards astern and slightly above. Three sections formed a 9-plane division, also in a vee, with trailing sections 175–200 yards astern of the lead. Three divisions formed a squadron, similarly arrayed in the vee, with trailing divisions 440–880 yards astern of the lead. Each carrier had a single squadron of Zero fighters, Val dive-bombers, and Kate torpedo bombers. When multiple squadrons from two or three carriers formed for a single strike, the squadrons of the same type grouped together. Though the fighters fought by sections, the bombers maintained their division integrity through the attack.[57]

IJN pilots were highly proficient at the outbreak of the war. The phases and skills covered in their training did not differ radically from U.S. naval aviator training. Most pilots were enlisted aviators who accumulated more than 250 hours before undergoing a year of intense training in a fleet squadron. In December 1941, the most junior fully qualified fighter pilots in the IJN had been flying about two years, roughly equivalent to the junior pilots of VMF-221. Most leaders from sections on up had flown in combat in China.[58]

On the eve of war VMF-221 was fairly ready to fulfill its role in the Pacific Fleet's strategy. All its junior aviators save one had at least a year's experience. Three had more than ten years, and five had at least five years. The squadron mustered a full complement of ground crew. The high proportion of senior noncommissioned officers suggests the squadron was well poised to train its junior marines.

The squadron had fourteen F2A-3 fighters. Though the Buffalo was not the Bureau of Aeronautics' preferred fighter, there is little evidence that it was significantly inferior to the F4F-3. The shortfall of four aircraft was a significant issue, but if the bureau could scrounge up another four aircraft, the squadron would have its full allowance.

VMF-221 could not help *Saratoga* in a fight. Only a handful of its senior aviators were qualified to land on carriers, and none had done so in the F2A-3. The squadron could launch from *Saratoga*—once—but not recover. VMF-221 could serve the Pacific Fleet only by reinforcing an island garrison.

Navy and marine aviation had published coherent doctrine, and VMF-221 had spent four months in San Diego progressing through the first two phases of operational training delineated by *USF-74*. Though Lieutenant Carl's account indicates the squadron had not yet progressed beyond section tactics, VMF-221 was poised to complete its operational training if given time.

The tactics outlined in *USF-74* appear suited to attacking Japanese naval bombers. With the Japanese emphasis on large formations and maintaining division integrity through the attack, American attacks by sections and divisions from multiple directions seemed a sensible tactic. However, the American tactics presumed friendly and adversary fighters would be roughly matched in performance and numbers. This was unlikely. The Zero was faster and more maneuverable, and Japanese carriers could mass more air power than the U.S. fleet. Japanese naval fighter pilots were at least as skilled as the pilots of VMF-221.

As *Saratoga* sailed out of San Diego Bay on 8 December 1941, the marines of VMF-221 may well have believed their squadron was ready to face the Imperial Japanese Navy, and that the Pacific Fleet had a plan to give them that chance.

2

★ ★ ★

December 1941–May 1942

Operational Context, December 1941

Although American commanders had intended to pursue an aggressive, active defense in the Pacific, the loss of ships and aircraft at Pearl Harbor curtailed their ambitions.[1] On 9 December Adm. Harold R. Stark, Chief of Naval Operations, canceled prewar plans and limited the Pacific Fleet's immediate tasks to raiding enemy sea communications and defending the Territory of Hawaii as well as Johnston, Midway, Palmyra, Samoa, and Wake atolls.[2]

These orders had significant implications for the Fleet Marine Force, which had marine defense units garrisoning the five atolls. Only Wake, 2,200 miles west of Pearl Harbor, had aircraft. Twelve Wildcats from MAG-21's other fighting squadron, VMF-211, had landed on Wake from the carrier USS *Enterprise* (CV 6) on 4 December.[3]

Zeros had destroyed every one of MAG-21's aircraft at Ewa Field on 7 December. A subsequent raid by bombers based in Kwajalein destroyed two-thirds of Wake Island's F4Fs on the ground. Fifty-four of MAG-21's ninety-one aircraft had been destroyed. The Fleet Marine Force was no longer ready to reinforce all five advance bases with aircraft. Until the Bureau of Aeronautics could replace MAG-21's losses or deploy MAG-11's squadrons from Virginia, the Pacific Fleet would have just one fighting squadron (VMF-221) and one scout bombing squadron (VMSB-231) to reinforce its advance bases.[4]

VMF-221 Operations, December 1941–May 1942

Saratoga's ferry mission was now a wartime sailing. In addition to carrying VMF-221's fourteen F2A-3s, *Saratoga* had her sixty-seven navy planes and another twenty-two aircraft as cargo. The Pacific Fleet was short of fighter aircraft, which was one reason VMF-221 and VF-2 still flew F2A-3s. *Saratoga*'s fighting squadron, VF-3, had just twelve F4F-3s.[5] Pfc. William F. Hall, an ordnance marine in VMF-221, recalled that *Saratoga*'s hangar deck was so crowded with extra aircraft that the marine F2A-3s were triced from the overhead.[6] Stowed as they were, the F2A-3s would have been of little help to *Saratoga* had she encountered the Japanese. Even if the aircraft could have been readied for action, few of VMF-221's aviators were carrier qualified. They could have launched from her flight deck but could not have recovered aboard her.

To escort *Saratoga*, the Pacific Fleet scrounged up three slow World War I–era destroyers. *Saratoga* did not get close enough to Hawaii to launch VMF-221 until 14 December. Twelve of the F2A-3s landed at Naval Air Station Kaneohe on Oahu, along with *Saratoga*'s navy aircraft. Two marine fighters remained aboard, presumably due to maintenance issues. The following morning, *Saratoga* eased into Pearl Harbor.[7]

As *Saratoga* sailed toward Hawaii, Adm. Husband E. Kimmel, Commander in Chief, U.S. Pacific Fleet, was planning how to employ *Saratoga* and VMF-221. The defense battalion on Wake Island and VMF-211's four remaining F4F-3s had repulsed one Japanese assault and withstood at least five air raids. Wake was in peril, and Kimmel was determined to relieve the garrison. He placed Rear Adm. Frank J. Fletcher in command of Task Force 14 and gave him *Saratoga*, three cruisers, eight destroyers, an oiler, and the seaplane tender USS *Tangiers* (AV 8). VMF-221's aircraft and aviators reembarked on *Saratoga*. The ground echelon and a group of defense battalion marines embarked on *Tangiers* along with radar, fire control equipment, and a month's supply of ammunition. Fletcher planned to sail to Wake and establish air superiority long enough to fly VMF-221 and a navy dive-bombing squadron ashore. While marine and navy fighters provided protection, *Tangiers* would unload her marines and cargo.[8]

The aviators of VMF-221 had mixed feelings about the mission. Captain Bauer recalled,

> I felt very sorry for the Marines at Wake and wanted to go to their aid but at the same time I could see the futility of it all. Wake would fall to the Japs whenever they wanted to make the necessary effort. It could not be protected by our surface vessels due to its distance from Pearl Harbor. We felt the Wake Garrison should be evacuated rather than send more lambs to the slaughter.
>
> We left Pearl Harbor aboard the USS *Saratoga* bound for Wake feeling that we were to be sacrificed but we were determined to do our bit for our country and were proud to be able to serve her even for such a small thing as Wake Island.[9]

The ensuing relief operation revealed the limitations harsh weather could impose on carrier task forces. A prudent commander would sail into a fight with his destroyers fully fueled, and they required fuel every thirty hours. As Task Force 14 neared Wake, heavy seas delayed refueling. Fletcher's oiler slowed the task force to thirteen knots. The threat of Japanese aircraft in the Marshalls forced Fletcher to set a circuitous course to the north. Task Force 14 would be in position to relieve Wake on 24 December as planned (23 December Hawaii time), but no earlier.[10]

With few qualified carrier pilots, VMF-221 did not participate in combat air patrols over the task force. It did not help that McCaul's ground support marines and equipment were on *Tangier*. With VMF-221 unable to help protect *Saratoga*, VF-3's twelve busy Wildcats alternated in six-plane combat air patrols.[11]

On 22 December, aircraft from the carriers *Hiryū* and *Sōryū* had struck Wake Island, revealing that Japanese carriers were nearby. On 23 December, the day before Fletcher planned to fly VMF-221 ashore, a Japanese amphibious force assaulted Wake. This time, Wake fell. The new acting commander of the Pacific Fleet, Vice Adm. William S. Pye, briefly considered striking the Japanese carriers with *Saratoga*'s air group. But Task Force 14 was no match for *Hiryū* and *Sōryū*, particularly with VF-3 at half strength and VMF-221 unable to pitch in. Pye ordered Fletcher to abandon Wake and take his marines to Midway.[12]

On Christmas Day, VMF-221's fourteen F2A-3s and an escort of three SBD Dauntless dive-bombers launched 258 miles from Midway. "Needless to say the Marines and other inhabitants of Midway considered our arrival as the best Xmas present they had ever received," Bauer wrote in his diary.[13] The squadron commenced two-plane section and four-plane division patrols until dark. The following day, *Tangier* arrived with the remainder of the squadron.[14]

Midway offered an austere, isolated home, but not a miserable climate or harsh living conditions. The atoll consisted of two islands: Sand Island, which had a small harbor and a seaplane base, and Eastern Island, where VMF-221 operated. The air station on Eastern Island had a 5,400-foot crushed coral runway and a large parking apron. The marines lived next to their aircraft in sandbagged dugouts. A chow hall served two starchy, unappetizing meals a day. The marines had plenty of sea water for showers and laundry and enough foul-smelling fresh water to drink. There was electricity and a small post exchange.[15]

For the rest of December the squadron focused on three tasks: combat air patrols, bore-sighting guns, and digging entrenchments. Pilots manned their aircraft in ground alert by dawn, and the squadron maintained a four-plane air patrol until 0800. Two-plane sections rotated until 1600, when the squadron launched a four-plane dusk patrol and resumed ground alert with the balance of the squadron.[16]

When the squadron first arrived, the marines found plenty of room to disperse aircraft, but the site offered little protection from an aerial attack or naval bombardment. Pilots aloft easily spotted the parked aircraft against the white coral. To provide a modicum of camouflage, the marines cut out hollow spaces in the island's scrub, then dug revetments for aircraft and dugouts for personnel. It was slow, laborious work until a bulldozer scrounged up in mid-January helped to complete the revetments.[17]

Midway was now the forwardmost American base in the central Pacific. At the end of December, the new commander in chief of the U.S. Fleet, Adm. Ernest J. King, issued the new commander in chief of the Pacific Fleet, Adm. Chester W. Nimitz, two primary tasks: hold Midway and maintain sea lines of communication to Australia.[18]

On 2 January Nimitz and his staff prepared a formal estimate of the situation. Nimitz assessed that the Japanese would focus on conquering the Philippines and Malaysia, possibly also Burma and northeast India, and then advance toward Australia. In the central and southern Pacific, the Japanese would conduct carrier raids against U.S. bases, interdict lines of communication to them, and attempt to seize some or all of them, including Midway, which was particularly vulnerable. To counter these actions, Nimitz had to rely on his four carrier task forces. Rather than dispersing his carriers across the Pacific and exposing them to destruction, Nimitz kept them in reserve for a counterpunch.[19]

In addition to VMF-221, Midway's defenses included VMSB-231 and the 6th Defense Battalion. Marines had been fortifying Midway for nearly a year with seacoast artillery and antiaircraft guns. VMSB-231 had preceded VMF-221 there, flying its 17 SB2U-3 Vindicator dive-bombers 1,137 miles from Oahu to Midway on 17 December. On 9 January, Lt. Col. William J. Wallace, who had lectured on "Fighting Aviation" at Quantico, took command of the detachment of two squadrons. The marines operated under the naval air station's commanding officer, Cdr. Cyril T. Simard.[20]

Radar and Fighter Direction

The marine defense battalion on Midway operated three SCR-268 radars and one SCR-270 radar, which Wake Island had lacked. The SCR-270 on Sand Island could detect a bomber at five thousand feet at fifty miles and provide the operator with range, azimuth, and altitude.[21] The aviation detachment operated a second SCR-270 on Eastern Island.[22]

Wallace implemented a simple air defense. The aviation detachment had dug out a command post in the sand and reinforced its walls with imported redwood logs. When radar detected unidentified aircraft, sirens on the command post's roof and on a truck alerted aircrews. A single black ball run up the signal mast directed all aircraft to take off, fighters first. Two balls indicated the enemy was too close to launch bombers; only fighters took off. No balls meant the enemy was so close that aircrew should man antiaircraft guns or seek shelter in the bunkers. No one on Midway was trained in fighter direction, so the marines improvised. The command post had three small rooms and a fighter direction center. Marines covered a card table in the fighter direction center with graph paper and laid out gradations for 360 degrees around Midway. They affixed a pivot arm to the center of the table and marked distances out to 150 miles. With azimuth, distance, and altitude of enemy and friendly aircraft provided by radar, the command team could plot the attackers' locations, calculate intercept courses, and radio instructions to the fighters.[23]

Combat

Midway's defenders did not rely on radar alone. Aircraft scouting missions were an essential component of the atoll's defense against Japanese ships and submarines. On 7 December 1941, two Japanese destroyers had bombarded Midway, killing four marines and sailors and wounding ten more.[24]

VMF-221's F2A-3s were well suited to the patrol mission. The Buffalo could cruise almost 1,200 miles—slightly farther than VMSB-231's SB2U-3s—and carried two 100-pound bombs to strike targets of opportunity.[25]

These patrols brought VMF-221 pilots into their first action. On 27 January and again on 8 February, a submarine shelled Sand Island. Both attacks occurred during twilight. Both times the submarine approached from the south, where deeper water enabled it to approach Midway submerged and then escape into the darkness.[26] After the second attack, VMF-221 adjusted its patrols and kept two aircraft aloft until dark.[27]

On the second night, the dusk patrol paid off. At 1800 on 10 February 1st Lt. John F. Carey and 2nd Lt. Philip R. White spotted a submarine three miles south of Sand Island. Wasting no time, they attacked. The submarine's deck gun had fired just two rounds when Carey's and White's bombs exploded alongside it. The two marines recovered, whirled about, and strafed the submarine until it submerged. Although the pilots could not swear to any damage, no submarines tested Midway's defenses again for months.[28]

VMF-221 had its first aerial combat on 10 March. When Midway's radar detected an aircraft heading toward the atoll, Captain Neefus led a four-plane division aloft. The fighter director vectored the division to an intercept point, where the marines spotted a twin-engine Mavis. Neefus led the division above and off the left wing of the Mavis and commenced a high side deflection run. His .50-caliber guns scored hits on one or both engines, which trailed smoke. The burning Mavis dove for a cloud bank. Lt. Charles W. Somers Jr. and Lt. Francis P. McCarthy each completed an overhead pass. Marine Gunner Robert Dickey approached the Mavis from astern and for his effort received seven holes in his engine and one in his shoulder, likely from the 20-mm cannon in the flying boat's tail. Neefus conducted a second gunnery pass and then dropped below the cloud bank, where he spotted a fire and aircraft remnants on the water. Dickey returned safely to Eastern Island but never flew in combat again.[29]

Training New Aviators

In addition to the constant patrols and an occasional skirmish, VMF-221 had to train its aviators. Marine aviation had expanded rapidly following the attack on Pearl Harbor. On 31 December 1941, the Marine Corps had 13 squadrons and 659 aviators. By 30 June 1942, it would have 31 squadrons and 1,369 aviators.[30] In the first half of 1942, marine aviation had to reconcile two conflicting missions: it had to defend the fleet's advance bases, and it had to train the corps' new aviators—and it had to do both using the same aircraft.

Brig. Gen. Ross E. Rowell, the commanding general of the Second Marine Aircraft Wing, faced a conundrum. Newly winged aviators reported aboard with about two hundred hours, but with none in the aircraft they would fly in combat and without operational training. The aircraft they needed experience flying were defending the advance bases in the Pacific. On 8 January 1942, Rowell outlined his dilemma in a letter to Halsey: "I have now accumulated 35 second lieutenants in various stages of advanced training. . . . If ComAirBatFor approves and you want some half-baked flyers, send me a dispatch to that effect." ComAirBatFor approved; Halsey directed Rowell to push half-baked flyers out to squadrons like VMF-221.[31]

Halsey's decision triggered a sequence of transfers that diluted marine squadrons over the short term. As inexperienced aviators reported to advance bases, experienced aviators departed to Hawaii and California to form new squadrons. VMF-221 lost two majors and gained one, lost six captains and gained two, lost three first lieutenants and a gunner and gained none, and gained sixteen second lieutenants. Despite all its flying at Midway, the give-and-take left VMF-221 with a far less experienced cohort at the end of May.[32]

Before Major Bauer departed in February, he characterized Midway as "an ideal spot to train a new squadron."[33] However, several factors prevented VMF-221 from maximizing the opportunity. From December 1941 through May 1942, the squadron flew 219 patrols and 32 calibration flights, but only 49 gunnery practice missions and 75 flights practicing tactics.[34] The defense battalion marines relied on the calibration flights to integrate their radar and antiaircraft guns into an accurate defensive system. While patrols and calibration missions gave the pilots more hours, this was not the training *USF-74* delineated. Less than 30 percent of the flights were dedicated to improving fighter pilot lethality.[35]

The impact of these defensive duties on combat readiness was not lost on senior commanders. On 21 May 1942, Vice Adm. Wilson Brown Jr., Commander, Amphibious Force, Pacific Fleet, highlighted the inability of squadrons defending islands to train. Brown recommended that Nimitz subject these defensive assignments to Brown's approval and transfer three marine aircraft groups back to California to train.[36] However, events in May precluded Nimitz from releasing marine squadrons from Midway. The marines on Midway had to squeeze training flights in when other missions did not crowd out the flight schedule.

VMF-221 recognized the imperative of training its new pilots. An acceleration in training in April and May coincided with the arrival of the first two cohorts of second lieutenants. And though the squadron flew just ten gunnery sorties in each of these months, and several of these consisted of dummy runs due to a shortage of .50-caliber ammunition, the focus of gunnery training was on these new lieutenants.[37] Nonetheless, ten lieutenants who reported at the end of May had virtually no opportunity to train. According to Major McCaul, they were "fresh out of flight school."[38] These aviators flew familiarization hops on 27 and 28 May. The squadron conducted section and division tactics on 28 and 30 May that the inexperienced pilots likely joined.[39]

USF-74 included detailed instructions regarding escorts for bombers, but the two squadrons conducted little integrated training.[40] Wallace had instructed students at Quantico that fighters should protect the home base, and bombers should not expect fighters to escort them.[41] Wallace practiced what he preached, and VMF-221 did not practice escorting bombers.

Changing Commands and Commanders

The rapid expansion of marine aviation also brought changes in organization and leadership. On 1 March, Wallace's detachment became MAG-22. The Marine Corps bisected the two Midway squadrons that same date, assigning half of VMF-221's pilots, aircraft, and ground crew to the new VMF-222 under Captain Haynes. The SB2Us and personnel of VMSB-231 were divided into two new scout-bomber squadrons, VMSB-241 and VMSB-242; VMSB-231 was reconstituted at Ewa Field. The seaplane tender USS *Curtis* (AV 4) delivered eight F2A-3s on 28 March, bringing the group's strength to twenty-one fighters.[42]

The plan to build up all four squadrons on Midway was short-lived. On 12 April, all VMF-222's aircraft and personnel except Captain Haynes, Captain Dobbin, and twenty-two marines rejoined VMF-221. Captain Haynes and his marines returned to Ewa Field to form VMF-222 there. VMSB-241 absorbed VMSB-242's aircraft and personnel. Going forward, MAG-22 consisted of VMF-221 and VMSB-241.[43]

In a final flurry of changes, the Marine Corps replaced all three commanders. On 17 April, Maj. Lofton R. Henderson took command of VMSB-241.[44] On 19 April, McCaul turned VMF-221 over to Captain Neefus and moved up to MAG-22 as its executive officer.[45] On 20 April, Maj. Ira L. Kimes relieved Wallace as the group commander, and Wallace returned to Ewa to command MAG-23.[46]

On 16 May, Maj. Floyd B. Parks took command of VMF-221 from Neefus, who also departed for Ewa. Parks had served as a destroyer sailor before earning an appointment to the Naval Academy. He had played water polo at the academy and served as a seagoing marine before earning his wings in 1937. Since then, Parks had flown bombers and fighters and instructed at Pensacola. His academy yearbook described him as a good-humored charmer, more interested in girls than academics. It also indicated he earned a "Black N" sweater, an article awarded unofficially to midshipmen who committed severe disciplinary infractions.[47]

Parks may not have shed his casual attitude toward regulations by May 1942. On his first morning alert, after receiving the order to stand down, Parks taxied out of his revetment instead, accelerated down the runway, and took off. Perplexed, the group assumed the worst, and the garrison went to red alert. Major McCaul grabbed the phone and called the duty officer at VMF-221, Lieutenant Carl, who could not explain why Parks had taken off. McCaul ordered Carl to have Parks report to group operations as soon as he landed. After completing a short circumnavigation of the atoll, Parks landed and duly reported to McCaul. His excuse was that he did not believe in warming up an aircraft without flying it, but he also ceased the unscheduled hops.[48]

The Perils of Overwater Flight

Ocean patrols provided the pilots considerable experience with overwater navigation. In 1942, navy and marine fighters and dive-bombers had only a rudimentary radio navigation system, the YE-ZB homing system. A pilot equipped with a ZB receiver could determine the course to the YE beacon based on the combination of Morse code letters he was receiving. He could then "fly the beam" back to his base or carrier. The system was effective out to 275 miles for an aircraft at 15,000 feet. Because it used a double-modulated VHF signal, the Japanese were unable to exploit the system with direction finders.[49]

Keeping up with navigation was difficult enough in a one-man aircraft on patrol. Without the YE-ZB system, a fighter pilot might well survive a disorienting dogfight and yet lose track of the course home. Once out of sight of land, a pilot relied on dead reckoning, which required him to estimate his position by calculating the distance and azimuth flown since his last known position. He had to factor in variables such as wind speed, which experienced aviators estimated from the direction and appearance of waves.[50]

Final Preparations for Battle

The aircraft transport USS *Kitty Hawk* (AKV 1), which brought the final cohort of lieutenants on 26 May, also brought seven F4F-3 Wildcats. As *Kitty Hawk* could not recover or launch aircraft at sea, she had hoisted the aircraft aboard at Pearl Harbor and then craned them onto the pier at Sand Island at Midway. Marines rolled the aircraft over to the seaplane apron and gassed them up. Pilots conducted short-field takeoffs from the tiny apron, flew the short distance across the lagoon, and landed on Eastern Island. As Captain Carey and two members of his division, Captain Carl and Captain McCarthy, had flown F4F-3s, Major Parks assigned the Wildcats to Carey.[51] *Kitty Hawk* also delivered sixteen SBD-2s for VMSB-241 and a platoon of light tanks, a 3-inch antiaircraft group, and two companies of marine raiders assigned to the defense battalion. This reinforcement brought MAG-22's strength to 28 fighters (21 F2A-3s and 7 F4F-3s in VMF-221) and 36 dive-bombers (19 SBD-2s and 17 SB2U-3s in VMSB-241).[52]

Although VMF-221 had just received a significant reinforcement of aircraft and aviators, the squadron did not fly any training missions the first three days of June. VMSB-241's pilots did not even have the opportunity to get check rides in their new SBD-2s because MAG-22 curtailed training due to a shortage of fuel.[53]

McCaul's fuel headaches had begun on 22 May. In an act of extraordinary short-sightedness, someone had ordered emergency destruction demolition charges placed at the underground fuel storage on Sand Island. When one of the defense battalion batteries fired its 11-inch guns, sixteen of the island's thirty-one fuel tanks erupted in a spectacular explosion. Although no one was injured, the station lost 375,000 gallons of precious aviation fuel, and the blast destroyed the pipeline to Eastern Island.[54] A marine gunner named Dorn E. Arnold—whom the Marine Corps official history asserts was "exonerated on the spot of any responsibility for the mishap"—obtusely commented, "Well, that proves that the damn thing works, anyway."[55]

Eastern Island's storage capacity was about 165,000 gallons: 100,000 in the main stowage system, 51,000 in a reserve tank, and about 14,000 gallons in 55-gallon drums. After the 22 May explosion, sailors and marines on Sand

Island had to pump fuel into a 15,000-gallon barge, float the barge across the lagoon, and then pump the fuel up into Eastern Island's main stowage system. McCaul recorded that daily fuel consumption leapt from 3,000 gallons on 26 May to 15,000 the following day. The spike was due not to VMF-221's training flights but to scouting patrols by eleven PBY-5 Catalinas of Patrol Squadron 44 (VP-44). During the last three days of May, the arrival of four army air force B-26 Marauders, seventeen B-17 Flying Fortress bombers, and sixteen amphibious PBY-5As at Eastern Island, and their incorporation into the naval air station's patrols, spiked fuel consumption even higher. The barge shuttled fuel day and night. McCaul nervously monitored the island's fuel supply. After the new arrivals guzzled 65,000 gallons on 31 May, Eastern Island's supply dropped to 21,000 gallons—not enough for a full day's operations. A resupply ship offloaded 165,000 gallons and averted a crisis, but the fuel arrived in drums. Half the group's marines and many of the raiders Nimitz had sent to Midway pumped fuel by hand into the army air force, navy, and marine aircraft.[56]

3

★ ★ ★

Battle of Midway, June 1942

By the end of May, army air force, navy, and marine aircraft crowded Eastern Island. Their arrival left little doubt among the garrison that their commanders expected trouble.

Plans and Final Preparations

Admiral Nimitz had inspected Midway's defenses on 2 May. During the visit he took a few minutes to pin medals on Captain Neefus, Captain McCarthy, and Lieutenant Somers for shooting down the Mavis on 10 March.[1] But Nimitz had not flown to Midway to pat fighter pilots on the back; he had come to ensure that Midway could repel invaders.[2]

By 15 May, Cdr. Joseph Rochefort, in charge of the code-breaking Combat Intelligence Unit at Pearl Harbor, had convinced Nimitz that the Japanese planned to attack Midway with at least four carriers.[3] Though Nimitz had already intended to reinforce Midway as a result of his inspection, the alarming intelligence accelerated *Kitty Hawk*'s departure.[4]

On 20 May, Commander Simard received a warning from his immediate superior, Rear Adm. David W. Bagley, the commandant of the 14th Naval District. Bagley warned Simard that Midway would be attacked after 25 May, possibly around 30 May during the full moon. He informed Simard that he was reinforcing Midway and charged him to "give them hell." Bagley did not mention the role Midway's aircraft should play in the coming battle.[5]

That same day, Nimitz sent King a message with his thoughts on land-based aircraft drawn from the recent Battle of the Coral Sea. He had concluded that the task force commander at sea and the land-based air commander ashore should coordinate operations, with land-based air supporting the task force at sea with fighter protection and strikes.[6]

Nimitz incorporated these views in his planning guidance to his staff. On 23 May, Nimitz wrote to his chief of staff, Capt. Milo F. Draemel, "Midway planes must thus make the CV's [aircraft carriers] their objective, rather than attempting any local defense of the atoll."[7] In an undated memorandum likely written about the same time, Nimitz reiterated his intent to Capt. Arthur C. Davis, his air officer: "Balsa's [Midway's] air force must be employed to inflict prompt and early damage to Jap carrier flight decks if recurring attacks are to be stopped. Our objectives will be first—their flight decks rather than attempting to fight off the initial attacks on Balsa. . . . If this is correct, Balsa air force . . . should go all out for the carriers . . . leaving to Balsa's guns the first defense of the field."[8]

Nimitz laid out his plan to ambush the Japanese fleet in Operation Plan 29-42, issued on 27 May 1942. The Pacific Fleet was "to prevent the capture and occupation of Midway by enemy forces." Task forces organized around the aircraft carriers USS *Yorktown* (CV 5), USS *Enterprise* (CV 6), and USS *Hornet* (CV 8) would take position northeast of Midway to "inflict maximum damage on enemy."[9]

The tasks Nimitz assigned to Captain Simard are revealing. Simard's ultimate task was to hold Midway. To support the task forces at sea, Simard was to conduct aerial searches and inflict the maximum possible damage on the enemy. But Nimitz also admonished Simard to take every precaution to guard against the destruction of his own forces on Midway.[10] The order from Pacific Fleet, discussions between Nimitz and his senior commanders, and memoranda between Nimitz and his staff reveal conflicting priorities for Simard and the joint air force on Midway. They also suggest contradictions in the intent Nimitz expressed for the coming battle. Was Nimitz's intent for Midway's air force to "inflict maximum damage" or was it to "prevent the capture and occupation of Midway"? The very explicit language Nimitz used in memoranda to his staff—that Midway's aircraft "should go all out for the carriers . . . leaving to Balsa's guns the first defense of the field"—is not reflected in his operations order. How Simard and Kimes understood Nimitz's intent would significantly influence how they employed VMF-221.

Though Nimitz may have shorted Simard on guidance, he was generous with aircraft. Simard commanded an armada of 122 aircraft, more than the captain of an aircraft carrier: 17 B-17s, 4 B-26s, 31 PBYs, 6 navy TBFs, 28 marine fighters, and 36 marine dive-bombers. On 30 May, Nimitz placed all aircraft on Midway under Simard's tactical control, with Cdr. Logan C. Ramsey acting as Simard's air operations officer. Nimitz also sent Simard a naval base air defense detachment to help coordinate the defense of Midway.[11]

Ramsey's ability to coordinate this large air force from the naval air station command post on Sand Island was limited. According to McCaul, the marines "ran their own show" on Eastern Island. The marine aircraft group did not command the army air force bombers and navy torpedo planes. The marines provided the visitors with services such as refueling and minor maintenance, but tactical direction of these aircraft came from Ramsey on Sand Island, often via the MAG-22 command post and out to the flight line by messenger. Neither Simard nor Kimes appears to have attempted to integrate the army air force bombers, navy torpedo planes, and marine aircraft group into a cohesive force.[12]

On Eastern Island, bulldozers scraped revetments out of the coral for the B-17s and PBY-5As. But the marines quickly ran out of space on the small island and had to park excess aircraft wherever they could. Two revetments were designated rapid rearming and refueling points for fighters. Marines dug additional bunkers with overhead protection for themselves and aircrews. To augment the defense battalion's antiaircraft guns, the marine squadrons emplaced eight water-cooled .50-caliber machine guns. Marines affixed spare air-cooled .50- and .30-caliber aviation machine guns through holes drilled in the top of fuel drums. Each squadron formed a provisional rifle company to augment the raiders. Though exhausted from servicing all the extra aircraft and fortifying the airfield, the ground side of MAG-22 was ready to fight.[13]

The navy's code-breakers had not been resting while the marines prepared for battle. On 26 May, Rochefort's team concluded that the Japanese did not plan to attack Midway until 4 June.[14] This intelligence was passed to Simard and his marines.[15]

The PBYs had begun patrolling on 14 May. The searches paid off on 3 June at 0904. The ships they discovered were too far away for the marines' aircraft to strike them but were within the range of the B-17s and PBYs. Simard launched daylight strikes with six B-17s followed up with four PBYs after dark. Though the army air force bombers claimed hits, not one ship suffered damaged. A torpedo dropped by a PBY in the night attack damaged a Japanese tanker. Thus ended the first day of the battle.[16]

MAG-22's plan for 4 June assumed Sand Island's radar would provide sufficient warning. Prior to dawn, the two marine squadrons would warm up their aircraft. VMF-221 would launch six fighters to protect the PBYs and B-17s during takeoff. Once the bombers and patrol aircraft were on their way, the six fighters would recover, refuel, and wait. If the radar detachment reported unidentified aircraft, the command post would alert VMF-221 and VMSB-241 by siren, mast signal, and telephone to scramble. The fighters would take off first and get an intercept command by radio. The dive-bombers would rendezvous twenty miles east of the atoll and stand by to attack Japanese carriers. Either MAG-22 would vector the dive-bombers to their targets by radio, or the dive-bombers would follow the Japanese aircraft back to their carriers. The dive-bombers would attack without a protective escort because every fighter would be engaged in intercepting the incoming Japanese strike.[17]

Major Parks organized VMF-221's twenty-eight fighters into five divisions. Parks, Capt. Daniel J. Hennessy, and Capt. Kirk Armistead led divisions of six F2A-3s. Capt. Robert E. Curtin led the remaining three F2A-3s, and Captain Carey led the seven F4F-3 Wildcats.[18]

First light at Eastern Island would come at about 0500 on 4 June. The skies over Midway would be partly cloudy and clearing, with visibility between twelve and thirty miles. The Japanese carriers to the northwest would enjoy concealment offered by the cloudier conditions and occasional rain squalls—as would American search and strike planes.[19]

At 0355, Captain Carey's division of F4F-3s, short one Wildcat, took off and provided cover for the PBY-5As and B-17s. Kimes' plan soon began to unravel. Captain Carl's section joined up with Carey and his wingman, but Captain McCarthy's section had radio trouble and did not. Carey and the three F4F-3s with him landed at 0500 while McCarthy continued to patrol with his wingman, 2nd Lt. Roy A. Corry Jr.[20]

At 0520, a PBY reported enemy carriers 180 miles from Midway. MAG-22 alerted its aircrews to man their aircraft and warm up their engines. At 0555, Midway's radar detected a large Japanese strike on a bearing of 310 degrees at 93 miles and 11,000 feet. MAG-22's siren wailed.[21]

VMF-221, 4 June 1942

"There was no briefing, no coordination," Captain Carl recalled. "Just a mad scramble to get out from under whatever was inbound."[22] In Carey's division, 2nd Lt. Walter W. Swansberger's F4F-3 slid into a dugout. Wildcats and Buffalos taxied from their revetments and accelerated down Eastern Island's airstrip, many nearly colliding at the intersection of the two runways. Armistead's division, at the end of Runway 2, did not hear the siren over their engine noise and did not move until the squadron duty officer drove up in a truck and passed the order. Armistead took off at 0602. Swansberger, extracted from the dugout by some marines, joined Armistead's division twenty miles from Midway.[23]

VMF-221 had gotten airborne quickly, but not at full strength and not according to plan. One F2A-3 and one F4F-3 were not airworthy. McCarthy and Corry were still patrolling, unaware of the air raid. The engine of 2nd Lt. Charles S. Hughes' F2A-3 sounded rough, and he headed back hoping for a quick repair and relaunch. Second Lt. William V. Brooks struggled to keep up with Hennessy's division, unaware that his landing gear would not fully retract. Second Lt. William B. Sandoval's F2A-3 also lagged behind Hennessy's division.[24]

At 0605, MAG-22's fighter direction team ordered Parks' division of five Buffalos, Carey's division of three Wildcats, and Curtin's division of two Buffalos to intercept the inbound air strike, now reported on a bearing of 310 degrees at 12,000 feet. The group ordered Hennessy and Armistead, each leading a division of six Buffalos, out on the same bearing but to hold ten miles from Midway in case radar detected another strike.[25] Visibility was excellent, with low-lying puffy clouds below and scattered cumulus high above.[26]

When McCarthy and Corry finally heard the reports of enemy aircraft, they were low on fuel and requested instructions. The Japanese had closed to thirty-five miles. MAG-22 ordered them to refuel and take off again. The two F4F-3s landed and taxied into the squadron's rearming and refueling pits. They took off at 0625 and headed into the fight.[27]

Carey was left with just three F4F-3s. The Wildcats circled for altitude. Each pilot reached down and pulled the charging handles on either side of his cockpit, cocking the four .50-caliber wing guns in turn. Carey had reached 14,000 feet when he spotted the Japanese formation at 0615.[28]

The Japanese strike consisted of 108 aircraft—almost as many as Midway's air force totaled. The strike included 36 Val dive-bombers and 36 Kate carrier attack aircraft from *Hiryū* and *Sōryū*, and 36 Zero fighters, 9 from each carrier. Lieutenant Joichi Tomonaga, the commander of *Hiryū*'s air group, led the strike from his Kate. Each 18-plane squadron flew within a vee of vees 440–880 yards in length. All aircraft flew in three-plane sections, Zero and Val squadrons in two nine-plane divisions and Kate squadrons in three six-plane divisions. The two squadrons of Kates led at 12,000 feet, with the Vals following, and the Zeros farther back and above them at 14,000 feet.[29]

Carey radioed to the squadron, "Tally ho, large formation of bombers!" And then added, "Accompanied by fighters!" He rolled inverted and executed a high side gunnery run from the right against one of the Val squadrons. Second Lt. Clayton M. Canfield followed. Carey targeted the lead Val and saw it explode in a fireball. Canfield engaged the third aircraft in the third section and watched it explode. Carey and Canfield dove through the formation and pulled up to position for a second overhead pass. During their second attack, a tail gunner's burst ripped through Carey's cockpit, smashing his right knee and piercing his left leg. Zeros caught up to the pair, and the marines hustled for a cloud five miles away. They evaded the Zeros and headed back to Midway.[30]

Carl, who had been unable to keep up with Carey, heard Carey's "Tally ho!" and watched Carey and Canfield attack. Carl made a high side gunnery

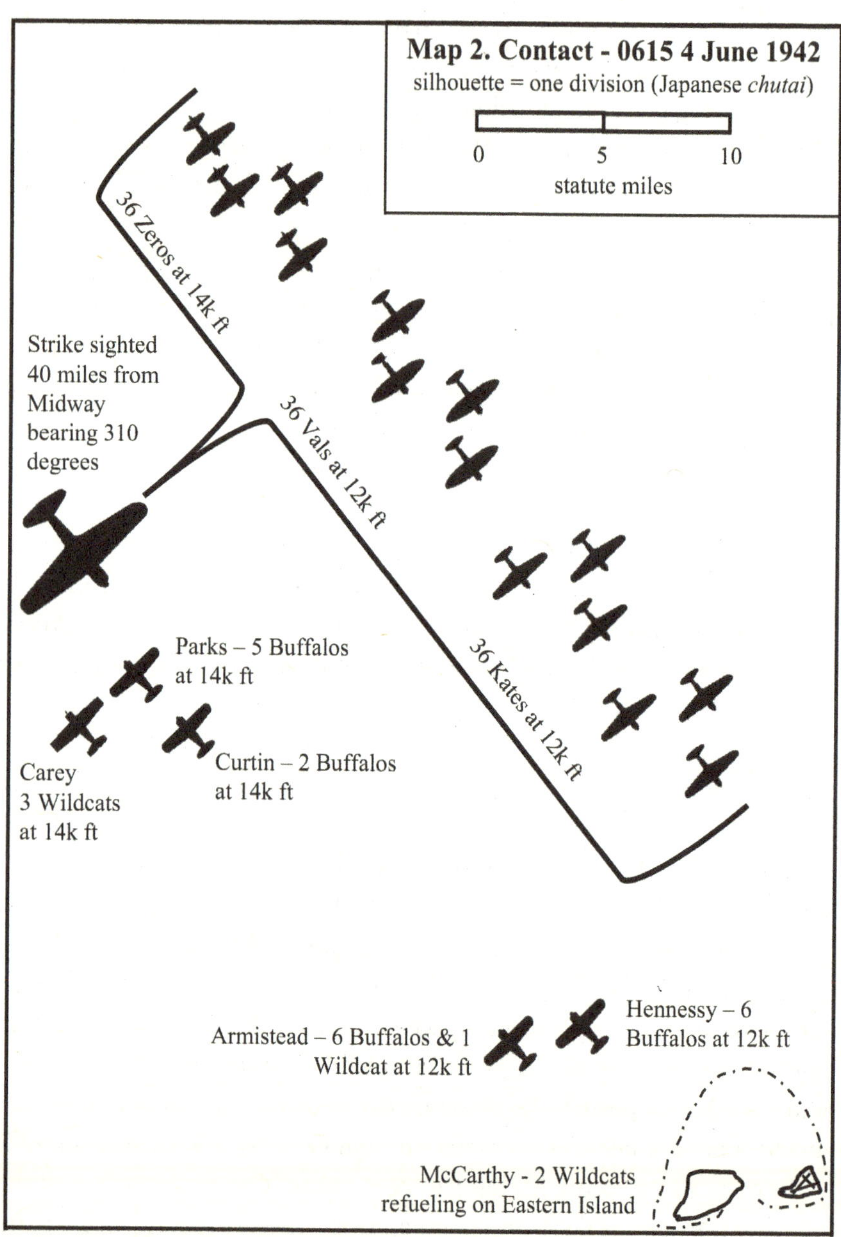

MAP 2. Contact—0615, 4 June 1942

pass on one of the Zeros, intercepting it. He fired as the target filled his gunsight, and then dove through the formation of bombers with several Zeros in pursuit. He continued diving to elude them, rolled 180 degrees, and headed away from Midway alone, reasoning the fighters would stay with the bombers.[31]

Carl climbed to 20,000 feet and started working his radio. Shortly he spotted another Zero on his tail. As the Zero chased him, firing bursts, Carl ducked into a cloud. He cut his throttle, stomped on his rudder, and threw the control stick in the opposite direction. The skid abruptly decelerated his Wildcat. The Zero overshot him and dove. Carl dove after it, but the negative gravitational force of his manezuver had fouled his ammunition belts. The Zero sped away while Carl manually cleared his guns.[32]

As he was arriving back at Midway near the end of the engagement, Carl spotted three Zeros below him. He made a diving gunnery run on one unsuspecting pilot and sent the Zero spinning into the ocean. The other two fighters did not appear to notice. When Carl recovered from his run, they had disappeared.[33]

Parks' five Buffalos engaged at nearly the same time as Carey's division. Parks commenced an overhead attack from 14,000 feet. Captain Curtin's division of two Buffalos had followed Parks up and attacked immediately thereafter.[34] These first seven Buffalos may have surprised the Japanese, whose accounts suggest that *Hiryū* lost at least three Kates to this initial gunnery pass.[35]

Before Parks' division could begin its second pass, the Zeros engaged. Only 2nd Lt. Darrell D. Irwin, Curtin's wingman, survived the action, and exactly how the other six pilots died is unclear. It is clear these seven fighters drew the attention of a large fraction of the thirty-six Zeros escorting the bombers. Irwin escaped by diving away and speeding back to Midway at full throttle, five hundred feet above the waves. Two Zeros took turns peppering the armored plate behind his seat. Irwin landed his rugged Buffalo amid the bombs falling on Eastern Island with Zeros still making passes at him.[36]

MAG-22 waited until 0624 to direct Hennessy and Armistead into the fight.[37] The two divisions did not attempt to coordinate their attacks.

Hennessy led his division to 15,000 feet and intercepted the formation of Kates. Armistead spotted the formation of Vals and climbed to position his division up-sun and well above them.[38]

Hennessy led his six Buffalos in an overhead gunnery attack on the Kates. It appears that all but one of Hennessy's division were shot down during or shortly after their first gunnery run.[39]

Bullets struck the right wing of Capt. Herbert T. Merrill's Buffalo and blasted his instrument panel as he pulled out of his dive. He dove and headed toward Midway. Zeros pursued him and struck his aircraft on two more passes. Merrill's aircraft caught fire, and he either jumped or was blown clear of the flaming aircraft. He got his parachute open before landing in the ocean, swam toward the atoll for two hours, and climbed onto the reef, where a PT boat found him.[40]

Captain White was climbing to make his third overhead pass when he spied a Zero climbing to get on his tail. "I rushed my stick forward as hard as I could," he recalled, "and went into a violent dive. When I recovered and looked around, I had lost the Zero Fighter." White heard the fighter direction center report an enemy aircraft departing on heading 310 degrees. White soon spotted it, a Val dive-bomber at just one thousand feet. White conducted a high side gunnery pass and watched the dive-bomber turn gently to its left and crash into the sea. White spotted another Val and may have damaged it before exhausting his ammunition.[41]

Armistead's six Buffalos, reinforced by Swansberger in an F4F-3, attacked the vee of dive-bombers from 17,000 feet. Armistead made a straight-in approach from directly ahead of the formation. Diving fast and at a steep angle, he targeted the leader of the fourth vee and watched his tracers pass through the Val and through the dive-bombers on the left side of the vee. Armistead looked back and saw two or three planes falling in flames.[42]

Capt. William C. Humberd followed Armistead into the attack and claimed one dive-bomber.[43] Second Lt. Charles M. Kunz aimed for a Val in the fifth division and watched it burst into flames and pull out of the formation. Swansberger followed Kunz; what became of him after that remains a mystery.[44] Sandoval and Brooks, who had lagged behind the division, made a gunnery run against the right flank of the fourth vee, claiming another dive-bomber.[45]

Armistead had begun to climb and position for another attack when he saw three fighters climbing steeply and very fast, gunning for him. Armistead commenced a violent split-S and dove. Three 20-mm cannon shells and about twenty 7.7-mm bullets ripped through his wings and engine cowling. His Buffalo corkscrewed, and he had difficulty controlling it. The Zeros did not pursue him, and he was able to slow down and level off.[46]

Humberd was starting his fourth approach when a loud bang and a large hole in the cowling of his aircraft alerted him to two Zeros behind him. He dove with one Zero in pursuit. Humberd stated afterward that he opened the distance between his F2A-3 and the pursuing Zero at full throttle until he had enough separation to whirl about and meet the Zero head-on. He claimed that he fired a long burst at three hundred yards and watched the Zero catch fire and crash.[47]

Kunz also attempted a second gunnery run, this time employing a high side approach. He set one Val on fire but then discovered a Zero tailing him. He dove and escaped, suffering a head wound and losing his radio and hydraulics to enemy bullets.[48] A pair of Zeros intercepted Brooks as he climbed to make a second attack. With his wheels still one-third extended, Brooks could not out-dive them. As they shot past him, he let loose a burst in their direction and then flew back to Midway, where the intense antiaircraft fire drove off the Zeros. While contemplating a landing, Brooks saw two aircraft apparently dogfighting. Despite his damaged, sluggish aircraft, he headed over to help out a fellow marine. When he neared the "dogfight," the aircraft—both Zeros—turned toward him. Brooks reported that he shook off one and fired a burst into the other as they passed him head-on. He spied another two Japanese fighters attacking a Buffalo and raced across the island to help but was too late. He watched the F2A-3 crash into the sea.[49]

The last marine fighters to get into the battle were the F4F-3s flown by McCarthy and Corry.[50] Corry's account is succinct and to the point. Eight Zeros intercepted them before they could climb to the bombers' altitude. Corry reported afterward that McCarthy shot down one fighter and then

Corry shot one off McCarthy's tail. The two Wildcats separated, and McCarthy was never seen again. Despite enemy fighters relentlessly shooting up his Wildcat and puncturing his fuel tanks, Corry claimed he shot down a lone Val near Eastern Island before he landed.[51]

Ten minutes after McCarthy and Corry had taken off, the Kates attacked Eastern Island from the east. After the Kates completed bombing runs on Eastern and Sand Islands, the Vals circled in from the north, also attacking from the east. The fighters that had not expended all their ammunition against VMF-221 strafed the installation. The antiaircraft guns of the marine defense battalion and the aircraft group's machine guns erupted as the Japanese aircraft crossed the island. Midway presented a nightmare of flak and automatic weapons fire to the lower dive-bombers and fighters. Marines shot down at least three and perhaps as many as five attacking aircraft and damaged many more. Japanese who survived the battle reported the marines' "accuracy is excellent, and the anti-aircraft fire is intense."[52]

The bombing lasted from 0635 until 0710. Four 500-kilogram bombs and ten 250-kilogram bombs hit Eastern Island, destroying the power house, command post, mess hall, and post exchange; cutting the telephone line to Sand Island; and severing fuel lines. There were three craters in the runways. Most catastrophically for VMF-221, one bomb struck the rearming and refueling point. The detonation triggered a secondary explosion of eight 100-pound bombs and ten thousand rounds of .50-caliber machine-gun ammunition. The four marines who had just refueled McCarthy and Corry's Wildcats—Pfc. Maurice A. Belanger, Pfc. Robert L. Holsbo, Pfc. Robert E. Mowrey, and Pfc. Abraham Zuckerman—never had a chance. Pvt. William A. Burke perished when the power house was hit, and a VMSB-241 marine died when a bomb struck near the squadron's engineering tent.[53]

As the Japanese headed back toward their carriers, the battered fighters of VMF-221 began to land. Brooks was one of the first, pulling up with seventy-two holes in his aircraft and one in his left leg.[54] Armistead landed his Buffalo safely despite its damaged hydraulic system.[55] Humberd, also losing hydraulic fluid, lowered his wheels manually and landed without flaps.[56] Kunz had lost hydraulics and his radio, and was dizzy from his head wound, but he brought his Buffalo down and staggered off to the dispensary.[57] Of the

F4F-3s, Carey, bleeding severely from both legs, ground-looped spectacularly. Corry's fuel tanks were hemorrhaging, but he touched down before running out of fuel and without immolating himself.[58] Canfield landed safely without flaps, but his Wildcat's wheels collapsed.[59]

Captain Carl and Captain White landed, taxied back to their revetments, and filled up with gas and ammunition. Though he could not raise his landing gear, Captain Humberd likewise rearmed and refueled. The three took off again before MAG-22 ordered them back.[60]

The Zeros had shot down thirteen of VMF-221's twenty-one F2A-3s and severely damaged another five. Two Wildcats were missing, and four were in no shape to fly. Of the three flyable fighters, one could not raise its landing gear. In his 1994 memoir, Carl described VMF-221 as "a shattered command" after the morning's combat. Not only had the squadron lost many aviators, but many of the survivors had lost confidence in their ability to go up against the Imperial Japanese Navy's fighters. "Our squadron fell apart," Carl recalled. "The senior surviving officer went to the first sergeant and asked if the NCO could run the outfit for the next few days. The career marine replied, 'Yes, sir,' as expected. With that, the senior captain walked out of the command post, went to a bomb shelter, and proceeded to get drunk. He had plenty of company."[61]

To a man, the fighter pilots had not hesitated to plunge into combat that morning. Fortunately, the rest of the day's action precluded any need to sortie their remaining two fighters.

VMSB-241, 4–6 June 1942

Immediately after VMF-221 sortied, the six TBFs from Torpedo Squadron Eight (VT-8) took off and headed alone toward the Japanese fleet.[62] The four B-26 Marauders, modified to drop torpedoes, took off next.[63] The navy and army air force bombers did not join up together or attempt a coordinated attack.[64] VMSB-241 took off last. Major Henderson, the squadron commander, led the sixteen SBD-2s. Maj. Benjamin W. Norris, the executive officer, led the twelve SB2U-3s. Both groups rendezvoused east of Eastern Island and then proceeded independently to intercept the carriers.[65]

The TBFs and B-26s both spotted the Japanese carriers shortly after 0700. The TBFs attacked *Hiryū* and *Sōryū* to the east. The B-26s attacked *Akagi*, more than three miles to the west. *Kaga*, several miles from *Akagi*, escaped attention. The four carriers had up to thirty-three fighters on combat air patrol. Unprotected by friendly fighters, Midway's TBFs and B-26s faced a string of gunnery runs by the nimble Zeros. The Zeros shot down five TBFs and damaged the sixth, killing one of its gunners. Two of the four B-26s escaped, both with holed fuselages and wounded crewmen. None scored a torpedo hit.[66]

The marine dive-bombers flew slower, took off later, and flew east before heading northwest, and so did not attack until half an hour after the B-26 and TBF attacks ended. When Henderson spotted the carriers about 0755, the combat air patrol had dropped to thirteen fighters.[67]

Henderson intended a glide-bomb attack from four thousand feet. At eight thousand feet, nine Zeros struck. The Japanese concentrated their fire against Henderson, and his SBD was quickly in flames. Capt. Elmer G. Glidden led the remaining SBDs into a cloud bank. When Glidden emerged, he spotted *Hiryū* below. The Zeros resumed their attacks as soon as the SBDs broke from the cloud cover. One by one, the marines released their bombs—and missed. Some came very close, fooling marines into thinking that they scored hits. But despite frightening *Hiryū*'s crew, this was a bloodless encounter. None of the marines' bombs struck the carrier, and none of the carrier's guns downed a dive-bomber. Air-to-air combat was a different matter. Six SBDs went down under the Japanese fighters' cannons.[68]

Before the SBDs completed their attack, fourteen B-17s arrived overhead. The B-17s dropped their loads from 20,000 feet, missing the ships but providing those aboard with a few more minutes of excitement.[69]

Major Norris and his eleven Vindicators were the last to arrive—after the SBD-2s had sped away but before the B-17s had completed their attack. The combat air patrol was twenty-six fighters strong upon their arrival and climbed to thirty-six by the time the last Vindicator ran for safety. At least three fighters completed gunnery passes before Norris commenced his attack. Starting from 13,000 feet, Norris dove through the clouds toward *Akagi*. When the dive-bombers emerged at 2,000 feet, there was no carrier below them. Instead, directly ahead was the battleship *Haruna*, which evaded every one of the marines' bombs. Like the SBDs before them, the SB2U-3s hugged the surface and set a course for Midway.[70]

Zeros had shot down four of the twelve SB2U-3s and eight of the sixteen SBD-2s, including Henderson. Just five SBDs and six SB2Us were still combat ready. On Eastern Island, meanwhile, marines filled in craters, bulldozed a Zero off the runway, and cobbled together a refueling system. VMSB-241 had suffered horrific losses but was still in the fight.[71]

While VMSB-241 was en route to the Japanese carriers and the Japanese air group was wrapping up its attack on Midway, the American carriers began launching their air groups. Roughly forty-five minutes after the last marine dive-bomber had fled, Japanese fighters and antiaircraft fire massacred the TBD Devastator torpedo bombers from all three carriers. The battle turned when SBD-3s from *Enterprise* and *Yorktown* arrived overhead. The dive-bombers scored fatal hits on three of the Japanese carriers, leaving only *Hiryū* untouched.[72]

For several hours, Midway's defenders had little idea of the battle's progress. At 1150, SBDs from *Hornet* landed, unable to reach their carrier after expending their fuel searching for the Japanese. This was the first indication for many of the island's marines that American carriers were nearby. At 1252 Midway learned *Yorktown* was under attack. To avoid being caught on the ground, the B-17s bypassed Midway and flew on to Oahu. "At this time," wrote Commander Ramsey, "things looked very black." The PBYs were ordered to prepare to withdraw to French Frigate Shoals, and the garrison began to wonder how soon Japanese battleships would appear over the horizon and blast their flimsy dugouts to smithereens.[73]

The two fleets traded carrier strikes that afternoon. *Hiryū*, the sole remaining Japanese carrier, had just thirty-eight operational aircraft: ten Zeros, eighteen Vals, and ten Kates. She would recover most of the twenty-seven fighters still aloft. *Hiryū* launched six fighters and all her dive-bombers against *Yorktown*, setting the American carrier ablaze just after noon. She launched a second strike at 1330 that included the remaining ten Kates and six Zeros. They hit *Yorktown* with two torpedoes, forcing her captain to order her abandoned.[74] Finally, at 1700, dive-bombers from *Enterprise* struck *Hiryū* with at least four 1,000-pound bombs, dooming the carrier.[75]

The mood in the Sand Island command post changed abruptly when Midway's patrol aircraft spotted the burning Japanese ships. At 1745, a PBY confirmed three carriers were burning.[76] Ramsey requested that MAG-22 attack them. Major Norris opted for a night attack, reasoning that burning ships would be easy to find in the dark and the danger from fighters and antiaircraft fire would be negligible. At 1905, Norris led a strike of five SB2U-3s and six SBD-2s into the moonless night. Squalls and low ceilings made visibility atrocious. The eleven dive-bombers found nothing. Ten dive-bombers returned safely, but Major Norris and his gunner did not.[77]

Through the night, MAG-22 marines, visiting raiders, and sailors from the PBY squadron hand-pumped 45,000 gallons from 55-gallon drums into aircraft. At 0630, a PBY reported two Japanese battleships 170 miles due west of Sand Island. MAG-22 ordered VMSB-241 to attack.[78]

The "battleships" were the cruisers *Mogami* and *Mikuma*, which had collided and were now trailing after the retreating Japanese fleet with an escort of two destroyers, within easy range of Midway.[79]

Captain Tyler, now leading VMSB-241, led the strike. The dive-bombers faced no fighters, but the cruisers' antiaircraft fire was heavy and accurate. All six SBDs dropped their bombs and swooped away, unhit but hitting nothing. The six SB2U-3s, gliding in from four thousand feet, presented an easier target. Capt. Richard E. Fleming released his bomb before his Vindicator burst into flames. The other five SB2U-3s dropped their bombs in close succession. One pilot claimed a hit, and several claimed near misses, but none hit either ship.[80]

Mogami and *Mikuma* escaped damage in a subsequent attack by B-17s. *Mikuma*'s luck ran out the following day. Strikes from *Enterprise* and *Hornet* damaged *Mogami* and crippled *Mikuma*. Fires raged, her torpedoes detonated, and she sank.[81]

The attack against the cruisers was MAG-22's last mission at Midway. As it became apparent the Pacific Fleet had achieved a spectacular victory, the marines turned their attention to counting the cost and writing their after-action reports.

4

★ ★ ★

VMF-221's Effectiveness at Midway

VMF-221's effectiveness at Midway can be assessed by an examination of the number of aircraft sortied, the number of enemy aircraft destroyed, the number of aircraft lost, and how well the squadron fulfilled the fleet commander's intent.

Sorties, Aerial Victories, and Aircraft Lost on 4 June

The squadron's sortie rate on 4 June was remarkably high. Twenty-six of VMF-221's twenty-eight fighters flew. As a full-strength squadron was normally allotted just eighteen aircraft, it is clear that the Marine Corps and the Pacific Fleet's Aircraft Battle Force had provided the squadron with an abundance of combat-ready aircraft and the marines, tools, parts, and supplies to maintain them.

The inability of VMF-221 to generate sorties after the first morning resulted from the high losses it sustained and the effect the fight had on its pilots. By 0800 on 4 June, the fighting squadron had just two combat-ready fighters: one F2A-3 and one F4F-3. A second F2A-3 could fly, but its wheels would not retract. MAG-22 did not order any fighters aloft for the remainder of the battle. The after-action reports of the group commander, group executive officer, and acting squadron commander are all silent on this decision, aside from expressing a lack of confidence in the F2A-3. Captain Armistead, who succeeded to command of VMF-221 as the senior survivor, assessed the F2A-3 as "sadly outclassed in all respects by the Japanese 00 (Zero) fighters."[1] The implication is that marine commanders believed ordering the two airworthy fighters into combat would amount to a suicide mission.

The evidence shows great discrepancies between the squadron's claims and Japanese aircraft actually lost. The variation is due not only to the difficulty of ascertaining victories in a few seconds of whirling action, but also to faulty calculus flavored by wishful thinking. Armistead's official report stated that he observed two groups of approximately forty dive-bombers each before VMF-221 began its attack. He further stated that a pilot from VMSB-241 on Eastern Island counted just eighteen bombers overhead during the strike. Though his pilots claimed only nine enemy aircraft destroyed, Armistead nonetheless reasoned that VMF-221 must have destroyed about fifty bombers in air-to-air combat.[2] Lieutenant Colonel Kimes used similar arithmetic to estimate Japanese losses at forty-three aircraft, which he admitted included "probable victories by missing fighter pilots" as well as claims by the tail gunners of VMSB-241.[3]

Japanese sources present a much lower number. Admiral Chūichi Nagumo's report admits just five aircraft lost to marine fighters on 4 June and eight more to tail gunners and U.S. carrier fighters. Naval historians John Parshall and Anthony Tully, after scrutinizing Japanese air group records, credited VMF-221 with just three aerial victories and credited another five to Midway's antiaircraft gunners. Parshall and Tully also noted sixteen aircraft that returned to their carrier but then ditched or landed but were too damaged to fly again.[4] The loss of these sixteen aircraft occurred out of sight of marine aviators and thus does not constitute aerial victories, but their loss nevertheless significantly reduced Japanese combat power at a critical time.

Hiryū suffered the most losses over Midway, with half of her twenty-four planes either shot down or recovered but too damaged to fly again. *Hiryū* was the only carrier to survive the U.S. carrier strike that morning, and thus was the only carrier to strike back. Her first strike included six fighters and eighteen dive-bombers. Her second strike, that afternoon, included just ten

Kates and six Zeros. VMF-221 and marine antiaircraft fire had removed ten of *Hiryū*'s Kates from the fight in the morning, cutting the potential strength of her second strike by half. The marines did not shoot down nearly as many aircraft as they claimed, but those they did eliminate from the fight were ones that mattered to the U.S. fleet—those from *Hiryū*.

When these Japanese losses are considered against the marines' losses, there is no doubt that VMF-221 got the worst of the fight. Twenty-three marine fighters had been shot down or were too damaged to continue, whereas the marine fighters had shot down or inflicted a mission kill on at best nineteen Japanese aircraft.

VMF-221 and the Fleet Commander's Intent

A marine squadron's effectiveness depends upon how it accomplishes the fleet commander's intent. Admiral Nimitz's intent at Midway is reflected in memoranda to his staff and in his operations order. Nimitz wrote explicitly that Midway's aircraft "should go all out for the carriers."[5] In his operations order, Nimitz directed Captain Simard to hold Midway but also to "inflict maximum damage on enemy, particularly carriers, battleships, and transports."[6]

Midway held. The marine aircraft group had not gone all out for the carriers, instead holding its fighters for the defense of Midway and failing to hit a single enemy ship. But an evaluation of VMF-221's effectiveness requires a deeper understanding of why Midway held and how MAG-22's modest performance contributed to the Pacific Fleet's destruction of the Japanese carriers.

The Japanese strike inflicted considerable damage to Naval Air Station Midway but did not neutralize it. VMF-221's interception disrupted the Japanese formation and brought down a few bombers. Midway suffered no more strikes because the threat to Midway evaporated when the Japanese lost their carriers. Nimitz's objective of holding Midway was accomplished with the destruction of the Japanese carriers, as was his intent to inflict maximum damage on the enemy fleet. MAG-22 played a minor but helpful role in the series of events that led to the destruction of those carriers.

As Parshall and Tully showed, the series of attacks from Midway that began shortly after 0700 and continued until sometime after 0830 helped create conditions that delayed the Japanese strike against the American carriers and made the Japanese carriers more vulnerable to subsequent attacks. Over these ninety minutes, the Japanese carriers maneuvered violently to dodge attacks by navy TBFs, army B-17s and B-26s, and VMSB-241's dive-bombers. Forty-five minutes after these attacks subsided, torpedo planes from the American carriers began their tragic attacks. Defending against these attacks required the carriers to launch and then recover fighters. Perhaps as important, the persistent attacks presented Nagumo and his staff with a series of menacing dilemmas that complicated their decision-making. All of these factors disrupted preparations for Nagumo's counterstrike. When the dive-bombers from *Enterprise* and *Yorktown* appeared overhead, the Kates and Vals were still on the hangar decks—fueled, armed, and waiting to spot on the flight deck for the strike against the U.S. carriers. These aircraft were not only lost in the resulting fires and explosions, but their fuel and ordnance amplified the destructive power of the American bombs.[7]

The damage MAG-22 directly inflicted on Japanese ships and aircraft was disappointing. Some of VMF-241's bombs aimed at *Hiryū* struck frightfully close. Had marine fighters protected the dive-bombers during their attacks, limiting the interference of the Japanese combat air patrol, VMF-241's aim might have improved. Missing *Hiryū* early in the day was a lost opportunity that cost the Pacific Fleet *Yorktown*.

But the cumulative impact of the marine, army air force, and navy aircraft launched from Midway and the torpedo squadrons launched from the carriers contributed indirectly to the destruction of the four Japanese carriers. As discussed above, the few Japanese aircraft that did strike the American carriers all flew from *Hiryū*, the one carrier unscathed that morning. VMF-221's fighters and the 6th Defense Battalion's antiaircraft guns had halved *Hiryū*'s torpedo-bomber strength, contributing directly to the protection of the American carriers.

Contributing Factors

Among the factors contributing to marine aviation's performance at Midway were the number and types of aircraft employed, doctrine and tactics, training and experience, command and control, intelligence and early warning, logistics, time, and Japanese capabilities.

Number and Types of Aircraft

MAG-22 started the battle with sixty-four aircraft, an abundant allocation. After it was clear in mid-May that Midway was threatened, the Pacific Fleet reinforced the aircraft group. *Kitty Hawk* delivered seven F4F-3s and sixteen SBD-2s on 26 May. It is worth examining whether the group might have received even more.

The Marine Corps had more squadrons that could have reinforced MAG-22. MAG-21 and MAG-23 at Ewa had at least three fighting squadrons and three scout-bomber squadrons between them, though their combat readiness was likely inferior to that of the squadrons at Midway.[8] In any case, reinforcing MAG-22 was not a simple operation.

Getting the aircraft to Midway would have been difficult but possible. The six TBFs that reached Midway on 1 June had flown from Oahu. This suggests the Pacific Fleet had no ships available to ferry aircraft to Midway. VMSB-231 made the flight in December 1941 in SB2U-3s. F2A-3s, F4F-3s, and SBD-2s could fly farther than Vindicators, and MAG-21 and MAG-23 could have reinforced MAG-22 by overwater flight.

Whether Midway could have accommodated more marine squadrons is another matter. Eyewitness accounts indicate Eastern Island had no room for additional aircraft on 4 June. Adding additional marine aircraft would have required Midway to offset that with a reduction in other types of aircraft.

This raises the issue of aircraft type. In their statements, the surviving marine fighter pilots highlighted the inferiority of their aircraft and gave the F2A-3s scathing reviews, as noted below.

Capt. Kirk Armistead: "The Zero Fighter is faster in level flight than the F2A-3. It is much more maneuverable than the F2A-3. It can outclimb the F2A-3. It has more fire power than the F2A-3."[9] In the final paragraph of the squadron's after-action report, Armistead concluded, "The F2A-3 is sadly out-classed in all respects by the Japanese (Zero) Fighters."[10]

Capt. John Carey: "The 'Zero' fighters out-maneuvered, out-performed and out-climbed the Brewsters and Grummans in [every] respect. The only advantage the Brewsters and Grummans [had] was in armor."[11]

Lt. Roy Corry: "The [Zero] fighter is by far the most maneuverable plane that exists at the present time. You cannot compare them with our service type ships."[12]

Capt. William Humberd: "Frankly, I think the F2A-3 does not compare with their type [Zero] fighters whatsoever."[13]

Lt. Charles Kunz: "As for the F2A-3 [or Brewster trainer], it should be in Miami as a training plane, rather than be used as a first line fighter."[14]

Lt. John O. Musselman: "What action I witnessed brought out the superiority of the Japanese [Zero] Fighter over our F2As and F4Fs."[15]

Lt. Hyde Phillips: "Brewsters and Grummans were no match for the Zero Fighters."[16]

Capt. Philip R. White: "The F2A-3 is not a combat airplane. It is inferior to the planes we were fighting in every respect. The F2A-3 has about the same speed as an Aichi 99 Dive-bomber. The Japanese Zero Fighter can run circles around the F2A-3. I estimated the top speed of a Zero Fighter, from what I saw, at better than 450 mile per hour. It is my belief that any commander that orders pilots out for combat in a F2A-3 should consider the pilot as lost before leaving the ground."[17]

Lieutenant Colonel Kimes was persuaded. In his 7 June report, Kimes concluded, "[I]t is recommended that F2A-3 and F4F-3 type airplanes be not assigned as equipment for use in combat but be retained for use at training centers only."

If Kimes was right, this was not good news for naval aviation. The next generation of fighters was a year away. The inferiority of marine aircraft troubled Nimitz to the extent that he recommended equipping marine squadrons with army aircraft.

> It has been our practice to complement Marine fighter squadrons on shore with planes of carrier type. This results in a distinct and unwarranted reduction in performance and ability to combat the enemy. Having adequate ground facilities, the Marine VF squadrons ought to be furnished

> with the very best fighting planes available to the country. Because of the limitations which carrier operation imposes on Naval planes, suitable fighters will naturally be Army air force types.[18]

In other words, Nimitz was ready to forgo marine aviation's ability to perform its secondary mission—to serve as a reserve for carrier aviation—in order to provide the marines with more capable aircraft.

However, there is evidence that Kimes might have been wrong. Notwithstanding the opinions of his pilots, there is evidence that neither the F4F-3 nor even the F2A-3 was to blame for VMF-221's poor performance. Marine and navy pilots would achieve far better results with the F4F in other actions. Captain Carl, one of the few pilots who did not criticize his squadron's aircraft, and probably the only one who shot down a Zero, believed the F2A-3 was as maneuverable and fast as the F4F-3. The Buffalo was a less stable gunnery platform, but it was otherwise comparable with the Wildcat.

A breakdown of each fighter's performance reveals the pilots of VMF-221 had some justification for their low opinion of the F2A-3. Japanese fighters shot down two-thirds of the F2A-3s, but only one-third of the F4F-3s. Less objectively—as VMF-221 only shot down three Japanese aircraft over Midway—the six Wildcat pilots claimed six aerial victories whereas the twenty Buffalo pilots claimed only thirteen victories.

In contrast, Finnish Air Force F2A-1 Buffalos destroyed 496 Soviet aircraft from 1941 to 1945 while losing only 19.[19] The Soviet air force was not of the same quality as the Imperial Japanese Navy, but the Finns' experience suggests that the F2A-3's inferiority was not the sole contributing factor to VMF-221's poor performance.

Doctrine and Tactics

How navy and marine commanders chose to employ marine aviation significantly impacted the squadron's performance. Their decisions were to some extent influenced by doctrine, but they also resulted from poorly communicated intent by Nimitz and Midway's inability to coordinate large air operations.

MAG-22 withheld all its fighters to protect Midway, denying VMSB-241 fighter protection. Neither Naval Air Station Midway nor MAG-22 coordinated VMSB-241's strike with the army air force and navy bombers. VMSB-241 was unable to coordinate its SBD-2 and SB2U-3 attacks. These failures enabled Japanese fighters to defeat each attack in turn.

Following the policy Wallace had advocated in his Quantico lecture, MAG-22 employed its fighters in "general support" and allowed them to be "on the prowl." Wallace had emphasized "general support wherever and whenever possible."[20] Wallace had commanded MAG-22 until April, so this bias likely influenced Kimes' decision to retain VMF-221 in general support on 4 June. In stark contrast, both the Japanese and American carrier task forces allocated fighter escorts to their strikes on 4 June, even though carriers were far more vulnerable to air attack than an island base. Commanders at sea provided strikes with fighter protection to ensure they achieved results against the enemy's fleet.

Nimitz wanted Midway's aircraft to "go all out for the carriers." Keeping fighters in a general support role was not an "all out for the carriers" move. Nimitz's orders to Simard did not include his intent that he go "all out for the carriers." He tasked Simard to "hold MIDWAY," with "inflict maximum damage on enemy, particularly carriers" included among other tasks. Given the competing tasks without amplifying direction, and likely influenced by a marine commander advocating general support, it is unsurprising that Simard did not direct Kimes to provide fighter escorts to his bombers.

Training and Experience

Surprisingly, experienced pilots were shot down at nearly the same rate as inexperienced ones. Twenty-seven pilots from VMF-221 flew on 4 June. Fifteen were shot down. One pilot was recovered after bailing out; the other fourteen went missing. Another three were wounded but brought their aircraft back. Six of the eleven experienced pilots were shot down and a seventh was wounded. Nine of the sixteen inexperienced second lieutenants were shot down and another two were wounded.

The loss of experienced and inexperienced aviators at similar rates may reflect the interdependence between section leaders and their wingmen. Experienced section leaders had to rely on inexperienced wingmen for protection. Additionally, an experienced section leader might have to rush to aid an inexperienced wingman in a dangerous predicament, making himself vulnerable. Pairing unready pilots with experienced section leaders likely placed both pilots in jeopardy.

In their after-action reports the eleven experienced aviators claimed six aerial victories, whereas the fifteen second lieutenants claimed just three.[21] However, as marines' claims exceeded the number of Japanese planes shot down, this measure of performance is imprecise.

Nevertheless, inexperience likely undermined the squadron's collective performance. Lieutenant Colonel Kimes thought that inexperience retarded the performance of both squadrons. In his report of 7 June 1942 he recommended that "replacement pilots should, prior to leaving the mainland, be given a short transitional training course in modern service aircraft. Such a course should cover training in gunnery, bombing, instrument flying, and basic type tactics."[22]

Command and Control

MAG-22's improvised fighter direction center worked, but it was not state-of-the-art. The Japanese flew straight in at high altitude, simplifying radar detection and MAG-22's intercept problem. Kimes recommended the Marine Corps acquire superior radar similar to that used by the Royal Air Force.[23]

Aviation command had not gone well. Neither Naval Air Station Midway nor MAG-22 coordinated the aircraft on Eastern Island into a unified strike. Simard and Ramsey were located in the air station command post on Sand Island, while Kimes and McCaul ran the aircraft group from their command post on Eastern Island. Communication between the two command posts was primarily by telephone and, after the air raid, by radio.

Coordination between Midway and the American carriers was nonexistent. After the Battle of the Coral Sea in early May, Nimitz had identified a need for land-based air commanders to support the fleet with strikes and fighter protection.[24] The Pacific Fleet's experience at Midway suggests that capability was still beyond its grasp in mid-1942. The carrier task forces struggled to coordinate strikes between squadrons from the same carrier, much less with the marine aircraft group ashore, which was unaware of the carriers' positions and intentions. "We had no idea how they were faring as far as other forces in the vicinity were concerned, or what our forces afloat were doing," Kimes noted.[25]

Intelligence and Early Warning

U.S. naval intelligence performed superbly, providing the fleet commander with sufficient knowledge of the enemy's capabilities and intentions to achieve surprise and warn Midway. Scouting PBYs and B-17s located the enemy fleet. Midway's radar provided MAG-22 sufficient warning to scramble its fighters and attack aircraft. Although MAG-22 was plotting hundreds of aircraft at one point on 4 June, the group interpreted the information and directed its fighters to a successful interception.[26]

Had the Pacific Fleet relied on MAG-22 instead of PBYs to scout, it is doubtful the marines would have detected the Japanese task forces as early as the navy patrol bombers did. PBYs could fly 3,100 miles. F2A-3s and SB2U-3s were limited to 1,200 miles, and the SBD could fly just 773 miles in its configuration as a scout plane. The F4F-3's range was just 925 miles.[27] A Navy PBY detected one of the Japanese task forces 700 miles from Midway on 3 June, well beyond the patrolling range of any marine aircraft.[28] This suggests that employing carrier aircraft limited marine aviation's utility as a scouting force.

One piece of crucial intelligence in the Pacific Fleet's hands played no role in the battle. Either it failed to reach VMF-221 or the marines failed to recognize its significance. The Fleet Air Tactical Unit had issued an intelligence bulletin nine months previously regarding the Zero's superior speed and maneuverability. Reports from the American Volunteer Group in China also warned of the Zero's speed and impressive climbing performance. Yet none of the accounts by VMF-221's pilots indicate anything but astonishment at the Zero's capabilities.[29] So, unaware of or indifferent to the Zero's superior flying characteristics, the marines made no effort to adapt their tactics to this emerging threat.

Logistics

Midway lay at the end of a long ocean supply line. Vessels like *Kitty Hawk* could moor alongside Sand Island's pier and discharge cargo, but getting to Midway from Pearl Harbor took four days at fifteen knots, and Pearl Harbor itself was eight days from the nearest West Coast port. This supply chain provided Midway with sufficiency but not abundance.

The fleet's failure to supply MAG-22 with two items in particular directly impacted VMF-221's performance: ammunition and fuel. On several occasions the squadron did not have enough .50-caliber machine-gun ammunition to conduct live gunnery practice. Fuel shortages curtailed training even more severely. The loss of 375,000 gallons in an own-goal on 22 May (as discussed in chapter 2) and the demands of the thirsty B-17s and PBYs left no fuel for the novice aviators to train.

Other aspects of logistics did not hinder operations. Though the army air force bombers arrived without ground support, the marines serviced them along with their own aircraft, even after bombs damaged the fuel system. The ground crews achieved an impressive sortie rate on 4 June and returned two damaged dive-bombers to operation. There is no indication that aircraft readiness was impaired by a shortage of tools, parts, or technical ability.

The airfield's three hard-packed coral runways enabled more than forty aircraft to take off minutes after the air raid warning. Revetments and bunkers provided sufficient protection for most of the marines and infrastructure.

Time

VMF-221 had abundant time to prepare for combat but was unable to utilize that time efficiently. The squadron had been at Midway for more than five months before the action on 4 June, but conflicting operational requirements, personnel turbulence, and logistical limitations impaired its preparations. When the first replacement aviators arrived, almost four months before the action, their training sorties were limited by the hours the squadron was tasked to devote to patrol and calibration flights. After the final replacements arrived in May, the short window before the action was insufficient to provide even a modicum of training, a problem exacerbated by the fuel shortages that limited flying hours.

Japanese Capabilities

The reverse side of the aircraft performance coin is the superior performance of the Zero. The surviving marines agreed on that point. A few recognized that the Japanese were better airmen as well. Lieutenant Musselman and Lieutenant Phillips, who witnessed the battle from the ground, acknowledged the Japanese pilots' "skill and daring."[30] Even the most junior Japanese naval fighter pilots had well over two years' experience, and many had previous combat experience in China, at Pearl Harbor, against the British, and at the Coral Sea.[31]

Armistead did not credit the Zero with being superior in every way, writing, "In general, the Japanese airplanes appear to be very vulnerable to .50 cal. gun fire. They burst into flame in nearly all cases upon receiving any bullets."[32] Lieutenant Corry observed the same weakness, reporting that "the Japanese planes seem to be very vulnerable if you are fortunate enough to bring your guns to bear."[33]

The Japanese coordinated a strike comprising more than one hundred aircraft from four carriers. In contrast, the Americans could not coordinate a strike of fewer than fifty bombers from a single airfield. The Japanese Combined Fleet's ability to mass air power had helped overwhelm VMF-221.

VMF-221 suffered grievous losses at Midway and failed to destroy many enemy aircraft outright, but nonetheless its actions helped achieve the fleet commander's intent. What little it destroyed—the aircraft from *Hiryū*—limited Japanese offensive power when it mattered most. The unprotected marine dive-bomber strikes against the Japanese carriers, though uncoordinated and causing no direct harm, contributed to the accumulation of delay, distraction, and poor decision-making on the Japanese carriers that facilitated the attacks of the dive-bombers from *Enterprise* and *Yorktown*.

Several factors inhibited VMF-221's performance. The relative inferiority of the F2A-3 in combat against the Zero is certainly among them. The poor employment of VMF-221 resulting from doctrinal bias and imprecise direction ensured that the dive-bombers attacked without protection. The inability of Naval Air Station Midway and MAG-22 to coordinate strikes enabled enemy fighters to defeat each in turn. Most of all, the relative inexperience of marine aviators prevented them from shooting down aircraft and staying alive. This inexperience had many causes, including the service's rapid expansion, an aircraft shortage, the competing demands of defending Midway, and logistical shortfalls.

On 19 June, the surviving pilots of VMF-221 boarded a transport and departed Midway. The Marine Corps would rebuild the squadron at Ewa and redeploy it to a new combat zone within the year. The squadron's next chapter would reveal how well the Marine Corps had learned the lessons of Midway.

PART TWO

★ ★ ★

THE SOLOMON ISLANDS, 1943

5

★ ★ ★

Refitting, Rearming, and Redeploying, June 1942–February 1943

Rebuilding, June 1942–February 1943

After Midway the Marine Corps brought VMF-221 back to Ewa to rebuild it. The squadron would be spared another tour of island defense and would not deploy again until February 1943, when it would sail for the South Pacific. Nonetheless, its reconstitution was not a simple matter of replacing combat losses followed by seven months of rigorous training. Competing demands placed on marine aviation in the latter half of 1942 hobbled the squadron's reconstruction. Marine aviation continued its accelerated buildup, growing from thirty-one squadrons at the end of June 1942 to sixty a year later.[1] The requirement to defend advance naval bases continued to pull squadrons forward, inhibiting the attempts of the Fleet Marine Force and Air Force, Pacific Fleet (the renamed Aircraft Battle Force, Pacific Fleet) to train, organize, and equip them. Most important, the victory at Midway enabled the Pacific Fleet to take the offensive. The battle for Guadalcanal that began in August 1942 would quickly become the focus of marine aviation.

Personnel Turbulence and Replacements

The marines of VMF-221 had all reached Ewa Field by the end of June as passengers on transport aircraft or logistics vessels. Even before the last echelon arrived, the Marine Corps began transferring many to other squadrons. By early August, every officer and most of the senior noncommissioned officers had departed. Of the 167 enlisted marines who fought at Midway, 102 remained on 1 August. The squadron would rebuild without a single pilot who flew at Midway and without the senior NCOs who had kept their aircraft flying.[2]

On 10 June 1942, the 2nd Marine Aircraft Wing published a new table of organization. Each fighting squadron would comprise 18 fighter aircraft, 2 trainer aircraft, 41 officers, and 242 enlisted marines.[3] The wing faced an acute shortage of pilots and ground crew in Hawaii and at its advance bases at Midway, Palmyra, and Samoa.[4] At the end of August 1942, VMF-221 was a still long way from its full complement. The squadron had just 7 aviators on hand, none of whom had flown at Midway, and 110 enlisted marines.[5]

Over the next three months, new pilots and enlisted marines joined the squadron as others transferred out in a confusing merry-go-round that defies comprehension. Between 1 September and 30 November, forty-six pilots joined VMF-221 and thirty-five transferred out. The need for fighter pilots in Samoa to guard the shipping lanes to Australia and Guadalcanal took priority. VMF-221 was stripped to a small cadre again. Not until December did the squadron's roster fill with aviators and ground marines who would train, deploy, and fight in its next action.[6]

The turnover among pilots was matched by a rotation of commanders. As the senior surviving officer, Captain Armistead had taken command on 4 June; but he left on 1 August, the last of the aviators who had flown at Midway. Fortunately for VMF-221, Capt. Robert R. Burns rejoined the squadron.[7]

Burns was an experienced fighter pilot and, according to one pilot who served under him in combat, "a marvelous person."[8] Burns had joined a marine aviation reserve unit in 1936 at Wold-Chamberlain Field in his hometown of Minneapolis, Minnesota. He served there for two years while studying aeronautical engineering at the University of Minnesota, graduating in 1938. Burns survived elimination flight training in September 1938 and reported to Pensacola that November. He earned his wings in October 1939.[9]

Burns had flown with VMS-2 at North Island for a year before he returned to Pensacola as an instructor. He joined VMF-221 in October 1941 and flew with the squadron until he moved up to MAG-22 as the group communications officer on 19 April 1942.[10] Throughout the Midway fight, Burns worked tirelessly aiding Lieutenant Colonel Kimes and Major McCaul. On 1 August he replaced Armistead as the commanding officer of VMF-221.[11]

Burns' first period in command lasted only a week until Maj. Luther S. "Sad Sam" Moore arrived from Palmyra Island and took command on 8 August. But the Marine Corps promoted Moore to lieutenant colonel within a week, and he detached on 6 October, turning over the squadron to Maj. Harold J. Mitchener.[12] Fortunately for Moore, Mitchener, and the squadron, Burns remained as the executive officer, providing the only continuity among the officers.

Mitchener had received a regular commission after graduating from Carnegie Technical College in Pittsburgh in 1936. He had attended The Basic School in Philadelphia and served at sea aboard the battleship USS *Mississippi* (BB 41) before going to flight school. He flew for several years with VMF-111 at Quantico until 1942, when he was assigned to MAG-13. VMF-221 was his first command.[13]

By 1 February, weeks before deploying to the South Pacific, the squadron had 30 pilots. Its ground echelon included 209 enlisted marines and 3 officers: an adjutant-intelligence officer, a transportation-mess officer, and a ground defense officer. The squadron also had a navy flight surgeon and 4 hospital corpsmen.[14] While this put the squadron at just 75 percent of its authorized officer strength, 30 aviators provided a healthy ratio of 1.6 pilots to each aircraft for an 18-plane squadron, and the ground echelon was at 87 percent of its authorization.

In addition to Mitchener and Burns, two experienced aviators reported on board just prior to deployment. First Lt. John S. Payne arrived on 8 December and was promoted to captain a week later. Capt. Sidney G. Bemis reported to the squadron with the final cohort of aviators on 29 January 1943.[15]

The other twenty-six pilots lacked experience. The twenty-four second lieutenants had all completed flight school as naval aviation cadets between April and September 1942. The two enlisted naval aviation pilots had also earned their wings in 1942.[16]

Of these twenty-six pilots, James "Jimmy" Swett had the most experience. Swett had enrolled in the Civilian Pilot Training Program in 1939 while he was a student at San Mateo Junior College in California.[17] President Roosevelt had authorized the program in 1938 to train 20,000 pilots for the armed forces.[18] By the time Swett joined the aviation cadet program in August 1941, he had accumulated 240 hours.[19] Due to Swett's high marks in intermediate training, the senior marine at Corpus Christi invited him to seek a commission in the Marine Corps, which he obtained on 1 April 1942.[20]

The Marine Corps ordered Swett to Quantico for communications school, where he earned a reputation for hijinks. The air station commander placed Swett under arrest in quarters for ten days for "Diving & Zooming over traffic on U.S. Route #1, below the altitude of 500 ft."[21] Swett reported to the 2nd Marine Aircraft Wing at San Diego in late July and was immediately sent to the Advanced Carrier Training Group.[22]

The Chief of Naval Operations had established Advanced Carrier Training Groups in Norfolk and San Diego in July 1941 to provide the operational training that had previously been the responsibility of fleet squadrons like VMF-221. Aviators assigned there were supposed to complete a seventy-five-hour syllabus that included fighter tactics and gunnery, bombing, overwater navigation, instrument flying, night flying, and carrier qualification. According to Lundstrom, the Advanced Carrier Training Groups struggled to train their aviators due to shortages of pilots and aircraft. Few qualified to land on aircraft carriers because the carriers were busy operating with the fleet.[23] From August to October 1942, the Advanced Carrier Training Group in San Diego had only 14–18 F4F fighters, 17–23 SBD dive-bombers, 8–10 TBF torpedo bombers, and 30–40 SNJ trainers to train all the navy and marine aviators rotating out to the Pacific. Not every aircraft could fly every day, and the training group also flew scouting patrols for the Western Sea Frontier Force, which detracted from its training mission.[24] Second Lt. Jefferson J. DeBlanc reported to the Advanced

Carrier Training Group in late July 1942 but spent most of his hours in SNJs and did not check out in an F4F until 28 September. DeBlanc deployed to the South Pacific with VMF-112 shortly thereafter.[25] As the navy winged an average of 875 aviators a month in 1942, even after those headed to patrol and utility squadrons are subtracted, it is clear that the Advanced Carrier Training Groups did not have enough aircraft.[26]

In addition to the lieutenants, the squadron acquired two naval aviation pilots, TechSgt. Calvin J. Voelker and SSgt. Jack Pittman. Unlike prewar naval aviation pilots such as Gunner Dickey who had flown for years, these noncommissioned officers had no more experience than the lieutenants. Voelker had served three years as an aviation mechanic before extending his contract to attend flight school. Pittman had flown as a radioman and gunner in dive-bombers and volunteered for flight school after witnessing the annihilation of his aircraft group during the Pearl Harbor raid.[27]

While the squadron would deploy with more senior NCOs than it had fought the Battle of Midway with, these were not grizzled sergeants with decades of experience. The most senior of them, MTechSgt. Carl N. Mason, the communications chief, had only about three years' time in service. Mason's only technical training had prepared him to install, maintain, and operate radios and radar, not to maintain airframes or power plants. The squadron no longer rated a first sergeant, and the other seventeen senior NCOs were technical sergeants and staff sergeants.[28] TechSgt. Martin Y. Andres and TechSgt. Victor A. Mroz Jr., the senior noncommissioned officers who had been at Midway, had been a sergeant and staff sergeant respectively during the battle. Of the twelve staff sergeants, six months earlier one had been a staff sergeant, three had been corporals, and eight had been privates first class.[29] Nine of the senior NCOs had completed aviation mechanic school, two had completed aviation ordnance school, and one had completed aviation metalsmith school.[30]

In a significant change, the squadron received a navy medical detachment. Flight surgeon Lt. Joseph H. O'Connell and seven pharmacist's mates and hospital apprentices attended to the squadron's health, particularly the pilots' fitness for flying.[31]

Aircraft by the Numbers

The squadron brought no aircraft back from Midway. To no one's disappointment, VMF-221 would never be issued another F2A Buffalo. The fluctuations in personnel were matched by an ebb and flow of aircraft. The squadron received forty-two F4Fs between July and September, but by mid-September the squadron had no aircraft at all. Only in December, after the squadron began to accrue pilots in significant numbers, did new fighters arrive. By mid-December the squadron had nineteen F4F-4s, one over its allowance. Due to operational losses, when the squadron deployed in late February it had sixteen F4F-4s and two SNJs, two fighters short of its authorized strength.[32]

The revolving door of aircraft complicated maintenance as well as training. When aircraft were assigned to the squadron for only a few weeks, the ground crews had fewer opportunities to identify the nuances of each aircraft. When mechanics knew that the aircraft they were working on one day might be taken away the next, it became more difficult to embrace ownership and take pride in the plane's upkeep.

The F4F-4 had five new features the F4F-3 lacked: standard armor protection, self-sealing fuel tanks, folding wings, drop tanks, and two additional machine guns. The folding wings reduced the wingspan from thirty-eight to just fourteen feet, enabling carriers to embark more fighters.[33] The two 58-gallon drop tanks increased the fighter's range to 1,275 miles,[34] though its actual combat radius overseas would prove to be less than half that distance. The additional guns increased the number of rounds a pilot could fire in a burst by 50 percent while providing some insurance against all his guns jamming in a fight.

But these modifications added weight. The folding wings came with a heavy hydraulic system. The F4F-4, heavier than the F4F-3 by 210 pounds, lost 10 mph in top speed (dropping to 320 mph) and 2,600 feet in its service ceiling (dropping to 34,900 feet). Full drop tanks added another 787 pounds.[35] VF-6 aboard *Enterprise* tested the climb rate of the F4F-4 and determined that it took 10 minutes to reach 15,000 feet.[36] Though the tanks could be dropped when the fighters encountered the enemy, they were gone for good, and replacing them proved terrifically difficult at sea and at advance bases.[37]

Ammunition was usually belted in a "one-one-one" sequence: one tracer round, one incendiary round, and one armor-piercing round. This sequence proved highly effective against the Zero.[38] But the additional two guns not only added weight, they also robbed the wings of ammunition space. Instead of 430 rounds per gun, the F4F-4 carried just 240 rounds per gun, cutting firing time by almost half when all six guns were fired. Some navy pilots who flew the F4F-4 in combat from *Enterprise* in October 1942 recommended the navy revert to a four-gun fighter with 430 rounds per gun.[39] Not all veterans agreed. After becoming an ace at Guadalcanal, Maj. Frederick Payne asserted, "I'd rather have six guns with 250 rounds than four guns with 400."[40]

The chief of the Bureau of Aeronautics, Rear Adm. John H. Towers, had attempted to mitigate the F4F-4 weight problem in February 1942 by advising commanders to choose either a full load of fuel or six fully loaded machine guns.[41] In other words, Towers told pilots to pick their poison: fight without enough ammunition, fight without enough fuel, or fight without optimum performance. Until the United States produced a better fighter, navy and marine fighter pilots would need to adjust their tactics to fight and survive.

In addition to the carrier aircraft VMF-221 had encountered at Midway, the squadron would face land-based aircraft in the South Pacific. Foremost of these would be the Mitsubishi G4M3 Model 34 "Betty" twin-engine navy bomber. The Betty could reach 325 mph at 20,000 feet and carry nearly 5,000 pounds of bombs or torpedoes. The bomber bristled with armaments: 20-mm cannons in both the top turret and the tail as well as 7.7-mm machine guns in the nose and on either side.[42]

Training and Tactical Changes

The twenty-six new pilots accumulated between four and eleven months' experience after flight school before the squadron departed Hawaii. All had learned basic fighter tactics and passed gunnery qualification in either F2A Buffalos at Miami or F3F biplanes at Corpus Christi. Frank B. "Baldy" Baldwin, William V. Moore, Walter J. Schocker, William N. Snider, and Swett all accrued time in F4Fs at the Advanced Carrier Training Group, but Warner O. Chapman and John F. Connelly had never flown an F4F before reporting to VMF-221. With a full complement of aircraft and two months to train the new pilots, the senior aviators wasted little time. Chapman estimated that all the new pilots got in at least a hundred hours before the squadron sailed on 21 February 1943.[43]

The squadron's war diary and history recorded that the squadron conducted "normal flight operations" or "flight training" nearly every day in December 1942 and January 1943, and gunnery and division tactics during the first week of February. Though an aggressive schedule is apparent, what tactics the new aviators were practicing must be inferred. VMF-221's training likely mirrored that of another fighting squadron in MAG-21, VMF-213; both squadrons received new pilots during this period, and they deployed together in February. VMF-213 predominantly flew gunnery practice missions in December and January, practicing section and division tactics and instrument flying.[44]

VMF-213 conducted several sessions of gunnery practice at 20,000 feet, which required pilots to fly on oxygen. Inexperienced pilots tended to misjudge distance at high altitude. In many cases, the oxygen mask fit so high on the pilot's face that he had to fly with his goggles pushed up on his forehead to preserve his line of vision. This was not a significant handicap with the windshield closed—until metal and glass began hurtling around the cockpit.[45]

The tactics and training syllabus published in *USF-74* in March 1941 still provided the foundation for the fleet's fighting squadrons. Since then, however, navy and marine fighter pilots had gained battle experience at the Coral Sea, Midway, and Guadalcanal. While the tactics developed in other F4F squadrons may not mirror what VMF-221 was training to do, they illustrate the innovations and adaptations that fleet fighting squadrons were incorporating.

Around the same time Mitchener was preparing VMF-221 for the South Pacific, Maj. Joseph N. Renner was already there preparing VMO-251 for combat. Although designated an observation squadron, VMO-251 was a fighting squadron. Renner had been assigned twenty-two dive-bomber and observation pilots who were eager to fight, but he had only about three and a half weeks to train them. Nevertheless, he was prepared for the job. He had been on Guadalcanal and had absorbed a great deal from the squadron commanders there. Renner's accelerated syllabus included section and division tactics and gunnery. He insisted that wingmen stick with their section leaders. Training dogfights were similar to real one-on-one engagements, but with two four-plane divisions maneuvering against each other and wingmen staying with their section leaders throughout the fight. With little time for his men to master gunnery, Renner focused on the overhead pass, which enabled a fighter pilot to shoot first and then get away quickly. The fighter started well above the target, dove at high speed, engaged, and then continued past without giving the enemy an opportunity to fire back.[46]

The commanding officer of VF-3 at Midway, Lt. Cdr. John "Jimmy" Thach, had developed a tactic to mitigate the Zero's superior speed and maneuverability. In Thach's "beam defense," Wildcat sections flew abreast, each watching the other's rear. When a fighter pilot saw a Japanese fighter maneuvering against his wingman, he turned toward his partner. Thus signaled, his partner likewise turned into him, forcing the Japanese fighter either to face the guns of the first fighter or break off the attack. The navy incorporated the tactic into training publications and films in late 1942 and 1943.[47] Aircraft, Pacific Fleet highlighted the "Thach Weave" in a tactical bulletin published on 20 February 1943.[48] As this memorandum is located in the archives of MAG-12, which served as Fighter Command, Solomons, it is reasonable to assume that the aviators of VMF-221 learned the Thach Weave not long after they reached Guadalcanal in late March, but likely not before they left Pearl Harbor on 21 February.

While it is unclear whether Mitchener, Burns, and the other pilots at VMF-221 received a heads-up about Thach's beam defense tactic, it is clear that marines in combat adopted something like it. In a postwar interview Renner described the tactic as follows:

> In order to knock Zeros down the Grummans stuck together, and each pilot paid less attention to the man on his tail than to the Zero on somebody else's tail. The Grumman fighters tried to stay in the same air, as we called it; once the dogfight started, we all revolved about in the same area. If a Zero dived out from the dogfight, our instructions were not to follow him but to swing back into the middle of the merry-go-round. In swinging back, you look for a Zero on some other Grumman's tail.[49]

At Midway VMF-221 had fought in divisions as large as seven aircraft, but four-plane divisions were now the norm.[50] Though this organization left two of the eighteen aircraft unassigned, it made it easier for a division's two sections to protect each other.

Innovative tactics aside, VMF-221's training in Hawaii in December and January appears to have been primarily internal. The only indication that the squadron trained with any outside organization is a reference in the Marine Corps Air Station Ewa war diary noting that VMF-221 was tasked with standing alert in conjunction with the army air force from 29 to 31 December 1942. The island's fighter direction center scrambled the marines several times each day, which provided some useful experience operating under army command and responding to a fighter direction center. Otherwise, VMF-221 appears to have trained on its own. There is no indication the squadron practiced escorting bombers.[51]

Though the war diary characterized the squadron's flying as "normal," mishaps did occur. On 3 September one of the pilots walked away from a crash that severely damaged his F4F-4. On 13 October the landing gear on an F4F-3 loaned by VMF-214 collapsed upon landing, and the Wildcat was quickly engulfed in flames. The pilot escaped with bruises and cuts, but the aircraft was lost. On 25 January 2nd Lt. Wallace H. Hallmeyer was unable to get his F4F-4 airborne on a takeoff run and ran off the end of Ewa's runway. Hallmeyer escaped with minor injuries, but his aircraft was demolished. Six days later Hallmeyer was less lucky. While flying through a thunderstorm off the coast of Oahu at about noon he went into a spin from which he was unable to recover. His buddies looked for him after he bailed out but could not find him in the rough weather, and the squadron finally called off its search at 1900. At 0200 the following morning, a sentry patrolling Oahu's windward side found Hallmeyer, still alive, tangled in a barbed-wire barrier on the beach. Hallmeyer was hospitalized for exposure and shock but rejoined the squadron on 1 February.[52]

On 4 February, the squadron suffered its first fatality in eight months. Captain Bemis, an experienced aviator, was making a gunnery pass against another section when his aircraft came apart in midair. The squadron stood down that afternoon for a safety lecture but was right back at gunnery practice the following day. On the squadron's last flying date before embarkation, 1st Lt. Gale W. Roberts landed his SNJ in a strong crosswind and skidded, damaging the aircraft's right landing gear. Roberts was unhurt, and the aircraft was repairable.[53]

On the eve of deployment, VMF-221 lost yet another experienced aviator: its commander. Major Mitchener fell ill—"very, very, ill," according to Swett—and was hospitalized on 19 February.[54] With Mitchener gone, it fell on the shoulders of Captain Burns to embark the squadron's aircraft, equipment, and personnel; deploy to the South Pacific; and lead VMF-221 into combat. Burns was twenty-six years old and had been a naval aviator for just over three years.[55] Except for Captain Payne, all Burns' pilots had graduated flight school less than a year before.

Voyage to the South Pacific

At this stage in the war, the Pacific Fleet could no longer tie up fleet carriers like *Saratoga* shuttling land-based squadrons like VMF-221 overseas. Bombers like the B-17 and patrol aircraft like the PBY could hop from island base to island base across the Pacific, but fighters had to embark aboard ships. To get squadrons overseas, the Secretary of the Navy approved conversion of twenty-four merchant vessels into aircraft auxiliary vessels. In an astounding feat, the Seattle-Tacoma Shipbuilding Corporation launched USS *Nassau* (APV 16; later CVE 16) on 4 April 1942, scarcely three months after laying her keel as a merchant vessel. *Nassau* had less than a third of *Saratoga*'s displacement and just over half her length. By utilizing all of her flight and hangar deck space, she could squeeze ninety aircraft aboard, but due to her shorter flight deck they required assisted takeoffs with hydraulic catapults.[56] On 21 February 1943 *Nassau* was moored at Ford Island in Pearl Harbor, having completed a week of repair and refit, awaiting MAG-21.[57]

VMF-221 began packing up on 9 February. Mechanics overhauled every aircraft and vehicle. An advance party of twenty-nine junior marines under Lt. Augustine B. Reynolds Jr., the squadron's ground defense officer, sailed aboard the seaplane tender USS *Wright* (AV 1) on 11 February.[58]

On 20 February VMF-221 flew the short hop from Ewa to Ford Island. *Nassau* hoisted the squadron's sixteen F4F-4s and two SNJs aboard along with aircraft from VMF-213 and VMF-214. Burns, Payne, and eighteen other pilots; the squadron's plane captains, first mechanics, and leading NCOs; the flight surgeon; and a pharmacist's mate embarked *Nassau* as well.[59] As she slipped her mooring late on 21 February, bound for Espiritu Santo in the New Hebrides, a navy band played "The Marines' Hymn."[60] Six officers and twenty-seven marines and sailors from VMF-221 sailed the following day aboard the troopship SS *President Tyler*, a former ocean liner.[61]

The first two days at sea proved pleasant, though Chapman recalled that the ship was "vastly overcrowded." The marines slept topside, enjoying the balmy breeze and starlit sea. But at midday on 24 February, *Nassau*'s escort, the destroyer USS *Sterett* (DD 407), reported a sonar contact. *Nassau* went to general quarters and began a radical zigzag. *Sterett* dropped three depth charges. Three days later, *Sterett* established another sonar contact and *Nassau* repeated the drill. This occurred three more times on 28 February and twice on 2 March.[62]

According to 1st Lt. Charles C. Winnia of VMF-213, the marines found the frequent general quarters a nuisance rather than something to worry about.[63] But the vulnerability of *Nassau* and her embarked aircraft group to a submarine attack was quite real. A few weeks after delivering VMF-221 to Midway, *Saratoga* suffered a torpedo hit from a Japanese submarine and took another torpedo east of the Solomon Islands in September 1942. Though the carrier survived both torpedoes, converted merchant vessels like *Nassau* were not constructed with the same degree of armor and watertight integrity. Just nine months after VMF-221 sailed aboard *Nassau*, a Japanese submarine sank another converted merchantman, the escort carrier USS *Liscome Bay* (CVE 56), with a single torpedo. She sank quickly, taking 644 of her crew and air group down with her.[64]

Nassau reached Espiritu Santo safely on 3 March. It took five hours to catapult all MAG-21's embarked fighters. One VMF-213 F4F-4 stalled on takeoff and spun into the sea. *Sterett* swiftly recovered the pilot.[65] The pilots of VMF-221 survived their catapult launches and landed at the airfield code-named Buttons.[66]

The squadron was still dispersed in three echelons. *Wright* deposited Lieutenant Reynolds and his advance party on Guadalcanal, 560 miles to the northwest. The detachment aboard *President Tyler* did not arrive at Espiritu Santo until 9 March.[67]

Espiritu Santo was out of range of the Japanese aircraft based at Rabaul, but close enough to Guadalcanal to reinforce Henderson Field. An anchorage enabled deep-draft vessels to discharge troops, equipment, and supplies. Seabees—naval construction battalion engineers—were completing wharves to expedite unloading. A crushed coral road led from the landing to the airfield where MAG-21's fighters landed.[68]

The Seabees had bulldozed the airfield on a former coconut plantation, the typical crop grown on the flat areas of volcanic islands in the South Pacific. Buttons consisted of four airfields: Bomber 1, Bomber 2, Fighter 1, and Fighter 2. MAG-21's personnel moved into four-man tents near the fighter strips adjacent to Pallikulo Bay. The food was good, and the marines slept on cots. The camp had showers, and the marines could swim when time allowed. It would have seemed a tropical paradise but for the frequent rainstorms that liquified the ground and the flies and mosquitos that tormented the marines.[69]

On 9 March VMF-221's pilots got back in their cockpits. For the next week the squadron's four divisions practiced fighting as teams. On 16 March, the pilots boarded a marine R4D, which flew them to Guadalcanal to relieve VMF-123.[70]

6

★ ★ ★

Air War in the South Pacific, March 1943

When the pilots of VMF-221 disembarked at Henderson Field, they reentered a war vastly different from the one the squadron had left after Midway. Prior to Midway the Japanese Combined Fleet had held the initiative in the Pacific. The Pacific Fleet's victory there enabled the United States to take the offensive.

Operational Context

On 2 July 1942 the Joint Chiefs directed Nimitz to seize and occupy the Santa Cruz Islands and Tulagi as the first step toward seizing the Japanese stronghold at Rabaul. The airfield on Guadalcanal emerged as the key to success in that first step. The Japanese conceded defeat at Guadalcanal and withdrew the remnants of their landing force by 9 February 1943. Wasting no time, American soldiers and marines seized the unoccupied Russell Islands thirty miles northwest of Guadalcanal on 21 February. In the Southwest Pacific Area commanded by Gen. Douglas MacArthur, American and Australian troops repelled a Japanese overland attempt to seize the Allied base at Port Moresby in late 1942. Army air force and Australian bombers annihilated a troop convoy in the Bismarck Sea on

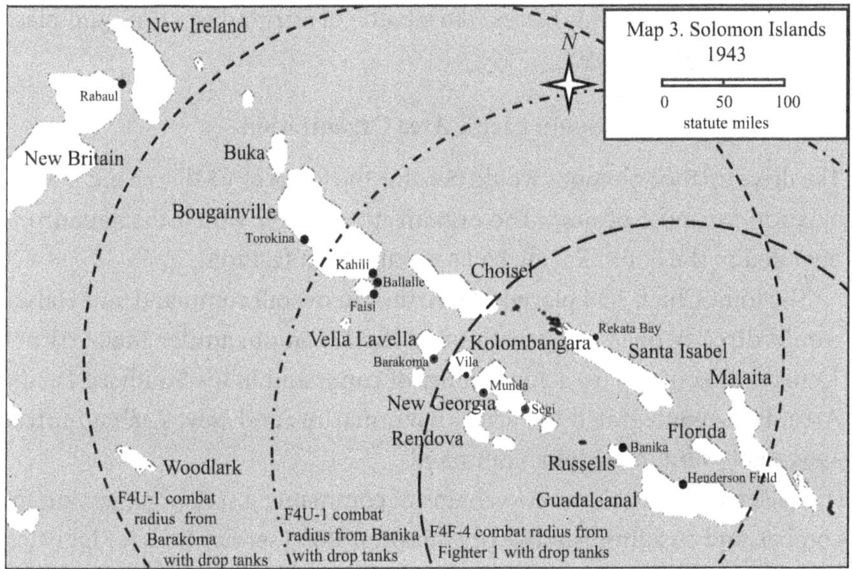

MAP 3. Solomon Islands, 1943

2–3 March, preventing the Japanese from reinforcing their bases on the north coast of New Guinea.[1]

On 28 March, with Guadalcanal and Papua New Guinea secure, the Joint Chiefs issued broad strategic guidance to MacArthur and Nimitz. MacArthur, in overall command, would seize bases on the northeast coast of New Guinea and on islands offshore. Halsey, now commanding the Third Fleet and the South Pacific Area, would seize the Solomons, including the southern portion of Bougainville. With these objectives accomplished, the Allies would encircle Rabaul, and Allied aircraft could overwhelm and neutralize the Japanese stronghold there.[2]

In the Joint Chief's language, the purpose of the campaign was "to inflict losses on Japanese forces, to deny these areas to Japan, to contain Japanese forces in the Pacific Theater by maintaining the initiative, and to prepare for ultimate seizure of BISMARCK ARCHIPELAGO."[3] The Bismarck Archipelago included the island of New Britain and the air and naval base at Rabaul. Control of the Bismarck Archipelago would enable MacArthur to move toward the Philippines. Perhaps as important, it would force Japan to commit its naval and air forces into a battle of attrition at a time and place the United States chose.[4]

South Pacific Area Organization

The drive up the Solomons would become the focus of VMF-221 and marine aviation for most of 1943. The organization under which the squadrons operated in the South Pacific had several salient features.

The Joint Chiefs had placed MacArthur in overall command, but Halsey would directly oversee operations in the Solomons under MacArthur's "general directives."[5] To achieve unity of command in the Southern Pacific Area, Halsey integrated the army, navy, marine, and New Zealand forces assigned to him into a joint command.

Halsey's force required two chains of command: a task organization for combat, and an administrative organization along service lines for logistics. The commander of Aircraft South Pacific, Vice Adm. Aubrey W. Fitch, commanded all army, marine, navy, and New Zealand squadrons. Those in the Solomon Islands were under Fitch's subordinate, Rear Adm. Marc A. Mitscher, commanding Air Command Solomon Islands, or "AirSols."

When the pilots of VMF-221 arrived on Guadalcanal on 16 March, they fell under the command of Col. Edward L. Pugh and his Fighter Command, Solomons. Pugh had graduated from the University of Maryland in 1926 and become a marine aviator in 1928. He flew fighters before the war and had served as executive officer of VMF-1 at Quantico.[6] Halsey had placed all army, marine, and navy fighters under Pugh. The arriving VMF-221 aviators found they were relieving the pilots of VMF-123, who told the newcomers they had not seen a single Zero during their combat tour.[7]

In mid-March, Colonel Pugh had 125 fighters under his command: 13 marine F4U Corsairs, 59 marine and navy F4F Wildcats, 21 army air force P-38 Lightnings, 16 army air force P-39 Airacobras, and 16 army air force P-40 Warhawks.[8] All the squadrons flew from the Fighter 2 airstrip at this time. The historic Henderson Field, named to honor VMSB-241's commander at Midway, primarily served Bomber Command, Solomons due to its longer runway.[9] The marine squadrons included VMF-214, which arrived a week ahead of VMF-221, and VMF-124, the first marine squadron to convert to the F4U Corsair. Service Squadron 12 and the ground echelon of VMF-122 maintained the aircraft at Fighter 2. The navy F4F squadrons were VF-6, VGS-11, VGS-12, and VGS-16.[10]

Aviation Maintenance in the South Pacific

On paper, Air Force, Pacific Fleet assigned all navy and marine aircraft, matériel, and aviation and directed the training of all squadrons. Air Force, South Pacific, located on Espiritu Santo, performed those same functions within Halsey's Southern Pacific Area. Fleet Aircraft, South Pacific, located in Noumea on New Caledonia, was responsible to Air Force, South Pacific for aviation supply and maintenance in the Southern Pacific Area. Marine Aircraft Wings, South Pacific trained, organized, and equipped marine squadrons for combat but did not direct combat operations. Of note, I Marine Amphibious Corps, which included the 1st and 3rd Marine Divisions, exercised no authority over marine aircraft units in the Southern Pacific.[11]

In practice, the logistics was even more muddled than this complicated organization suggests. By the spring of 1943, maintenance of naval aircraft could be separated into three echelons. Basic maintenance consisted of servicing tasks such as refueling and ordnance loading, and routine maintenance such as engine and preflight checks. These tasks did not require the marine or sailor who performed them to have technical training or years of experience. They were intended to be performed by a squadron's personnel. Specialized maintenance included overhauling accessories, instruments, and propellers; changing engines; minor repair to the airframe and power plant; and salvaging parts from damaged aircraft. Marines with such expertise were divided between the aircraft squadrons and the aircraft group service squadrons.[12] More advanced work, such as engine overhauls and major repairs, was completed by a navy unit such as a Carrier Aircraft Service Unit or an Aviation Repair and Overhaul Unit.[13]

From September 1942 to April 1943, 10–25 percent of 1st Marine Aircraft Wing's planes were continuously grounded awaiting minor repairs. Aircraft requiring repairs that should have taken five or six days sat idle for eight to ten weeks.[14] When VMF-221 joined Fighter Command, Solomons, F4F daily operational readiness was 78 percent, up from 60 percent the month before. This was far better than F4U readiness, which was just 46 percent—down from 70 percent in February.[15]

In April 1943, the Bureau of Aeronautics sent Cdr. Seldon B. Spangler, the head of its power plant design section, on an inspection tour to determine why aviation commands were struggling to get planes in the air. His report illuminates the issues that plagued marine squadrons in the Solomons.[16]

The trouble began with the transportation of personnel, equipment, and supplies across the Pacific. Spangler observed that throughput at Noumea and Espiritu Santo was mind-numbingly slow: "I was reliably informed that there were enough ships in the harbor up there [at Espiritu Santo] to account for over a year of unloading at the rate they were able to put stuff ashore."[17] An army transportation command determined which ships to unload. Once material was unloaded, no one inventoried or tracked supplies. There were not enough trucks to move supplies, as many were hauling coral to keep the muddy roads surfaced. All manner of material was cached under trees in the hope that the unit that ordered it, or at least one that needed it, would discover it.[18]

Transportation snarls and other problems impeded aviation readiness in numerous ways. Carrier Aircraft Service Unit 3 in New Caledonia, for example, was assembling newly arrived aircraft under canvas tents that blew down in rain squalls.[19] Fleet Aircraft, South Pacific established a base that could overhaul two hundred engines each month, but it was in "the middle of the wilderness and mud." Highly trained mechanics were assigned to camp guard, camp sanitation, and camp maintenance details. Due to the harsh climate and rough living conditions, the navy expected aviation mechanics to work only a six-hour shift per day.[20] Sailors of one maintenance command arrived on Guadalcanal, but their tools, housing, and supplies were offloaded at Espiritu Santo and Noumea.[21]

Spangler discovered that squadrons received little or no support from the Carrier Aircraft Service Units and were maintaining aircraft on their own. The squadrons were doing ingenious work, salvaging parts from wrecks and performing advanced power plant maintenance—such as valve replacements—that should have been done by the Carrier Aircraft Service

Units.[22] A marine salvage unit at Guadalcanal recovered aircraft parts from wrecks, inventoried them, boxed and crated them, and cached them by the beach for shipment to naval aviation depots. However, to minimize his vessels' exposure to enemy air attacks, the amphibious force commander insisted ships land troops and supplies and then depart immediately. The salvaged parts sat on the beach, unused.[23]

The marine and navy mechanics Spangler encountered impressed him with their attitude:

> There never was a serious complaint, by anyone on where he lived or how he had to live—the real basic complaint they had was that they had to do too many things with their bare hands. They wanted more tools, more equipment, more shops, more machinery. And those are the things we're not getting for them. They're being sent out of here, all right; but they're not getting to the squadrons.[24]

Major Renner in VMO-251 shared his perspective on the problem. Wing and group commanders sent squadrons up from Espiritu Santo to Guadalcanal with reduced complements of ground support when they should have been reinforced. There was more maintenance work necessary at a combat airstrip, and marines became fatigued quickly in the harsh conditions.[25]

VMF-221's aircraft and support marines remained in Espiritu Santo. The maintenance of the fifty-nine F4Fs and thirteen F4Us at Fighter 2 fell primarily on the shoulders of the mechanics in Service Squadron 12 and VMF-122.

Operating from the austere airfields was hard on aircraft and men alike. The metal Marston matting engineers laid over soft ground as crude runways tore up tires and tail wheels. Covering the matting with dirt or coral and growing grass under it mitigated the problem somewhat, but spare tires and tail wheels were always in short supply.[26]

Tropical diseases exacerbated the challenge of getting pilots in cockpits and aircraft in the air. In mid-April, the 1st Marine Aircraft Wing's medical officer reported that from September 1942 to March 1943, the wing evacuated 4,995 personnel due to disease—1,300 more than it had evacuated with combat wounds.[27]

In response, Maj. Gen. Ralph J. Mitchell, the 1st Marine Aircraft Wing's commanding general, ordered his commanders to tighten up sanitation and mosquito protection measures. Mitchell directed every unit to erect screens around its galleys, heads, messes, and garbage cans, and to cover its Lyster bags, burn its garbage, and spray its latrines with waste oil. Sleeping under mosquito netting in shirts and trousers—despite the oppressive heat and humidity—was mandatory. He directed every commander to detail a squad to the medical officer to eradicate mosquito breeding areas. Mitchell ordered medical personnel to supervise their marines to ensure they swallowed their Atabrine.[28]

It was one thing to order the wing to battle malaria, but another to make it happen. Malaria hit all units ashore in the South Pacific. The same logistics snarls that impeded maintenance retarded the fight against malaria: there was not enough netting, screening, and medicine to protect all the soldiers, sailors, and marines in New Caledonia, Espiritu Santo, and the Solomons.[29]

Guadalcanal

Living conditions at Fighter 2 on Guadalcanal had improved considerably since the brutal fighting from August 1942 to February 1943. No longer a battlefield, Guadalcanal was now an advance naval base, a vast supply depot, a busy port, a cluster of airfields, and the command post of AirSols.[30] All hands were quartered in tents.[31] An outdoor theater screened Hollywood movies. Some nights a Japanese bomber orbited overhead and dropped a few bombs. The marines considered these raids no more than a nuisance, but they contributed to the general fatigue that accumulated as the days passed on Guadalcanal.[32]

Temperatures were not yet brutally hot in March and April, rising to no more than 84 degrees Fahrenheit, but Guadalcanal was no tropical paradise. It rained two days out of three, ten to eleven inches per month, and nothing ever dried out in the high humidity.[33]

Food was plentiful, but without refrigeration it was limited to canned meat, canned stew, canned hash, powdered eggs, powdered milk, occasional fresh Australian mutton, and coffee. Meals were served on greasy metal trays that never seemed to get clean. Most marines contracted dysentery, an unpleasant affliction that sucked energy from the already tired men.[34]

Actual Performance of Aircraft

Commanders discovered that not only were their marines not performing optimally in the South Pacific, neither were their aircraft. Lt. Col. Nathaniel S. Clifford, who took command of MAG-21 in the Russell Islands in May 1943, recorded the actual performance of the F4F-4s in the Solomons. The maximum speed he recorded, 287 mph at 20,000 feet, was considerably lower than the Bureau of Aeronautics' specification of 320 miles per hour at 18,800 feet.[35] Even accounting for the variation in altitude, this suggested around a 10 percent loss in speed, with corresponding loss of efficiency at other altitudes and in climbing.

To calculate the combat radius, Clifford subtracted the amount of fuel required for 20 minutes of combat at high throttle and 20 minutes of reserve at cruising speed and came up with 230 miles.[36] Less experienced pilots were not achieving even that in combat. Commander Spangler noted a relevant point during his inspection: the pilots were operating at higher power, higher speeds, and richer fuel mixtures than recommended, in part due to lack of education and in part to gain an edge in combat. Spangler found a common lack of understanding among aviators about the difference cruising at higher speeds made: "They think because we say 160 knots that 200 knots won't make a lot of difference in fuel consumption. Well, actually the miles per gallon at 200 knots are only about half of what they are at 160 knots. And nobody has ever taken the trouble to explain that."[37]

Spangler had identified a serious training oversight. But another factor curtailing the actual combat radius of fighters was the drop tanks. Regardless of how many miles the tanks extended the aircraft's range, the pilot had to drop them upon enemy contact. He then had to have enough internal fuel to fight, get home, and maintain a reserve to fly around adverse weather or fight unexpected contacts.[38]

Third Fleet Plans

Determined to avoid the shoestring nature of the previous year's Guadalcanal landing, Halsey began Operation Drygoods in February 1943. His intent was to stock 50,000 tons of supplies and 80,000 barrels of gasoline on Guadalcanal to support an amphibious assault on New Georgia.[39]

The purpose of assaulting New Georgia would be to capture the airfield at Munda.[40] The Japanese were using the field to stage attacks on Guadalcanal and Tulagi. Seizing Munda would not only deny the airfield to the Japanese but would also enable American fighters to achieve air superiority over Bougainville. Fighters flying from Bougainville would have the range to control the skies over Rabaul.[41]

But Halsey could not move against New Georgia until he had enough troops, ships, aircraft, and supplies assembled at Guadalcanal. While Drygoods stocked depots around Henderson Field, Pugh's Fighter Command protected the buildup from Japanese interference. To degrade Japanese air power, Air Search and Attack Command, Solomons (primarily marine and navy squadrons) and Bomber Command, Solomons (predominantly army air force medium and heavy bombers) struck resupply vessels and airfields, escorted by the squadrons of Fighter Command. Halsey's destroyers bombarded Japanese airfields, intercepted resupply vessels, and laid mines off New Georgia. Halsey tasked AirSols to conduct scouting and combat air patrols to protect the task forces.[42]

Southeast Area Fleet Plans

Japanese military commanders correctly assessed that American forces would advance on Rabaul in a two-pronged offensive via the Solomons and New Guinea. The army and navy general staffs divided the defense of Rabaul along service lines. The defense of New Guinea, opposing MacArthur, was assigned to the 18th Army and 6th Air Division. Defense of the Solomons was assigned to Vice Admiral Jinichi Kusaka's Southeast Area Fleet, which included the land-based naval aircraft of the Eleventh Air Fleet and the ships of the Eighth Fleet.[43]

To delay Halsey's offensive, Kusaka's superior, Admiral Isoruku Yamamoto, directed a preemptive air offensive called Operation I. The offensive would begin against the American base at Guadalcanal and then follow up against MacArthur's forces in New Guinea. Yamamoto joined Kusaka at Rabaul and reinforced the Eleventh Air Fleet with the air groups from the carriers *Hiyō*, *Junyō*, *Zuihō*, and *Zuikaku*. By the beginning of April, Yamamoto had a naval air force at Rabaul of approximately 182 fighters, 92 dive-bombers,

72 medium bombers, and a few torpedo planes—a force larger than the one that had struck Pearl Harbor.[44]

To face the Eleventh Air Fleet, on 1 April Fighter Command could muster 93 operationally ready fighters: 56 F4F-4s and 8 F4Us from navy and marine squadrons and 9 P-38s, 10 P-39s, 7 P-40s, and 3 P-70s from army air force squadrons.[45]

Early Warning and Fighter Direction

AirSols relied upon an integrated network of radar, coast watchers, and fighter direction to detect enemy air attacks and control Fighter Command's interceptions. The principal marine radars were SCR-268 and SCR-270 search radars at Banika Field on the Russell Islands and at Henderson Field on Guadalcanal. Eight miles east of Henderson Field at Koli Point, the Royal New Zealand Air Force erected a ground control intercept radar (GCI) that provided more accurate altitude measurements than the American search radars.[46]

The SCR-268 and SCR-270 radars proved less effective in the Solomons than they had been at Midway. Maj. Frederick Payne, who had served with VMF-221 on Midway until February 1942, had helped calibrate the marine radar there. After flying with VMF-212 from Guadalcanal in 1942, he observed that the numerous islands northwest and north of Guadalcanal created false echoes on the operator's scope. It took a sharp operator to tell the difference between an island and a flight of aircraft.[47]

Fortunately for Fighter Command, Australian coast watchers stationed across the Solomons provided early warning far beyond the range of Allied radars. Due to the great distance from Rabaul to Guadalcanal, Japanese aircraft flew in a direct line, passing right over coast watchers on Bougainville, Kolombangara, Rendova, and southeastern New Georgia. These Australian naval reservists and their Melanesian partners evaded Japanese patrols and radioed reports of aircraft and ships to the coast watcher liaison on Guadalcanal. The coast watchers could provide Fighter Command with ninety minutes of warning.[48]

Pugh's fighter direction center assigned missions to fighting squadrons and directed the fighter launches and intercepts. Maj. John P. Condon, Pugh's operations officer, spent nearly all of his time in the command post along with a team of communications, operations, and administrative staff.[49] To direct the fighters, Pugh and Condon needed to know where enemy aircraft were and where friendly aircraft were, and had to communicate with the aircraft, radars, and coast watchers. By this point in the war, the navy was installing airborne recognition sets in its aircraft. These sets received radar transmissions and responded with an Identification Friend or Foe (IFF) transmission that enabled radar operators to distinguish friendly aircraft among the many aircraft on their screens. The operations team used the information reported by the radar operators to plot friendly and enemy aircraft on a circular plotting board. Pugh and Condon directed fighters to intercept based on this plot.[50]

Doctrine advised Pugh and Condon to keep their fighters in between incoming aircraft and the base and within thirty miles of the base to ensure communication. Fighters were directed to fly as high as possible, but altitude was limited by climbing speed and time available, visibility, and the oxygen supply of intercepting aircraft. Pacific Fleet doctrine considered it more than twice as effective to attack with eight aircraft at once than with two four-plane divisions at separate times.[51]

With early warning and adequate radio communication, Pugh and Condon could get their fighters in an advantageous position to intercept incoming raids. From that point, it was up to the pilots of VMF-221 and the other squadrons to spot the enemy aircraft and shoot them down.

7

★ ★ ★

First Combat Tour, Guadalcanal, 16 March–3 May 1943

Patrols and Escorts, 17–31 March

Even before their first combat, VMF-221's aviators began to suffer the cumulative effects of the harsh conditions in the Solomons. The day after its arrival, the squadron began flying combat air patrols over Guadalcanal and the Russells. The patrols proved uneventful for the first two days, but a series of mishaps occurred after that. In the predawn darkness of 19 March, 2nd Lt. Paul T. Coe crashed two hundred yards from shore after takeoff and was killed. The squadron suspected Coe had experienced engine failure. The next day Lieutenant Schocker's landing gear was caught in soft sand during a landing and his F4F-4 ground-looped and flipped onto its back. Shocker walked away, but his aircraft was severely damaged. One day later, one of Lieutenant Chapman's landing gear dropped down during flight. Chapman could not get the gear to lock, so he ditched rather than risk a belly landing on the runway. The Wildcat flipped on its back when it hit the water, but Chapman struggled free before it sank. That same day a P-39 taxied into one of the F4F-4s, damaging a wing. Five days after Chapman ditched, his oil pump quit while he was 22,000 feet over the Russells. He managed to glide to a deadstick landing. One day later, the fuel tank on 2nd Lt. Eugene

Dillow's F4F-4 malfunctioned, forcing him to ditch. A PT boat retrieved Dillow and returned him to Guadalcanal.[1] Eleven days into its first combat tour, the squadron had not laid eyes on an enemy aircraft but had lost three aircraft and one pilot.

AirSols replaced the squadron's lost aircraft in short order. On 24 March the hard-working ground crews presented the squadron with a new plane they had assembled from parts. On 29 March the squadron received three F4F-4s from VMF-213, which was still in Espiritu Santo transitioning to the F4U Corsair.[2]

While the frequent mishaps were troubling and the lack of enemy contacts may have disappointed most of the fighter pilots, the squadron was accumulating experience working with Fighter Command as well as the torpedo and dive-bomber squadrons. Pilots flew almost every day, sometimes twice. Local patrols over Guadalcanal lasted two hours, and patrols over the Russells and missions to Munda could run more than three hours.[3] The pilots also gained familiarity with the geography of the southern and central Solomons.

Though the squadron had not encountered any enemy aircraft, it had seen some action. Within four hours of their arrival on Guadalcanal, Fighter Command had briefed the pilots of VMF-221 on the types of missions the command was conducting: combat air patrols, fighter sweeps, strikes, and bomber escorts. They learned about Japanese concentrations in the Solomons and the early warning they could expect from the Australian coast watchers. The following day Major Condon had given the squadron a detailed lecture on fighter tactics.[4]

From 17 to 31 March the squadron's divisions took turns flying combat air patrols over Guadalcanal and the Russell Islands. On 19 March, the day Coe perished, two divisions of VMF-221 joined another sixteen fighters from other squadrons to strafe Munda airfield on New Georgia. The following day Lieutenant Swett and his four-plane division escorted a flight of SBDs to strike Munda. On both missions the squadron encountered only light antiaircraft fire. On 21 March the squadron escorted two PBY seaplanes that inserted a group of marine raiders off Segi Plantation. The raiders linked up with Melanesian guides working with an Australian coast watcher named Donald G. Kennedy and began scouting enemy positions, beaches, and terrain around New Georgia. A week later, two divisions led by Captain Burns and Captain Payne escorted TBF strikes on Munda and on nearby Kolombangara at Vila, and 1st Lt. Albert E. Hacking and his division escorted SBDs to strike forty-five Japanese troops who had gotten a little too close to the coast watcher on Rendova Island. On 30 March Burns and Schocker with their two divisions escorted SBDs on strikes against a seaplane base at Rekata Bay on Santa Isabel Island and Munda on New Georgia.[5]

One thing the F4F-4s could not do was escort bombers all the way to Bougainville. On five occasions during the last two weeks of March, B-17s and B-24 Liberators from Bomber Command conducted daylight raids against airfields at Kahili on Bougainville and nearby Balalae.[6] The Japanese airfields at Vila and Munda lay at the extreme operating range of the F4F-4s at Fighter 2 on Guadalcanal.

Eleventh Air Fleet Fighter Sweep, 1 April

On 1 April, prior to Yamamoto's Operation I, Eleventh Air Fleet launched a fifty-eight-plane fighter sweep in two waves, with the first wave comprising thirty-two fighters and the second, twenty-six.[7] Overall U.S. fighter strength outnumbered the Japanese fighters two to one, but Fighter Command could not sortie all its fighters at once.

At 1035, a coast watcher near Buka Passage on the northern end of Bougainville reported twenty-six single-engine planes headed toward Guadalcanal. The marines' radar on the Russells detected a large group of aircraft at 1022 while the Japanese were still 155 miles from Henderson Field. The radar could not provide the number of aircraft, their type, or their altitude. Fighter Command had a division of navy F4Fs already aloft over the Russells and scrambled two more divisions of navy F4Fs. The fighter direction center put one division at 22,000 feet, another at 15,000 feet, and a third at 10,000 feet.

At 1110, the twelve Wildcats reported spotting between fifteen and thirty Zeros (actually thirty-two). Recognizing the serious threat, Fighter Command scrambled two divisions of F4Us from VMF-124.[8]

Though outnumbered, the dozen navy F4F-4s attacked the thirty-two Zeros. Amazingly, the F4Fs brought down three enemy fighters and lost just four of their own. The survivors returned to Fighter 2. The rest of this

Japanese formation may have retired; by noon, the seven F4Us had taken up combat air patrol over the Russells and had not yet encountered the enemy.

At 1202, the radar at Henderson Field detected an unknown aircraft (a "bogey" in fighter direction terminology) 142 miles distant. Fighter Command vectored a four-plane division under Captain Burns and a VS-27 division from combat air patrol over vessels anchored at Tulagi to join the F4Us over the Russells. At the same time the fighter direction center scrambled two four-plane divisions of F4F-4s from VMF-221 under Lieutenant Gale W. Roberts and Lieutenant Schocker along with seven P-38s and directed them into the fight over the Russells.[9] Meanwhile, another division from VMF-221 under Swett patrolled over Henderson Field.[10]

The second bogey was the second wave of twenty-six Japanese fighters. Fighter Command put thirty fighters up against them. Burns and his division, 23,000 feet over the Russells, spotted Zeros below them and attacked. Lieutenant Snider, flying on Burns' wing, conducted an overhead pass against two Zeros in column and sent both down in flames. When he spotted a third Zero below him at 10,000 feet, he continued his dive and torched that fighter too. Roberts and Schocker, climbing through 13,000 feet, observed the dogfight above them and attacked. Lieutenant Chapman destroyed a Zero looping to get behind Schocker. Staff Sergeant Pittman shot down a Zero tailing his wingman, 1st Lt. William E. Walker.

While the F4Us and F4F-4s tangled with the Zeros above the Russells, the P-38s dove on the Zeros from 32,000 feet. When the fight ended, the Americans claimed another fifteen victories, for a total of eighteen, while losing just two aircraft: an F4U and a P-38.[11] The postwar Japanese operational history reported the loss of only ten aircraft.[12]

In its first combat in the Solomons, VMF-221 claimed seven aerial victories. Chapman and Pittman each claimed one fighter while Lieutenant Dillow claimed two. Snider, in his first action, claimed three Zeros. All twelve of the squadron's fighters returned without a single bullet hole.[13]

While reported Japanese losses were just over half of what Fighter Command's pilots claimed, they markedly exceeded the six lost by Fighter Command.[14] AirSols recovered three of its downed aviators, while all the Eleventh Air Fleet's downed pilots perished.

Operation I: 7 April

For the next few days, VMF-221 resumed routine patrols without encountering enemy aircraft. If Technical Sergeant Voelker's log is representative of the squadron, the pilots were now flying one day on, one day off, but flying between two to three patrols each day on.[15] Brig. Gen. Francis P. Mulcahy, commander of the 2nd Marine Aircraft Wing, stopped by on 2 April to congratulate the squadron on its performance the day before. On 4 April, VMF-213, which had remained behind at Espiritu Santo, landed on Fighter 2 sporting new F4U Corsairs.[16]

Maintenance issues continued to pop up at inconvenient moments. On 6 April, 1st Lt. John W. Kellog's troublesome propeller and carburetor forced him to land early. A broken oil line forced Lieutenant Moore to land at Koli Point Field on the opposite side of Henderson Field from Fighter 2.[17]

Fighter Command was receiving excellent intelligence on the Eleventh Air Fleet's buildup in the northern Solomons. At 0800 on 6 April, army air force F-5 Lightning reconnaissance planes photographed twenty-two fighters and four medium bombers at Buka and Kahili and eleven floatplanes at Faisi near Bougainville. The central Solomons airfields at Vila and Munda were empty, as was Balalae.[18]

The seventh of April would see one of the largest air battles of the Pacific War. For this day's operations, Fighter Command could count on only 69 fighters, 24 fewer than it had on 1 April: 30 F4F-4s, 10 P-38s, 10 P-39s, 4 P-70s, and 6 P-40s. Despite the arrival of VMF-213, there were just 9 F4Us available; VMF-124 had departed at the conclusion of its combat tour.[19] To bolster Fighter Command, VMF-213 received 6 additional F4Us from Espiritu Santo early on 7 April.[20]

The Eleventh Air Fleet would put up 158 fighters and 67 dive-bombers, giving the Japanese a more than two-to-one advantage in fighters. The attackers would be led by 2 fighter groups from Buka: 27 Zeros from Air Group 204 and 21 Zeros from Air Group 253. Four strike groups from Balalae and Kahili formed around the carrier air groups from *Zuikaku*, *Hiyō*, and *Junyō*, and Eleventh Air Fleet's Air Group 582 would follow. Zeros from *Zuihō* reinforced each group, bringing their strength to 15–18 Vals and 23–26 Zeros each.[21]

AirSols did not wait for the Japanese to bring the fight to Guadalcanal. Two B-17s bombed Kahili and Balalae in the early-morning hours. Fourteen SBDs and four TBFs escorted by eleven F4F-4s struck Vila at 0615.[22] For VMF-221, the day started with a two-division escort for six TBFs and six SBDs on a search-and-attack mission. They found no ships, so they struck the seaplane base at Rekata Bay just after noon; one bomb hit a four-engine flying boat. Afterward the aircraft returned to Guadalcanal.[23]

AirSols' strikes had little effect on the Eleventh Air Fleet. At 1030, American aerial photographs revealed 247 single-engine aircraft on southern Bougainville,[24] a dramatic increase over the previous 24 hours.

Fighter Command was soon awash in intelligence. At 1145, AirSols received a warning from Pacific Fleet headquarters at Pearl Harbor to expect a Japanese air attack that afternoon against the Russells or Guadalcanal. Less than an hour later, coast watchers on Bougainville reported a force of forty-eight fighters; ten minutes after that they reported a second group of fifty aircraft.[25]

Pugh now anticipated an attack of nearly one hundred aircraft at 1400. Condon began stacking fighters over the Russells. A division of four F4Us over Henderson was ordered to the Russells and back-filled by a division of F4F-4s. Guadalcanal's fighter direction center scrambled additional fighters and pushed them up to the Russells. MAG-21's fighter direction center there took control and positioned them to intercept the incoming formation.[26]

AirSols launched a group of B-17s and TBFs that had been warming up on Guadalcanal for another strike on Kahili. With the escorting fighters busy and the Japanese aircraft aloft, the bombers flew east to avoid the incoming strike.[27] Although three American cruisers and six destroyers at Tulagi likewise got underway, at least three dozen vessels remained in scattered flotillas between Tulagi and Guadalcanal. These included the tender USS *Niagara* (PG 52) and her fifteen motor torpedo boats, the tanker USS *Kanawha* (AO 1), the transport USS *Stratford* (AP 41), six small coastal transports (APCs), eight amphibious assault ships (LCTs), the New Zealand corvette HMNZS *Moa* (T233) refueling from the station tanker USS *Erskine Phelps* (YON 147), a minesweeper, and a mishmash of auxiliary vessels.[28]

At 1348, the radar on the Russells detected a large bogey 207 miles from Henderson Field, just north of New Georgia. The Russells operators estimated it included at least thirty aircraft. This group, likely *Junyo*'s air group, headed south across New Georgia.[29]

At 1400, the Russells radar detected a second bogey 148 miles from Henderson Field, about 85 miles northwest of the Russells, between 25,000 and 30,000 feet. This would place the aircraft east of New Georgia. Pugh concluded that this flight at higher altitude, approaching at 240 mph, was a force of fighters intended to draw his own fighters away from Henderson Field and Tulagi. These were indeed likely the forty-eight Zeros of Air Groups 204 and 253. The fighter direction center ordered MAG-21, "Suspect some bogey to draw off your fighter—save some for large bogey."[30] To all units in the area went the alert "Condition red."[31]

At 1418, the radar at Henderson Field detected a third flight at a lower altitude and slower speed just 90 miles away. This was probably *Zuikaku*'s air group and Air Group 582 heading for Tulagi Harbor. In 4 minutes the flight had closed the distance to 78 miles, indicating an airspeed of approximately 180 miles per hour.[32] Around this time, Guadalcanal updated its alert to "Condition *very* red."[33] At 1427, the radar at Henderson picked up the large flight that had cut across New Georgia. This flight was now due west of Henderson at a range of 115 miles.[34]

At 1435, the New Zealand GCI radar picked up the Japanese formations, and its crew began feeding more precise altitudes to the fighter direction center. The New Zealand operators informed the fighter direction center that the first group had split into two groups of 20–25 aircraft each (Air Groups 204 and 253) orbiting at 28,000–30,000 feet between the Russells and Savo Island, about 60 miles northwest of Henderson Field.[35]

Twenty minutes later, at 1455, the GCI detected the large formation closing on Henderson from the west. The GCI reported the formation's altitude as 25,000–30,000 feet and its range as 43 miles, less than 15 minutes away from the ships off Lunga, the target of *Junyo*'s air group. The GCI operators also alerted the marines that this large formation had altered course to the northeast and was descending.[36]

Pugh and his fighter direction team had a fairly good understanding of the situation, though it is not clear that Allied radar had detected all six Japanese attack groups. The strengths, dispositions, and units depicted in

Map 4 are informed by the available evidence but should not be taken as a definitive interpretation.

Air Group 582 had encountered severe weather on its flight south. One Val had aborted, five had become separated and joined *Zuikaku*'s air group, and eight could not locate the target. The latter dropped their bombs in the ocean before returning to base. This left Air Group 582 with twenty-one fighters but just four dive-bombers.[37]

Radar was tracking a large formation of dive-bombers and fighters—probably *Junyo*'s air group—approaching Guadalcanal from the west. Two groups of a couple dozen fighters each—Air Groups 204 and 253—were loitering sixty miles from Henderson Field at high altitude. A fourth group—probably the strikes from *Zuikaku* and Air Group 582—was approaching from the northwest. *Hiyo*'s air group, headed for Koli Point, may have trailed *Junyo*'s air group, or may have trailed *Zuikaku*'s.[38] Any of these groups could be over the anchorage at Tulagi, Henderson Field, or the Russells in ten to twelve minutes. Even if Pugh could get every one of his fighters into the battle at once—an impossible task—his pilots would be severely outnumbered.

At 1438, Fighter Command had sixty-two fighters aloft. All were well above the cumulus. Over the Russells, MAG-21 had control of four P-39s at 22,000 feet, four VMF-221 F4F-4s under 1st Lt. Howard K. Winfield at 25,000 feet, and six VMF-213 F4Us under Captain Humberd (who had fought at Midway with VMF-221) above 30,000 feet. A four-Wildcat division from VMF-214 was 25,000 feet over Savo Island. Eight P-38s were climbing through 18,000 feet in the same area. Four P-38s were 31,000 feet above Beaufort Bay on Guadalcanal's southwest coast. Eight VMF-214 Wildcats under Capt. John R. "Smiley" Burnett were positioned over Cape Esperance, also at 30,000 feet. Another four F4F-4s from VMF-214 patrolled 15,000 feet over Rua Sura Island east of Henderson Field. Four P-40s patrolled over the Tulagi anchorage at 25,000 feet. Two divisions of F4F-4s from VMF-221 under Lieutenant Swett and Captain Payne were climbing through 13,000 feet en route to Tulagi. The last two divisions from VMF-221, led by Lieutenant Schocker and Lieutenant Hacking, patrolled over Henderson Field at 25,000 feet. Four F4Us were returning to Fighter 2, low on fuel after a three-hour patrol over the Russells. Three more F4Us were on alert at Fighter 2.[39]

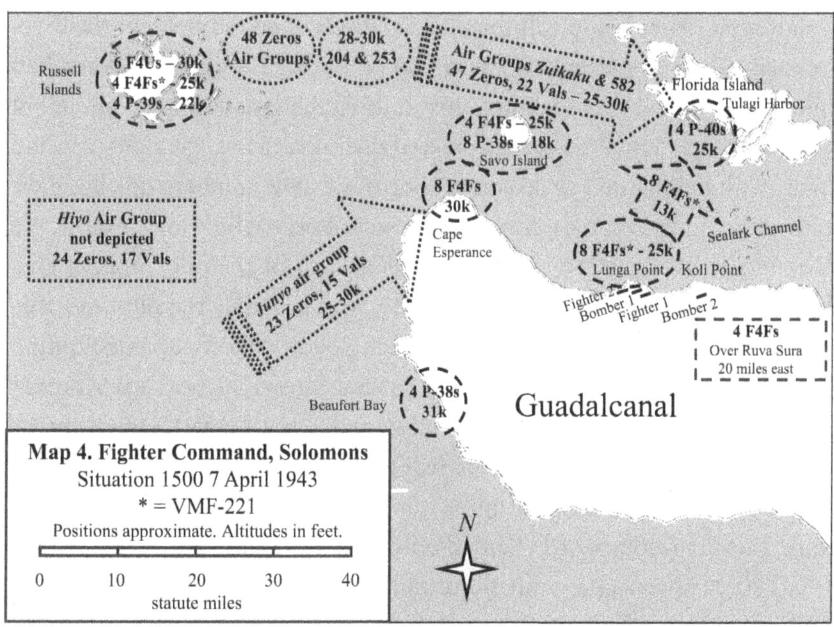

MAP 4. Fighter Command, Solomons Situation, 1500, 7 April 1943

At 1459, Captain Burnett over Cape Esperance sighted the Japanese formation approaching from the west. He hollered over the fighter channel, "Jesus Christ! There's a million of 'em!" He yelled, "Tally ho!" and attacked with his eight F4F-4s. Shortly thereafter he was heard to report, "There are Zeros and hawks all over me!"[40]

Each group of dive-bombers flew in a larger vee of three-plane vees. It is little wonder that Burnett reported Zeros all over him. His eight Wildcats were likely engaging *Junyo*'s air group of twenty-three fighters and fifteen dive-bombers. Burnett was shot down but survived and claimed one dive-bomber. The other seven F4F-4s survived the engagement. Two pilots claimed dive-bombers and a fourth claimed a fighter.[41]

Over Tulagi, Swett saw a large formation approaching the ships below him, likely the *Zuikaku* air group, Air Group 582, or both. The following narrative of Swett's actions in his first combat engagement is drawn primarily from two of his postwar accounts.

Gunning his F4F-4 to full throttle, Swett sprinted to intercept the dive-bombers. The other aircraft in Swett's flight followed, spread out over a half mile behind him. The escorting Zeros attacked the seven trailing F4F-4s, but Swett intercepted the Vals as they entered their dive. Making a right turn and diving with them, Swett closed on a group of six dive-bombers. The bombers were about 50 yards apart. Swett's guns were bore-sighted at 150 yards. He closed to 50 yards astern of the rear Val, aimed for the pilot, and let go a short burst. The gunfire killed the gunner and probably the pilot too. The Val caught fire and plunged toward the sea. Swett, soaked with perspiration in his first combat, closed to within 50 yards astern of the next Val. Another quick burst and it too caught fire and plummeted toward earth. Ignoring the 7.7-mm machine-gun fire from the rear gunners, Swett closed on the tail of a third Val. He let go another quick burst from his six .50-caliber machine guns. This dive-bomber too flamed quickly and went down.[42]

His plane approaching one thousand feet, Swett pulled up sharply over the anchorage and leveled off at five hundred feet. As he maneuvered amidst the enemy dive-bombers, at least one antiaircraft gunner mistook him for a Japanese plane. Swett felt a violent blow on his port wing. He glanced over and saw one of his machine gun barrels bent upward and protruding from a hole in the wing. The strike also destroyed his flaps. But the plane was otherwise undamaged, and he still had five working guns. Swett sped north over the harbor toward Florida Island, then east to avoid a layer of cumulus.[43]

Flying between the clouds and the jungle at five hundred feet, Swett emerged on the eastern side of Florida. To his surprise, he discovered "a whole flock of dive-bombers." These bombers had just attacked ships near Tulagi, and he had stumbled across their rendezvous point. As the dive-bombers were at the same altitude as Swett and were far slower, Swett was a fox in a chicken coop. He easily caught the nearest dive-bomber in a gentle left turn. Swett closed on its tail and shot it down with a quick burst. The next dive-bomber was ahead and to the right. Swett zigged right, zagged left, and positioned his fighter behind it. He fired a short burst, and this fifth Val went down too. Swett maneuvered behind a sixth, shot it down, and a seventh, and shot it down too. He tried for number eight but perhaps came too close. When he was between twenty-five and thirty feet from the dive-bomber's tail, the gunner fired his 7.7-mm machine gun and "knocked the living hell out of my windshield and my oil cooler and everything else." Swett got in a burst nonetheless that killed the gunner. He saw the aircraft trail smoke but did not see it go down. Alone, nearly out of ammunition, and losing oil pressure, Swett headed for Henderson Field.[44]

He recrossed Florida Island, but over Tulagi Harbor his engine froze. The Wildcat dropped. Without flaps to control its angle of descent, the aircraft landed hard on the water, bounced once, and plunged beneath the surface. Swett undid his seatbelt and shoulder harness, but as the aircraft sank, his parachute harness caught on the life raft release handle. The sinking fighter dragged Swett down. The water became colder and darker. At last, Swett freed himself and popped to the surface. His life raft emerged too, but only half inflated. Within fifteen minutes a coast guard picket boat recovered him.[45]

If Swett's colorful accounts are accurate, his gunnery was remarkable. He had claimed seven enemy aircraft and probably an eighth. With 240 rounds per gun, he had averaged just 30 rounds per gun against each victim, or 3 seconds of firing.

The rest of Swett's division did not fare so well. Staff Sergeant Pittman, Swett's wingman, claimed he shot down one dive-bomber before Zeros shot his plane full of holes. Pittman's landing gear collapsed at Fighter 2, but he walked away. In the second section of Swett's division, Lieutenant Roberts and 1st Lt. Edward A. Walsh were also shot down. Walsh claimed one fighter.[46]

Captain Payne's division jettisoned their wing tanks at ten thousand feet, and Payne led the four F4F-4s in a climbing, head-on attack in line abreast. Around two dozen escorting Zeros peeled away from the bombers and dove on Payne's division. Payne's wingman, 2nd Lt. Pitzer P. Pittman, claimed he brought down a dive-bomber before the fighters swarmed over his Wildcat and Payne's and shot them both down. Lieutenant Baldwin and his wingman, Lieutenant Hallmeyer, each claimed a Zero in the melee. Hallmeyer claimed another before his F4F-4 was struck fatally. Baldwin watched Hallmeyer bail out, leaving him alone in a sky full of Zeros. One behind him fired wild bursts, maneuvering to get directly astern for a kill shot. Baldy flew for his life. He remembered being told, "If you can see the adversary, you should never be shot down." Baldy twisted and turned, keeping the pursuing fighter in view. The technique worked, and Baldwin eventually evaded the Zero.[47]

Twenty-five thousand feet over the Russells, ten Zeros hit Winfield's division in an overhead attack. The four Wildcats evaded the attackers but took many hits and scored no kills.[48]

Over Koli Point, fifteen Zeros, likely from *Junyō*'s air group, attacked Schocker's division. The Zeros easily prevented the outnumbered marines from menacing the dive-bombers, which began bombing ships off Koli Point at 1512. Schocker and his wingman, Chapman, stayed alive by scissoring and exchanging bursts with Zeros for forty minutes over Henderson Field before running low on gas and ammunition. When he got back, Chapman counted more than thirty holes in his aircraft, "and the other 3 not too much better." Lieutenant Schocker, Lieutenant Chapman, and 1st Lt. Arthur T. Wood were each credited with downing a fighter, though it was unclear exactly who downed which Zero. The fighter direction center kept Hacking's division over Henderson Field, where it encountered no enemy aircraft.[49]

Out of Swett's division, only Staff Sergeant Pittman's severely damaged F4F-4 survived. All of Payne's division had gone down. VMF-221's other three divisions returned to Fighter 2, but the aircraft in Winfield's and Schocker's divisions were too severely damaged to fly right away. Only the four fighters in Hacking's division escaped unscathed.[50]

Fighter Command claimed forty-one aerial victories. VMF-221 claimed eight Vals and eleven Zeros shot down and another of each type probably destroyed.[51] The Japanese reported their actual losses as twelve Zeros and seven Vals, just under half of Fighter Command's claims. Another five Vals were lost either en route to Guadalcanal in bad weather or on the return flight out of sight of Allied observers.[52] VMF-221 lost seven Wildcats; VMF-214 lost another two; and XIII Fighter Command lost a P-39. As many as four badly damaged fighters returned safely only to be written off.[53]

Had the twenty-four aircraft that the Japanese reported lost all been shot down by Fighter Command, its pilots would have achieved close to a two-to-one loss ratio. However, antiaircraft guns aboard vessels and ashore were credited with destroying twenty-five Japanese aircraft, more than a third of the American claims. VMF-221's nineteen claims cannot be verified. In an exacting investigation of the available evidence, aviation historian Richard Dunn established that Swett should be credited with five aircraft at best and should share the credit for some of those five with antiaircraft gunners.[54] Michael Claringbould reviewed the same evidence and made a persuasive argument that Swett shot down just two or three dive-bombers.[55]

What is indisputable is that the Japanese lost one out of every eleven aircraft they committed to the strike. What is also certain, and more important, is the effect the raid had on Halsey's fleet.

More than half of the fifty-four bombs Val dive-bombers had carried when they reached Guadalcanal inflicted damage. U.S. ships suffered seven hits and twenty-seven damaging near misses.[56] The attackers sank three ships: the destroyer USS *Aaron Ward* (DD 483), the tanker *Kanawha*, and the New Zealand corvette *Moa*. Several minor vessels suffered damage. Though none of the airfields and supply depots had been hit, the command diary of the Pacific Fleet recorded on 7 April, "[O]ur air strength in the Guadalcanal area cannot prevent serious losses and damage to our surface forces in those waters." Fearing that he could not protect his ships in the central Solomons, Halsey temporarily relinquished sea control around New Georgia. The Third Fleet withdrew its cruisers, destroyers, and logistics vessels from the southern Solomons and postponed bombardment and minelaying operations in the central Solomons until it was clear that no further aerial attacks were coming.[57] Kusaka's Southeast Area Fleet exploited the opportunity and reinforced the defenders of New Georgia by barge and occasional nighttime destroyer sorties. However, Operation I's focus turned to New Guinea on 11 April. Kusaka failed to follow up with additional strikes against Guadalcanal, leaving Halsey to continue his logistics buildup. Naval historian Samuel Eliot Morison assessed that Operation I delayed the Third Fleet's New Georgia offensive by only ten days.[58]

Aircrew Survival and Recovery

As previously mentioned, a coast guard patrol craft pulled Swett from Tulagi Harbor fifteen minutes after he ditched. While Swett was recovering on Tulagi that evening, Walsh walked in, having banged his head on the gunsight when he ditched but otherwise healthy. On 9 April Hallmeyer returned to the squadron. Solomon islanders had picked him up and taken him by canoe to Tulagi. Later that evening the squadron learned Roberts had also been recovered, two days after he had bailed out. This left only Lieutenant Pittman missing from the 7 April action. On 14 April word came from Tulagi that Pittman was hospitalized there, recovering from a shrapnel wound in his leg.[59]

Air Force, South Pacific had recovered all but one of Fighter Command's nine downed aviators, whereas all but four of Eleventh Air Fleet's thirty-six downed aircrew were killed or captured.[60] Recovering aircrew was a priority for Air Force, South Pacific. This practice not only preserved trained airmen but also bolstered morale. The pilots of AirSols enjoyed the support of the local population, as Hallmeyer's rescue demonstrated. The PBYs of Air Search Unit, South Pacific could land and recover aviators at sea and along island coastlines. In contrast, the Eleventh Air Fleet had no similar capability and placed little emphasis on rescuing its downed pilots. Those shot down in the southern Solomons had no chance of being picked up.

Killing Yamamoto and the Limitations of Marine Aircraft

On 17 April, Third Fleet learned that Admiral Yamamoto would be flying into Balalae off the southern tip of Bougainville the following morning at 0945. Halsey directed Fighter Command to intercept the flight and shoot it down. Pugh and Condon quickly determined that only the P-38 fighters of XIII Fighter Command had the range to conduct the mission. Eighteen P-38s intercepted Yamamoto's flight and sent both Yamamoto's Betty and a second one down in flames. The commander of the Combined Fleet was dead.[61]

The 660-mile round-trip mission exceeded the combat radius of the marine F4F-4s and F4Us at Fighter 2. Not only were the carrier aircraft that the marines flew unable to match the range of the army air force P-38s, they could not even achieve the specifications determined by the Bureau of Aeronautics. Lieutenant Colonel Clifford reported that an F4F-4 with wing tanks could achieve an actual combat radius of just 230 miles in the South Pacific when flown efficiently.[62]

VMF-221 Operations, 8 April–2 May

On 8 April, Fighter Command could muster only eighteen airworthy F4F-4s. Four days later, that number surged to ninety-three Wildcats as ground crews repaired battle damage and Air Force, South Pacific pushed replacement aircraft and squadrons forward. Aerial photography revealed that Japanese strength in the northern Solomons had dwindled to fifty-one fighters, five medium bombers, and fifteen floatplanes.[63]

VMF-221's mechanics did not participate in this recovery. Beginning on 4 April, Marine Aircraft Wings South Pacific began transporting the squadron's ground echelon forward by ship, barge, and air transport from Espiritu Santo. They went not to Guadalcanal but to a new airfield in the Russells that Seabees had completed on 15 April. Most would remain there until 14 June, supporting other marine squadrons.[64]

The pilots of VMF-221 patrolled the southern Solomons for the remainder of this combat tour without encountering opposition. AirSols conducted strikes on Japanese airfields as far north as Kahili on the southern tip of Bougainville. The airfields around Bougainville lay outside the range of all Guadalcanal's fighters except the P-38s. B-17s, B-24s, and marine and navy TBFs struck these airfields, with little to show for it. SBDs and TBFs struck the airfields at Munda and Vila in the New Georgia area as well as the seaplane base at Rekata Bay on Santa Isabel Island during daylight, escorted by fighters of VMF-221 and other squadrons, but rarely found targets of value. Search planes and coast watchers reported barges and occasionally destroyers and transports in the northern and central Solomons, but AirSols was unable to exploit this intelligence. The Japanese grew adept at concealing barges in small coves, and carefully kept their destroyers outside the range of all but the army air force heavy bombers during daylight.[65]

On 22 April the squadron moved to the newly renovated Fighter 1 airstrip. The delighted pilots left behind their tents and moved into Quonset huts—prefabricated metal buildings that sheltered them from the weather and mosquitos. Despite more comfortable living conditions, however, malaria still took down marines. On 1 May, Lieutenant Schocker, 2nd Lt. Marshall R.

Tutton, Lieutenant Walsh, and the flight surgeon, Lieutenant O'Connell, were evacuated to Espiritu Santo for malaria treatment.[66]

On 2 May, VMF-112, an F4U squadron, landed at Fighter 2 to relieve VMF-221. On 4 May, eleven of the aviators flew their F4F-4s south to Espiritu Santo. The remaining pilots had joined them there by 8 May, catching rides on transport aircraft.[67]

8

★ ★ ★

Second Combat Tour, Russell Islands, 26 June–13 August 1943

VMF-221's first combat tour had lasted seven weeks. Afterward, following Marine Aircraft Wings Pacific policy, the aircrews rotated to the rear for rest.

Rotation, Rest, and Recreation, 9–21 May

Around this time, the medical officer of the 2nd Marine Aircraft Wing reported that some squadrons suffered from low efficiency, fighting spirit, and morale. He attributed this to flying too many hours per day, combat tours that were too long, rest periods that were too brief, harsh living conditions, and poor rations. The medical officer observed pilots in other squadrons returning for a third combat tour who had "recuperated so little mentally and physically that they were practically worthless."[1]

VMF-221 benefited from the remedies the command instituted. The Quonset huts at Fighter 1 were one obvious improvement at the front. The pilots appreciated the break from flying. They also enjoyed a rest period in Sydney, Australia, from 9 to 21 May. By most accounts, the people of Sydney, particularly pub owners and young women, enthusiastically welcomed them.[2]

New Fighters, New Pilots, New Commander

The pilots returned to Espiritu Santo to another improvement: F4U-1 Corsairs. Tests by Maj. William E. Gise of MAG-12 had shown that the F4U outclimbed the F4F-4, reaching 20,000 feet in less than half the time even when encumbered by full drop tanks. The F4U's operating radius with full tanks was 287 miles, 57 miles farther than the Wildcat's.[3] The first marines who flew the F4U against the Zero estimated the Corsair was as fast as the Japanese fighter, could keep up in a climb with it at 15,000 feet, and maneuvered at least as well as the Zero. They found that a Corsair pilot in a pickle could escape by making a steep right-hand turn and diving away.[4] In late 1944 the navy tested a captured Zero against the F4U and determined the F4U averaged 64 mph faster at all altitudes, outclimbed the Zero above 10,000 feet, and outdove the Zero. Above 230 mph, the Corsair outmaneuvered the Zero, but the slower the speed, the greater the Zero's advantage.[5]

The F4U was superior in many respects to the F6F Hellcat that the navy selected to replace F4Fs aboard carriers. Carrier landing experiments with the F4U had gone poorly. The plane's long nose obscured the pilot's view of the flight deck. Its rigid landing gear caused the aircraft to bounce. Tail wheels blew out on the hard flight decks. Most concerning to the fleet, there were no Corsair parts in the pipeline for the carriers. Land-based marine squadrons benefited from the navy's preference for the Hellcat.[6]

Burns, now a major, turned the squadron over to Maj. Monfurd K. Peyton on 1 June.[7] Shortly after that, Burns contracted malaria and returned to the United States for treatment.[8] Peyton, from Morgan County, Kentucky, had graduated from Asbury College in 1930 and coached high school basketball, baseball, and tennis for two years before enlisting as a private in 1932. After recruit training he remained at Parris Island and served as a drill instructor. In June 1938, while a corporal at the marine barracks in Washington, DC, Peyton received a regular commission. As a second lieutenant he attended The Basic School and served aboard cruisers in the Pacific Fleet before reporting to flight school in November 1940. He earned his wings in May 1941.[9]

Peyton had flown F4Us as the executive officer of VMF-213. On 25 April, Peyton led his four-plane division on a strafing attack against Vila. On the return leg, Peyton spotted sixteen Bettys and twenty or more Zeros. Though outnumbered nine to one, Peyton attacked. He shot down three Zeros and his division claimed another two, though VMF-213 lost two Corsairs and one of its pilots. Peyton returned with seventy-eight holes in his Corsair, one in his left shoulder, and another in his left knee.[10]

In late May, eight lieutenants joined the squadron. After Lieutenant Schocker returned on 20 June, Peyton organized his twenty-six pilots into six divisions.[11] The majority of the pilots, including all the division and section leaders, were now combat veterans.

The squadron had exactly thirty days to train before its second combat tour. For the first three weeks, pilots concentrated on familiarizing themselves with the new aircraft. During the final week they practiced gunnery, section tactics, division tactics, and night flying. Training time was shortened by the need to share a limited number of airworthy fighters with other squadrons. For the last three days of May, flying was suspended because there were no mechanics available to service the planes.[12]

Training mishaps took a toll of aircraft and men. On 24 May the veteran 1st Lt. Norman L. George spun in while attempting to land. He survived, but his injuries grounded him and the aircraft was lost. On 2 June, one of the new lieutenants ground-looped his Corsair, which flipped over and caught fire. He survived but was transferred to a dive-bomber squadron. On 8 June Lieutenant Wood, a veteran, also ground-looped and flipped his fighter. The following day 2nd Lt. Robert C. Hanckle, a new replacement, collided with an SBD during a practice interception and was killed.[13]

On 25 June, the squadron flew nineteen Corsairs first to Guadalcanal and then on to the new base in the Russells the following day. One trailing Corsair and the six surplus pilots joined them there. The pilots had missed rejoining their ground echelon by twelve days. Marine Aircraft Wings Pacific had rotated the majority of VMF-221's marines from the Russells to Guadalcanal on 14 June.[14]

D-Day on New Georgia, 30 June

Seabees had completed a 4,100-foot crushed-coral runway on Banika in the Russells in late June.[15] The new airfield extended the reach of fighters and relieved the congestion on Guadalcanal, which housed more than three hundred aircraft, often vulnerably parked wingtip to wingtip. Banika was home to Lt. Col. Raymond F. Hopper's MAG-21, which comprised VMF-121, VMF-214, and VMF-221. The squadrons found Banika to be a nicer home than Fighter 2. The fighter squadrons had Quonset huts on a shaded hilltop for their ready rooms, offices, mess halls, and billets. Seabees provided burgers and milkshakes to any aircrew who dropped in. Fighters were parked in hardened revetments.[16]

MAG-21's mechanics worked tirelessly, sometimes twenty-four hours a day. The F4U proved more difficult to maintain than the F4F. Parts were in short supply, and Banika had no boneyard of wrecked Corsairs where the mechanics could scavenge parts. Machinists often fabricated parts the group could not obtain. Pilots commonly flew missions in aircraft that would have been grounded in the United States.[17]

VMF-221's arrival preceded the Third Fleet's amphibious assault on New Georgia by four days. Halsey's offensive would stir up a hornet's nest of Japanese air responses. In the weeks prior, Fighter Command had crushed three attempts by the Eleventh Air Fleet to disrupt the fleet's preparations. Japanese losses were so heavy that Admiral Mineichi Koga, who had succeeded Yamamoto, stripped another 150 aircraft from his carriers at Truk and sent them to Rabaul to oppose Halsey.[18]

The squadron encountered no enemy aircraft during its first four days. For D-day at New Georgia, 30 June, AirSols had an astounding 455 aircraft available, including 213 fighters. All army, marine, and navy aircraft in the New Georgia area were controlled by the New Georgia Air Force, the forward echelon of the 2nd Marine Aircraft Wing. Fighters were initially directed by a fighter director group embarked aboard a destroyer, and later by a similar group ashore on Rendova. A lightweight SCR-602 operated by the New Georgia Air Force and SCR-268, SCR-270, and SCR-516 radars operated by 9th Defense Battalion supported the fighter direction center on Rendova.

Fighter Command tasked VMF-221 to rotate air patrols of sixteen fighters each over the amphibious force assaulting Rendova, beginning at 0545 with only an hour between patrols. Air Command New Georgia stacked fighters over Rendova between 5,000 and 20,000 feet, rotating them to conserve the pilots' oxygen.

Visibility was poor during the squadron's morning and midday patrols, and they sighted no enemy aircraft. A final afternoon patrol of sixteen F4Us went up into clearer skies. Captain Payne, Captain Swett, Lieutenant Winfield, and Lieutenant Schocker orbited their divisions 10,000 feet over a task force of 10 transports and 7 destroyers that was steaming south after offloading. The fighter direction center on Rendova alerted the Corsairs to a force of 26 Bettys inbound at 2,000 feet covered by 24 Zeros at 15,000 feet. The fighter director sent Corsairs from VMF-122 and VMF-213 as well as navy Wildcats from VF-21 to engage the Zeros, and then radioed VMF-221, "Go get 'em, boys. Protect your shipping!" All four divisions commenced diving attacks against the Bettys, which were arrayed in a vee of vees.

On his first diving pass Captain Payne shot down a bomber and set fire to a second that was already smoking. His wingman, 1st Lt. George S. Langston, raked the wing of another Betty with gunfire on his second run and watched it explode.

Lieutenant Baldwin caught a Betty closing on the ships and fired into it for ten seconds. He watched it burst into flames and fly into the water. After regaining altitude, he spotted a Zero making a gunnery pass at him and turned into him. The Zero dove into a cloud and Baldwin lost sight of him. He spotted another Zero pursuing a Corsair, caught that Zero in the top of a wing-over, fired into it, and watched it burn and spin in. Another Zero jumped on Baldwin's tail, forcing him to dive into a cloud. When he emerged, only one of his guns was still working; he got on the tail of a Zero and fired ineffectively at it from behind until the Zero hid in a cloud.

Swett and his wingman, the replacement pilot 1st Lt. Harold E. "Manny" Segal, each claimed a Betty on their first diving pass. Swett claimed another Betty and a Zero, which he attacked at the same time as a Wildcat. Segal watched a Wildcat pursue a Zero and then quit the chase. Seeing his opportunity, Segal followed the Zero and caught it over Kula Gulf between New Georgia and Kolombangara, fired into it, and saw it explode.

Lieutenant Walker caught one Zero on the top of a roll, fired, and watched it flame and crash. He chased another and thought it was smoking when it disappeared in a cloud. Lieutenant Dillow claimed one Betty before it dropped its torpedo, shot down a second after it dropped its torpedo, and damaged a third Betty and a Zero. Lt. John W. Kellogg also shot down a Betty making a torpedo run.

VMF-221's pilots claimed 13 Bettys and 3 Zeros destroyed along with 4 Bettys and 2 Zeros probably destroyed. U.S. claims totaled 26 Bettys and 32 Zeros. The Japanese actually lost 19 Bettys and 10 Zeros. Between losses earlier that day and damaged aircraft, the Eleventh Air Fleet's operational strength dropped from 134 on 30 June to 27 the following morning.[19]

Ten Bettys had survived long enough to attack the task force, scoring a torpedo hit amidships on the attack transport USS *McCawley* (APA 4) that killed fifteen of her crew. *McCawley* stayed afloat, but while she was under tow that night, American patrol boats mistakenly torpedoed her and she sank.[20]

Protecting the Landing Area, 1–10 July

Around noon on 2 July, Admiral Mitscher, commanding AirSols, withdrew fighter cover, including two divisions from VMF-221, due to the worsening weather. The New Georgia Air Force, concerned by the resulting gap in fighter protection, had Mitscher's order confirmed three times before it released the fighters. In an unhappy coincidence, a marine had disabled the 9th Defense Battalion's SCR-268 radar when he refueled it with diesel oil from a drum mistakenly labeled "gasoline." The battalion's SCR-270 and SCR-516 radars were not yet operational, and the New Georgia Air Force's SCR-602 radar was being refueled as well. During this window, between eighteen and twenty-five Bettys escaped detection and dropped fifty bombs on the beachhead at Rendova. The raid killed fifty-nine soldiers, sailors, and marines and wounded another seventy-seven.[21]

VMF-221 was not flying patrols two days later when eighteen Bettys and seventeen Zeros repeated the approach of 2 July while forty-nine Zeros protected them. Fighter Command had forty fighters aloft, and the anti-aircraft gunners of the ships and the 9th Defense Battalion were ready this time. Six Bettys went down. A seventh was damaged beyond repair. At least four Bettys dropped bombs among the Landing Craft, Infantry (LCIs) off

Rendova, damaging three of the vessels. The strike killed five sailors and marines while wounding thirteen.[22]

The raids of 2 and 4 July were anomalies. Though the landing beaches were just an hour from Japanese airfields on southern Bougainville, and the New Georgia Air Force sounded "Condition red" as many as four times a day for the next three weeks, bombers rarely got through Fighter Command in daylight. At night, bombers often dropped their loads around American bases throughout the Solomons but rarely inflicted damage.[23]

Due to American air superiority, Japanese warships were restricted to nighttime forays. The Eighth Fleet's cruisers and destroyers occasionally clashed with the Third Fleet around New Georgia while its transports were attempting to reinforce New Georgia under the cover of darkness.[24] On 6 July, two divisions, one led by Captain Payne and the other by Lieutenant Winfield, covered the destroyers USS *Nicholas* (DD 449) and USS *Radford* (DD 446), which had lingered in Kula Gulf to pick up 745 survivors of the torpedoed cruiser USS *Helena* (CL 50).[25]

Payne and Winfield and their divisions took off just after noon on 7 July for Rendova. Payne and Lieutenant Baldwin aborted because their engines were running rough. The remaining six fighters consolidated into a single division. Around 1350, the fighter director on Rendova directed Winfield's division and fighters from VMF-121 and VMF-122 to intercept a force of six Bettys. Over the northern tip of New Georgia at 22,000 feet, Winfield spotted what he thought was a dozen bombers approaching from the north 3,000 feet above him; the bombers were covered by an equal number of fighters 2,000 feet above them. As Winfield's division climbed for an attack position, a previously unseen group of what looked to the marines like 50 fighters swarmed down from 30,000 feet. The six marines began weaving defensively. For twenty minutes the Corsairs took turns driving Zeros off each other's tails. Despite being outnumbered, all six returned. Three VMF-221 pilots each claimed a Zero while the other squadrons claimed another seven Zeros along with six bombers. The Japanese reported their actual losses as only two Zeros and two bombers.[26]

Overcast and rainy skies prevented AirSols from striking Bougainville until 5 July. Beginning the following day, B-17s, B-24s, and B-25 Mitchells from Guadalcanal mounted day and night raids against the airfields there. VMF-221 escorted B-25s on 8 July without contact. On a similar mission on 10 July, VMF-221's eight F4Us failed to rendezvous with some B-25s, which proceeded without them and hit their target on Kolombangara without encountering enemy fighters.[27]

The Eleventh Air Fleet Strike, 11 July

On the morning of 11 July, two divisions from VMF-221 patrolling over Munda spotted a lone Mitsubishi Type 100 Ki-46 "Dinah" twin-engine reconnaissance aircraft at 30,000 feet.[28] Lieutenant Snider and Lieutenant Hacking pursued the aircraft. After several gunnery runs and maneuvers, Hacking made a climbing gunnery pass from astern, positioning his Corsair so that the Dinah's tail would mask him from the rear gunner's fire. Hacking fired into the port engine on the climb and then dove back, firing at the starboard engine. He closed for a third pass, firing into the cockpit. Hacking observed both crewmen slumped over before the aircraft exploded.[29]

At 0955, two divisions led by Captain Swett and Lieutenant Schocker took off to patrol over Rendova. En route to Rendova, Swett's division pulled ahead of Schocker's, and the two divisions became separated. The pilots were frequently frustrated by difficulty transmitting and receiving over their radios. The fighter director suspected a Japanese submarine spotted in the area was jamming the fighter direction net.[30]

Two hours into the flight, Lieutenant Dillow's engine stopped when he switched fuel tanks. His wingman, Lieutenant Kellogg, escorted him back to Banika. Swett did not notice they had departed, leaving him with only his wingman, Lieutenant Segal. When Segal shifted to high blower as they passed 20,000 feet, his engine began running rough and he could not keep up. Swett began weaving with Segal, which enabled Segal to keep up and provided mutual protection for both aircraft.

The mechanical gremlins continued their pranks. After two orbits over Rendova, Lieutenant Wood's motor burned out a magneto. Wood retuned to Banika, leaving Schocker with his wingman Chapman and 1st Lt. William E. Sage, a replacement. Sage, perhaps hearing a transmission from fighter direction, pulled alongside Schocker and pointed toward Kolombangara. Schocker led his division up to 30,000 feet and north to Kolombangara, where he would be between the Japanese airfields on Bougainville and the ships off Rendova.

After flying around a large cumulus cloud, Chapman spotted what he estimated as fifteen bombers, each escorted by two flights of eight Zeros, thirty miles away and five thousand feet below them. The raid actually consisted of eight Bettys and forty-seven Zeros. Though they knew they were outnumbered by the Zeros five to one (actually, nearly sixteen to one), Schocker, Chapman, and Sage attacked.[31]

The three Corsairs dove out of the sun at the vee of Bettys. Schocker missed on his first pass but downed one on his second pass. As Schocker and Chapman began their second pass, the Bettys jettisoned their bombs. Five of Chapman's guns jammed. As he attempted to charge them, he saw "a cloudlike formation" of Zeros with a sole Corsair maneuvering wildly in the middle. He presumed the Corsair was Sage's. Chapman evaded the Zeros with a turning dive, weaving at one point with another Corsair he encountered. Alone again, he headed for home. Fire from a pursuing Zero hit him several times. One 20-mm round exploded in his cockpit, wounding his heel. Machine-gun bullets peppered his tail, and hydraulic fluid covered his windshield. Chapman struggled to control the Corsair, but he escaped and managed an emergency landing at Banika.[32]

Around 1155, Swett heard radio transmissions describing Schocker's contact but could not hear where the fight was taking place. He and Segal were over New Georgia, about twenty-five miles southeast of Kolombangara. Segal's engine was still running rough, and Swett told him to head back to base, but Segal opted to stay with Swett rather than let him fight alone. They headed northwest and spotted the same vee of Bettys that Schocker's division had engaged at 20,000 feet over Kula Gulf. The accompanying Zeros were scattered about, covering the Bettys from above but no longer in a coherent formation.

Swett and Segal each made a single gunnery pass from astern. Swett set a Betty on fire, then dove for the clouds. Segal fired into a Zero maneuvering against Swett and watched it burst into flames. Segal lost track of Swett, so he made a gunnery run on the last Betty in the formation from astern and 100–200 feet above. Although he fired 100 rounds from each gun into the bomber, it did not burn or change course. Defensive fire from the bombers and then from two Zeros shot holes through Segal's F4U, and he dove from 25,000 feet to 6,000 feet to evade them. After escaping his pursuers Segal climbed back to 25,000 feet. He was too far away to attack the bomber formation again, but he saw ten Zeros below and only three miles away. There were no friendlies in sight. He called Swett on the radio but got no response. Segal noticed two Zeros separated from the other eight, just 4,000 feet below him, and pounced. He fired into the top Zero and saw it blow up. He added left rudder while still firing and saw the second Zero smoke, burn, and go down—his third claim this mission. Segal then felt bullets riddling his plane again. Three Zeros were approaching from the right. He immediately performed a split-S and dove evasively for the second time. Throughout the dive, Zeros continued to make gunnery runs on his F4U.

Segal leveled off at twenty-five feet just off Visuvisu Point, the northernmost spot on New Georgia. He stated afterward that his airspeed indicator registered 360 knots (414 mph), which he held for a couple of minutes to elude four Zeros pursuing him. As he headed south toward Segi, his airspeed dropped to 300 mph, then to 160 mph 10 minutes later. The oil pressure fell to 0, and the cylinder head temperature went "sky-high." Bullets splashed around him, then peppered his wings, and then he felt them hammer the armor plate behind his seat. He was still going more than 100 mph when he made a water landing.

Despite smashing his face into the dashboard, Segal remained conscious and escaped the sinking craft. He inflated his life preserver. The Zeros left without strafing him. He inflated his raft, climbed in, and drifted.

When Swett emerged from the clouds, he saw a Corsair on fire with a Zero on its tail. Swett wheeled behind the Zero and shot its wing off. Unsure of whom he had just helped, Swett radioed, "Smoking Corsair, get out of that thing." Diving through the clouds, he found a Betty skimming the surface with a single Zero flying top cover. He waited until the Zero was out of position and closed to within fifty yards of the Betty. The bomber nosed over and hit the water. Then a Zero he had not seen peppered his cowling and the engine sputtered. Swett lost fuel and oil pressure and glided into the sea five miles off New Georgia.

Swett exited the cockpit, dove into the water, and hid behind the exposed tail of his floating Corsair for about five minutes as two Zeros checked to see if he had survived. When they left, he inflated his life preserver and raft and retrieved his parachute, which had floated free of the aircraft. Swett paddled all afternoon and came ashore at Lingatu on the north coast of New Georgia.

Segal, meanwhile, had lost his paddles, so he drifted along with the current. Later that afternoon, an albatross landed on his leg. He trapped the bird with his other leg, wrung its neck, and kept it for food. He tried towing the raft while swimming and using the emergency sail but soon gave up and hoped friendly islanders or a passing aircraft would spot him. He covered himself with the sail and slept for a time, spending a miserable wet night off New Georgia, presumably with the dead albatross for company. The following morning a flotilla of four U.S. destroyers sailed by within a thousand yards of Segal and spotted him. One destroyer plucked him from the sea. A boat took Segal to Guadalcanal that afternoon, and he hitched a ride in a transport aircraft back to Banika.

Swett slept on the beach at Lingatu that night and then paddled through a lagoon most of the next day. Around 1500 he linked up with islanders who brought him to Kennedy, the coast watcher. Swett ate dinner with Kennedy and afterward traveled to the new American field at Segi on the southern tip of New Georgia. Swett spent the night aboard an LCT (Landing Craft, Tank) and next caught a ride in an APc-1 coastal transport over to Banika, where he was reunited with Segal. Sage was never found.

VMF-221 had lost three Corsairs (but just one pilot) and claimed the Dinah, two Bettys, and four Zeros. The Japanese reported losing the Dinah, one Betty, and two Zeros. Of most importance, perhaps, the attack by Schocker's division had caused the Japanese bombers to abandon their strike.[33]

AirSols Strike on Kahili, 17 July 1943

The next six days consisted of patrols without contact, but mechanical problems continued to plague the squadron.[34] On 14 July, Lieutenant Hacking's F4U began smoking and vibrating while he was over Viru Harbor on the southwest side of New Georgia. He bailed out, and a crash boat rescued him a short time later.[35]

Throughout July, the Eleventh Air Fleet based dozens of Zeros and Vals at Kahili, on the southern end of Bougainville and only minutes from New Georgia by air. On the morning of 17 July, at least three Japanese destroyers and several cargo vessels were in the harbor at Kahili. That morning over Visuvisu Point, 8 VMF-221 F4Us and 106 other fighters rendezvoused with an exceptionally large strike of 7 B-24s, 37 SBDs, and 25 TBFs. Their target was the vessels at Kahili.[36]

Seven B-24s bombed from high altitude followed by 37 SBDs and 25 TBFs. Lieutenant Snider's division was assigned high cover for the TBFs at 12,000 feet. They escorted the TBFs across the harbor and through the withdrawal without contacting enemy aircraft. Lieutenant Hacking's division provided close escort to the same TBFs and dove with them, spiraling down and leveling off at 2,000 feet. As they passed Kahili airstrip, Hacking observed dust clouds. Forty-six Zeros were taking off, but most were too late to intercept the strike. Each of the TBF's 6-plane divisions made a glide-bombing attack on a different vessel, releasing bombs between 1,800 and 3,000 feet. The TBFs then headed southwest and re-formed. Hacking's division remained with the TBFs.[37]

Hacking heard a TBF pilot call out, "Get the Zero off my tail!" and spotted a Zero tailing a straggling TBF. Hacking gave the Zero a short burst at four hundred yards, then his wingman, Lieutenant Dillow, appeared and blew the Zero apart.

Hacking veered up and right, looked back, and saw a Zero dive toward 1st Lt. Nathaniel R. Landon Jr., the tail-end fighter in his division. By his own account, Hacking "slid down on the Zero—blowing him out of the air." Hacking next dove on a Zero and a Mitsubishi A6M3 "Hap" fighter pursuing what Hacking thought was a Wildcat. He flamed the Zero and followed the Hap into a steep dive, pulling out just above the water and momentarily blacking out from the gravitational force. After more confused maneuvering, wild firing, and a near collision, Hacking joined some other Corsairs and headed home.

In the battle, 1st Lt. John F. Connolly and his wingman, Landon, had been separated from Hacking and Dillow. There were so many American fighters over the harbor, Connolly later reported, that he "tried twice to make runs on Zeros but couldn't get at them for the Corsairs. You had to stand in line for a shot at one." He finally got his turn when a Zero wheeled about three hundred feet below him. Connolly led the fighter by half a ring on his gunsight and set it on fire with a two-second burst. Landon watched the Zero burn and go into the water.

VMF-221 claimed six Zeros, four of them Hacking's. When they returned, none of the VMF-221 fighters had a single bullet hole. Other squadrons claimed another forty-seven Zeros and five floatplanes. Japanese records reported just nine aircraft lost. American losses amounted to one SBD, one TBF, two P-38s, and one F4U. The bombers had sunk the destroyer *Hatsuyuki* and damaged at least two more destroyers and a minelayer.[38]

Losing the Maintenance Battle

The following day the two squadrons escorted another strike against Kahili, this time by B-24s. VMF-221 encountered no enemy aircraft.[39] Around this time, the number of available aircraft plummeted. Earlier in July, magneto failure had forced numerous aircraft flying above 20,000 feet to abort. Now, thick sludge in the sump oil strainers prevented the squadron from flying on 19 July, limiting the aircraft to ground alert. Only two aircraft were operational on 20 July, and the divisions took turns with four aircraft on 21 July. That day, the ground echelon of VMF-221 returned to Banika. For the first time since March, the squadron's pilots, mechanics, and aircraft were at the same base. The availability of aircraft seemed to improve at this point, as the war diary recorded more missions flown each day, many with two divisions aloft at once.[40]

For the remainder of this combat tour, the squadron flew patrols over Rendova and escorted B-24s, SBDs, and TBFs on strikes against Kahili and Munda. No aircraft were lost in action, though Lieutenant Hacking made a forced landing at Segi Point on 24 July, and 1st Lt. Edwin G. Nelson wrecked an F4U borrowed from VMF-214.[41]

The squadron encountered enemy aircraft only twice more during this combat tour. On 30 July, divisions led by Lieutenant Winfield and Lieutenant Hacking escorted a B-24 strike to Kahili and Balalae. Hacking and his wingman, 2nd Lt. Milton E. Schneider, repelled an attack by Zeros on the return leg. A 20-mm shell ripped through Schneider's wing, but no aircraft were lost on either side.[42]

On 6 August, Lieutenant Schocker led eight fighters from VMF-221 and eight F4Us from VMF-214 to escort an army air force F-5 Lightning reconnaissance plane on a photographic mission around Shortland Island. The F-5 approached Shortland at very low altitude and then surprised the fighters escorting it when it began a series of violent maneuvers. The sixteen F4Us took evasive action to avoid colliding with trees, the F-5, and each other. The marines lost sight of the F-5 and began looking for it. Schocker led his division across Shortland and then down the west coast before giving up and heading home. Dillow's path took him by several Japanese floatplanes, which he and his section strafed, leaving two burning.[43]

Dillow spotted a division of VMF-214 F4Us ten miles south of Shortland and joined them. Someone warned over the radio of Zeros at nine o'clock. Dillow's wingman, Segal, looked up and saw "a whole cloud of them up there. Next I heard everyone saying, 'Let's get out of here!'" With six fighters attacking them, Dillow and Segal began weaving violently. Dillow spotted a Zero climbing straight up and followed him, firing, until his Corsair nearly stalled. He rolled over and dove, almost hitting the water before pulling out. This gave Segal a clear shot. Segal poured fire into the Zero until it smoked and flamed. Segal then felt the impact of bullets on his aircraft. The plane shook violently, and half the left aileron disappeared. Segal raced for a cloud and found himself face-to-face with another Zero. He fired a burst and saw flames under the cockpit before he entered the cloud. After some cat-and-mouse maneuvers with Japanese fighters, Segal dove to sea level and headed toward home.[44]

Dillow had lost sight of Segal, so he began scissoring with another F4U. He spotted a formation of three Zeros off to his right and closed to within 150 yards before opening up. He saw the Zero burn and evaded another attack by speeding into a cloud.[45]

On 13 August, after forty-eight days in combat, the pilots of VMF-214 and VMF-221 turned their Corsairs over to VMF-123 and VMF-215 and boarded transport aircraft for Guadalcanal. The ground echelon remained at Banika.[46]

A Brewster F2A-3 Buffalo fighter, 2 August 1942. *NARA NH 97540*

Midway Atoll, 24 November 1941. Eastern Island is in the foreground. *NARA 80-G-0357177*

Capt. Marion Carl was likely the only VMF-221 pilot who shot down a Zero at Midway. *NARA 80-G-F-15823*

Maj. Floyd Parks commanded VMF-221 at Midway. *NARA 412883*

VMF-221 survivors after Midway, 14 July 1942. *Front row, left to right:* William Brooks, John Musselman, Phillip White, William Humberd, Kirk Armistead, Herbert Merrill, Marion Carl, Clayton Canfield. *Back row*: Darrell Irwin, Hyde Phillips, Charles Hughes, Roy Corry, Charles Kunz. *NARA 80-G-357094*

Capt. Robert Burns led VMF-221 through its first combat tour in the Solomon Islands. *Jim Burns*

The F4F repair shop at Fighter 2 in February 1943 *NARA 52801A*

VMF-221 aviators, 18 May 1943, probably just after returning to Buttons from Sydney. *Back row, left to right:* Edward Walsh, Jack Pittman, Jimmy Swett, Pitzer Pittman, William Snider. *Front row:* Frank Baldwin, Robert Burns, Donald Balch. *NARA 54760*

First Lt. Donald Balch after landing his damaged F4U-1 at Banika, 7 July 1943
Cdr. Peter Mersky, USN (Ret.)

On 9 October 1943, Maj. Gen. Ralph Mitchell presented Capt. Jimmy Swett with the Medal of Honor at a ceremony on Efate. *NARA 65176*

Marine mechanics work on an F4U-1's 2,000 h.p. Pratt and Whitney R-2800-8 power plant on Munda, 26 August 1943. *NARA 59975*

F4U-1s taxi at Banika in the Russell Islands, 6 September 1943. *NARA 61335*

Maj. Nathan Post commanded VMF-221 during its final combat tour in the Solomon Islands. *NARA 413087*

Maj. Roscoe Nelson briefs VMF-221 pilots on their role protecting the landing at Torokina in the squadron ready room at Barakoma on 31 October 1943. *NARA 65922*

The fighter squadrons' ready room on Barakoma, 1 November 1943 *NARA 65926*

F4U-1s prepare for takeoff from Barakoma on L-day of the Bougainville landing, 1 November 1943. *NARA 65923*

VMF-221 aviators, November 1943: *Back row, left to right:* William Walker, Manny Segal, Nathan Post, John Payne, Jimmy Swett, William Snider, Frank Baldwin, William Moore. *Front row:* Warren Duncan, Jack Pittman, Walter Schocker, Albert Hacking, Eugene Dillow, Warner Chapman. NARA 66111

Maj. Edwin Roberts commanded VMF-221 aboard USS *Bunker Hill.* NARA 46960

First Lt. Ralph Glendinning was one of the pilots in Captain Swett's division in 1945. *NARA 46419*

First Lt. Dean Caswell, credited with seven aerial victories, was the Marine Corps' leading carrier ace. *NARA 45759*

F4U-1Ds prepare to launch from USS *Bunker Hill*, 17 March 1945. *NARA 312608*

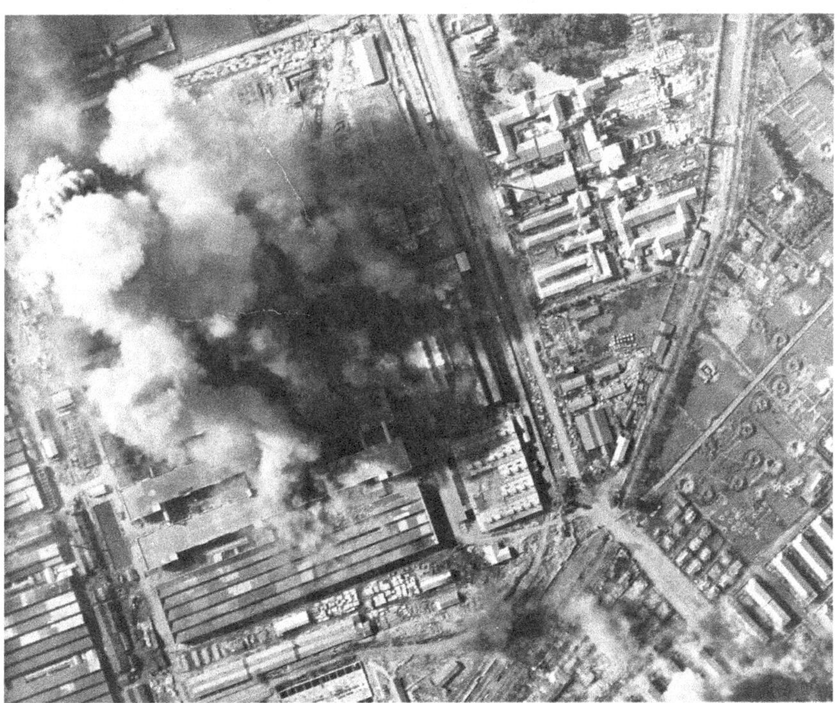

An F6F-5P escorted by Lt. George Johns and Lt. William Pemble photographed the strike on the Nakajima Tama Airport Engine Plant on 16 February 1945. *NARA NH 58152*

A Corsair fires its rockets over Okinawa on 6 May 1945.
NARA 126420

Bunker Hill burning, 11 May 1945. *U.S. Naval Institute photo archive*

9

★ ★ ★

Third Combat Tour, Vella Lavella, 10 October–19 November 1943

Before their third combat tour in the Solomons, the pilots of VMF-221 enjoyed another week in Sydney.

More Training, More Replacements

After their week in Australia the pilots reassembled at their new base at Efate, south of Espiritu Santo. Their ground echelon rejoined them there on 21 August.

Major Peyton had detached on 1 August to take command of the airfield on Espiritu Santo, leaving Captain Payne in charge for the month.[1] On 30 August, Maj. Nathan T. Post took command. Post had graduated from the Naval Academy in 1938, where—like Parks—he had been awarded a Black N by his classmates for having excessive demerits. Post's academy yearbook suggests he was more of an artist than an athlete. He attended The Basic School before flight training and earned his wings in 1941. While he was executive officer of VMF-122 on Guadalcanal in December 1942, flying alone, Post attacked three Nakajima E8N "Dave" seaplanes. Though wounded in the fight, Post downed all three.[2]

Eight more aviators joined the squadron at Efate. Fortunately, not all were untested. Capt. Alonzo B. Treffer had flown in combat with VMF-213. First Lt. Warren P. Nichols had achieved three victories, and 1st Lt. George E. Moore had scored one with VMF-124. By the time VMF-221 returned to combat, it had thirty aviators, or one and a half pilots per aircraft, and all but five were veterans. Post organized his pilots into seven divisions, with two aviators as spares.[3]

From 4 September to 10 October the squadron trained for combat. After familiarization flights the squadron practiced gunnery and interception problems when weather permitted and instrument flying in SNJs. Unlike the two previous training periods, the squadron suffered no mishaps. On 9 October, the squadron stayed on the ground and formed ranks as Major General Mitchell presented Captain Swett with the Medal of Honor for his aerial feats on 7 April.[4]

On 11 October the pilots returned to Banika by transport aircraft, leaving their ground echelon and aircraft in Efate. Two days later they rode another transport to Munda airfield on New Georgia, now in U.S. hands.[5]

Bougainville Operational Situation

Halsey had set 2 November as D-day for Bougainville. The purpose of the Bougainville operation was to establish airfields from which AirSols, now under Maj. Gen. Nathan F. Twining, USAAF, could join the long-range bombers of Gen. George C. Kenney's Fifth Air Force in strikes against Rabaul. Twining commanded 301 fighters—which included 116 navy and marine F4Us—as well as 162 navy and marine dive-bombers and torpedo bombers, 138 army air force and navy medium and heavy bombers, and 11 night fighters (6 navy F4U-2s and 5 marine PV-1s). Counting patrol, reconnaissance, and utility aircraft, Twining commanded more than 700 aircraft.[6]

Japanese strength at Rabaul reached 600 aircraft in November, but these were divided between army aircraft opposing the Fifth Air Force and navy aircraft opposing the Third Fleet. In anticipation of Halsey's offensive, Admiral Koga stripped 173 aircraft from his carriers at Truk and alerted the Twelfth Air Fleet in Japan to reinforce the 212 aircraft of the Eleventh Air Fleet.[7]

Twining's AirSols would fulfill three familiar roles: scouting; protecting the fleet and landing force; and striking Japanese vessels, bases, and troops. Prior to D-day, AirSols and the Fifth Air Force would neutralize Japanese airpower in the northern Solomons and around Rabaul. Air Command North Solomons, the forward echelon of the 1st Marine Aircraft Wing, would control aircraft in the Bougainville area beginning on D-day.[8]

The Battle for Air Superiority, 10–31 October

VMF-221's return to the Solomons coincided with AirSols' offensive against the Eleventh Air Fleet. After four days of testing aircraft inherited from other squadrons, routine patrols, and escort missions, the action began for VMF-221 on 17 October. Major Post led his division to Kahili, hoping to lure Zeros aloft, where fourteen F4Us of VMF-214 lurking at high altitude could pounce on them. Lieutenant Snider and his wingman linked up with VMF-214; the other two aircraft of Snider's division took off late and failed to rendezvous.[9]

As Post circled Kahili at 10,000 feet, the enemy took the bait. Maj. Gregory "Pappy" Boyington, commanding officer of VMF-214, led his eighteen F4Us down from 20,000 feet to meet the climbing Zeros. By the time they reached 7,000 feet, Boyington and his flight had lost sight of the Zeros, so they climbed back to 18,000 feet. After orbiting Kahili, Snider spotted thirty to forty Zeros approaching from the south at the same altitude. The Zeros and F4Us attempted to outclimb each other. When Boyington realized the Zeros were edging above his squadron, he attacked into the middle of the formation; Snider and the rest followed.[10]

Snider's first gunnery pass was a head-on engagement. He hit the Zero but did not see it go down. He dove evasively and then climbed for a second run. Snider and his wingman attacked three Zeros. One climbed and two dove. Snider elected to dive. He shot down one of the diving fighters at 200 yards with a 30-degree deflection shot, then made a right-hand dive, the standard tactic F4Us employed to evade Zeros. After escaping, Snider leveled off, climbed, and spotted the belly of a Zero above him. Snider executed a climbing, 60-degree deflection pass, firing a long burst that sent the Zero spiraling into the sea. In addition to Snider's two victories, VMF-214 claimed a dozen fighters. The Japanese reported losing only two Zeros and another two damaged. All the marine pilots returned home.[11]

That afternoon the squadron flew from Munda to Barakoma on Vella Lavella. The Third Fleet had seized Vella Lavella in mid-August, and Seabees had completed an airfield there on 27 September. VMF-221, joining MAG-14, was the first squadron based there. Barakoma was just a hundred miles from Japanese airfields on southern Bougainville, guaranteeing MAG-14 plenty of action.[12]

The squadrons at Barakoma suffered from poor maintenance support. Lieutenant Chapman recalled that the squadron struggled to keep eight aircraft operational each day because spare parts were in short supply and "the ground crews were not as skilled."[13] VMF-215 operated alongside VMF-221 in October and November. Maj. Herbert H. Williamson, VMF-215's commander, attributed the ground crews' unsatisfactory performance to three factors. First, the Carrier Air Service Unit did not report to the squadron commander, but to the air station. Second, the ground unit had no experience or training on the F4U-1, neglected simple duties such as cleaning windshields and checking tire pressure, and showed little desire to remedy the situation. "The attitude of the unit as a whole indicated neither a desire to learn or embarrassment at the poor performance turned in," wrote Williamson. Third, the Carrier Air Service Unit was short of tools and parts.[14] The Air South Pacific war history admits that "certain Carrier Air Service Units were so incompetent that drastic means had to be initiated to build them up to the standards of a good automobile garage in a small town."[15] These logistical and command problems would increasingly degrade the readiness of VMF-221's aircraft at Barakoma.

The day after the squadron's arrival at Barakoma, Major Post and Captain Swett linked up with Major Boyington and three divisions from VMF-214 to try the bait-and-ambush tactic again. The F4Us orbited Kahili at 18,000 feet. The marines counted sixty Japanese aircraft sitting on the ground, but none took off. Trying to force the issue, Boyington taunted the Japanese on a channel they were known to monitor: "Come on up and fight, you yellow bastards!" That did the trick. The Zeros obliged. When they reached 6,000 feet, the 20 marines dove. With the altitude advantage, the F4Us employed overhead gunnery passes and dove away. Major Post shot down one climbing Zero in such a run. After recharging his jammed guns, he returned to the fight and shot a second Zero down from behind. Swett also claimed one Zero in the initial dive and a second in a stern attack. Captain George E. Dawkins damaged a Zero with a 90-degree deflection shot. Pursued by three Zeros, he rejoined Swett and the two began a weave, after which the three Zeros disengaged. Jack Pittman, now a lieutenant, exploded two Zeros in a diving run from astern. He followed another Zero in a diving turn to the left and then a climbing, 180-degree turn to the right. The Zero rolled on its back, and Pittman saw smoke burst from the aircraft. Pittman made an overhead pass on a fourth Zero, but his guns jammed. Lieutenant Segal also wrestled with jammed guns. Captain Treffer's blower, which boosted power for a dogfight, malfunctioned. Lieutenant Schneider crashed when a Zero on his tail riddled his aircraft with 20-mm cannon fire. He did not survive. VMF-221 claimed six victories and two probables; VMF-214 claimed another two Zeros destroyed. The Japanese reported four Zeros lost and four damaged, one of which was written off.[16]

The malfunctions frustrated Major Post and his pilots, who were unimpressed with the F4U-1s they had inherited. Post ended his after-action report for the 18 October mission with a sobering comment: "The planes assigned to VMF-221 are definitely not suitable for combat due to excessive hard usage and poor upkeep. The majority need major overhauls. The guns have not been kept up properly. Some of the wing tanks do not draw, so that they are impossible to empty. The blowers do not function properly. Apparently, the newest planes in this area are used for training in the rear areas and the oldest ones are left in the combat area."[17] Between the poor condition of the aircraft and the inadequate support from the Carrier Aircraft Service Unit, the squadron rarely operated more than one division at a time between 19 and 25 October.[18]

On 22 October Captain Payne led three aircraft of his division and one from VMF-215 to strafe aircraft parked on Kara airfield near Kahili. As Payne approached at one hundred feet, he saw twenty-five to thirty aircraft parked wingtip to wingtip. The four Corsairs opened up at seven hundred yards and continued firing until they pulled away twenty feet above the target. Payne estimated they had destroyed eighteen aircraft. Japanese records reported eight burned on the ground.[19]

For the rest of October VMF-221 escorted bombers to the northern Solomons without encountering enemy aircraft. On 30 October, Major Post escorted six B-25s with five VMF-221 fighters and four from VMF-212 to strike shipping northeast of Bougainville. Post spotted two supply ships on the flight north. B-25s were extremely effective at strafing enemy surface vessels, but the B-25 crews could not hear Post's radio calls and returned without engaging any targets. On the return leg, Post and his fighters took turns strafing the supply vessels, a gunboat, and several barges, leaving the ships burning. Antiaircraft fire struck Payne's engine, and he lost oil pressure. Payne ditched and climbed into his inflatable raft sixty miles from Barakoma. Lieutenant Pittman used his IFF to guide a rescue boat to the location.[20]

Protecting the Amphibious Force, 1–17 November

From 1 to 3 November the squadron protected the Bougainville landing at Cape Torokina. D-day had begun with a rude awakening when a lone Betty dropped six 60-kg bombs near the airfield at 0505.[21] The squadron could put up only twelve aircraft that day: two divisions in the morning, one at midday, and two divisions (flying the aircraft from the morning mission) in late afternoon.[22] Though the Eleventh Air Fleet struck the task force twice while VMF-221 fighters patrolled the landing area, none were vectored to intercept. Aviation historian Michael Claringbould has written that the fighter direction center sent two divisions from VMF-221 in the wrong direction. Neither D-day strike hit any ships off Torokina, but the attacks did cause the warships to get underway, interrupting ship-to-shore movement.[23]

With the landings in progress, Koga committed his carrier air wings, bringing the total Japanese strength around Rabaul to 550 aircraft, including more than 390 fighters. Koga also ordered a task force of two heavy cruisers, two light cruisers, and six destroyers to attack the American transports off Bougainville on the night of 1–2 November. A Third Fleet task force of four cruisers and eight destroyers sank one cruiser and one destroyer in the ensuing night action at the cost of one destroyer badly damaged. Dawn saw the Japanese task force retreating toward Rabaul, but the American task force was still exposed to Japanese air strikes. Just before 0800, a strike force of more than one hundred aircraft attacked.[24]

Two aircraft in Jimmy Swett's division could not take off that morning, and the fourth had aborted, so he joined three P-38s. The mixed division attacked 20 Japanese dive-bombers and fighters from 30,000 feet, but the dive-bombers released their bombs before the Americans could reach them. Swett chased two Vals and claimed he shot both down. He came to the aid of a P-40 with a Kawasaki Ki-61 "Tony" on its tail. The Tony was slightly faster than the Zero at 356 mph and mounted two 12.7-mm machine guns or 20-mm cannons in its wings and two 7.7-mm or 12.7-mm machine guns in its fuselage. Swett saw the Tony begin to smoke before he noticed tracers whipping past him. He dove out of the fight and headed home. In addition to the two Vals Swett claimed, the P-38s, eight F6Fs, and four New Zealand P-40s claimed another six. Antiaircraft gunners also claimed many. The Japanese reported the loss of six dive-bombers. The Vals scored only two hits, both on the light cruiser USS *Montpelier* (CL 57), that wounded one sailor and inflicted minor damage. The task force was spared further attacks as heavy bombers from the Fifth Air Force compelled the Eleventh Air Fleet to keep much of its fighter strength over Rabaul.[25]

The squadron sortied two divisions on the morning of 3 November and a single division at midday to patrol above the task force. None made contact.[26] On 4 November, a bomb on Barakoma's runway—possibly one of those dropped by the Betty three days earlier—exploded while being defused. The blast killed nineteen personnel, wounded fifteen, and destroyed an SBD and a TBF. VMF-221 relocated to Munda on New Georgia while engineers repaired the runway.[27]

That same day, a Fifth Air Force B-24 spotted a task force of nineteen Japanese navy cruisers and destroyers approaching Rabaul, just a few hours' sailing time from the transports at Empress Augusta Bay. This task force could overwhelm the Third Fleet's cruiser force and wreak havoc among the amphibious ships. After the war, Halsey wrote, "This was the most desperate emergency that confronted me in my entire term as Commander, South Pacific." Halsey ordered *Saratoga* and the light carrier USS *Princeton* (CVL 23) up from the southern Solomons to strike the Japanese cruisers the following day. He ordered AirSols to protect the carriers to enable the carriers to throw all of their aircraft into the strike. On 5 November, VMF-221 patrolled over the carriers without encountering enemy aircraft. The carriers' pilots severely damaged six cruisers and two destroyers, eliminating the threat to the amphibious transports.[28]

From 6 to 16 November, VMF-221 patrolled over Torokina and escorted patrol and bombing missions without encountering enemy aircraft. On 11 November, Halsey ordered a second carrier strike on Rabaul, adding the air groups from USS *Essex* (CV 9), USS *Bunker Hill* (CV 17), and USS *Independence* (CVL 22) to those of *Saratoga* and *Princeton*. The Fifth Air Force added its heavy bombers to the strike. Rabaul was out of range for the F4Us on Vella Lavella but within reach of the carrier aircraft. VMF-221 maintained two divisions over the carriers from 0500 until 1515 and one division until 1640. The next morning the squadron repeated the patrols. Halsey was disappointed with the strikes' results, but at least cooperation between carrier and land-based air had improved drastically since Midway.[29]

The Japanese relied on barges to resupply their island garrisons. The small craft moved by night to avoid American aircraft patrols and concealed themselves in coves and rivers by day. After covering a strike by SBDs and TBFs against the airfield at Kara on 15 November, Captain Hacking and Captain Moore scoured the Shortland Islands for barges. They found several unprotected by antiaircraft guns and burned five of them in what they called a "strafer's heaven."[30]

The squadron's last day of combat in the Solomons, 17 November, began with tragedy. At 0349, under the illumination of a parachute flare, a Betty dropped a torpedo that hit the high-speed transport USS *McKean* (APD 5), which was en route to Bougainville with 185 marines. *McKean* sank in 28 minutes, taking 116 of the 338 men aboard with her.[31] The ugly scene demonstrated that Air Command North Solomons' protective umbrella often folded up at night.

After sunup, Major Post's division patrolled over Torokina. Around 0820, an enemy strike of thirty-five fighters and bombers arrived. Air Command North Solomons vectored most of the air patrol against different elements, leaving just Major Post and Lieutenant Segal protecting the ships. When a group of twin-engine Yokosuka D4Y Suisei "Judys" arrived, Post and Segal had them all to themselves. The Judys were very fast, with a top speed of 361 mph, but Post and Segal dispatched them easily. In stern attacks at 15,000 feet, Post shot three down in flames while Segal covered him. Segal then did the same to three closing on the task force down at 5,000 feet. No ships suffered damage. In addition to VMF-221's six Judys, American pilots claimed two Tonys, one Val, and one Kate. A Japanese postwar account stated that four bombers and six fighters failed to return.[32]

It would take MacArthur and Halsey another four months to neutralize Rabaul. When marine squadrons began flying from Torokina in December, VMF-221 was not with them. On 19 November the pilots had boarded transports and flown first to Guadalcanal and then on to Efate, where they rejoined their ground echelon. On 14 December the squadron embarked the Dutch troopship MS *Sommelsdijk*, arriving in San Francisco on the last day of 1943.[33]

10

★ ★ ★

VMF-221's Effectiveness in the Solomons

An assessment of VMF-221's effectiveness in the Solomons must consider its sortie rate; the damage it inflicted; its losses; and the damage inflicted by Japanese aircraft on the ships, bases, and aircraft the squadron protected.

Sorties

The squadron's war diary for November 1943 tabulated the number of combat flying hours and sorties flown by each pilot in the Solomons, presented here in Table 1. VMF-221's authorized strength was eighteen fighters on each combat tour. The data indicate that the squadron could generate only about two-thirds as many flying hours and sorties per day after it transitioned to F4U-1s. It averaged better than a sortie every day for each authorized F4F-4, but only sortied three quarters of its authorized F4U-1 strength.

Other ways to measure the squadron's ability to put up aircraft include the number of times a four-plane division launched short an aircraft, the number of times an aircraft aborted from a mission, the number of mishaps, and the number of aircraft lost due to mishaps. Table 2 provides a monthly breakdown of these factors.

TABLE 1. VMF-221 Combat Hours and Sorties, 1943

Combat tour	Total combat hours	Average combat hours per day	Total combat sorties	Average sorties per day
First tour, 1 16 March–2 May (F4F-4)	2,597	55.3	996	20.7
Second combat tour, 26 June–12 August (F4U-1)	1,794	38.2	650	13.5
Third combat tour, 12 October–17 November (F4U-1)	1,377	38.3	502	13.6

Note: Data for aviators who perished or detached before the third tour are omitted from the VMF-221 war diary for November 1943. The squadron average was used to estimate hours and sorties for these pilots for the days they were present.

TABLE 2. VMF-221 Air Strength Shortfalls in Combat, 1943

Month	Days in combat	Divisions sortied understrength	Aircraft aborts	Mishaps	Aircraft losses from mishaps	Mishap fatalities
First combat tour, 16 March–2 May (F4F-4)						
March	15			7	4	1
April	30	1	5	9	2	
May	2			0*	0*	0*
Second combat tour, 26 June–12 August (F4U-1)						
June	4			1	1	
July	31	4	19	3	1	
August	12	1	1	1	1	
Third combat tour, 12 October–17 November (F4U-1)						
October	19	8	8	2		
November	17	2	1	2	1	

* One F4U-1 was lost in a fatal mishap before the combat tour started in May.
Source: VMF-221 war diaries, March–November 1943.

Damage Inflicted by VMF-221

VMF-221 claimed 76 aerial victories across its 3 combat tours in the Solomons: 25 during its first tour, flying Wildcats out of Guadalcanal (17 fighters and 8 bombers); 35 flying F4Us out of Banika in its second tour (20.5 fighters and 14.5 bombers); and 16 flying F4Us from Vella Lavella in its third tour (8 fighters and 8 bombers). The squadron claimed another 18 probable aerial victories, 18 fighters and 2 seaplanes destroyed on the ground, 2 supply ships, and 8 barges.[1]

It is important to keep in mind that U.S. claims consistently exceeded the losses reported by the Japanese. A comparison of Japanese reported losses with U.S. aerial victory claims for 15 of VMF-221's 17 engagements is helpful. In these 15 engagements, U.S. airmen claimed 259 aerial victories. Japanese records reported the loss of 86 aircraft for the same engagements, or 33 percent of the total U.S. claims. Applying this ratio to VMF-221's 76 claims suggests the squadron probably shot down about 25 Japanese aircraft in 1943.[2]

VMF-221 Losses

VMF-221 lost 23 aircraft and 4 aviators in the Solomons.[3] Two aviators and 11 aircraft were lost in combat, and 2 aviators and 12 aircraft were lost in mishaps. The squadron claimed seven aerial victories for every combat loss. Factoring for mistaken claims, the squadron probably outperformed its adversaries in aerial combat at a ratio more like 2.5 to 1.

Damage Inflicted by Japanese Aircraft

It is more difficult to quantify the damage inflicted by Japanese aircraft on ships, bases, and aircraft the squadron protected. VMF-221 was part of a larger force. Attributing all damage inflicted by Japanese aircraft in the Solomons during each of its combat tours to this squadron would misrepresent the squadron's performance. An examination of the damage inflicted by Japanese aircraft on bombers the squadron escorted and vessels and bases over which the squadron patrolled provides a more helpful assessment.

On 7 April, VMF-221 was tasked to intercept a large Japanese strike. More than half of the Japanese dive-bombers inflicted damage on U.S. vessels, sinking the destroyer *Aaron Ward*, the tanker *Kanawha*, and the New Zealand corvette *Moa*. No airfields or supply depots suffered damage. On 30 June, while VMF-221 protected a task force, a Betty's torpedo hit the transport *McCawley*, killing fifteen sailors. On 2 July, between eighteen and twenty-five Bettys escaped detection and dropped fifty bombs on the Rendova beachhead, killing fifty-nine soldiers, sailors, and marines while wounding another seventy-seven. VMF-221 had been providing a combat air patrol over the beachhead but was withdrawn by Admiral Mitscher. On 4 July, while VMF-221 was limited to flying test hops from Banika, eighteen Bettys and twenty Zeros struck the Rendova beachhead, killing five and wounding thirteen. On 2 November, while VMF-221 protected a task force, dive-bombers hit the light cruiser *Montpelier* twice, wounding one sailor and inflicting minor damage. Aside from these actions, the squadron flew more than two thousand combat sorties in 1943 during which the Third Fleet lost no vessels. The evidence suggests that the squadron consistently prevented the Japanese from hurting the Third Fleet.

VMF-221 and the Fleet Commander's Intent

Translating VMF-221's performance into effectiveness first requires an examination of the fleet commander's intent and the tasks assigned to the squadron.

During the first combat tour, Halsey's intent was to build up supplies in the southern Solomons to support an amphibious assault on New Georgia. AirSols tasked Fighter Command, including VMF-221, to protect the ships and bases around Guadalcanal and to escort strikes against Japanese airfields and vessels to limit reinforcement and resupply of the garrison on New Georgia. In this combat tour, the Eleventh Air Fleet failed to substantially interfere with Halsey's plans. Though Morison concluded that Operation I-Go delayed the landing on New Georgia by ten days, and the withdrawal of warships from Guadalcanal may have enabled Kusaka to reinforce New Georgia, neither factor prevented the outcome of the assault. The protection afforded by VMF-221 and the other squadrons of Fighter Command accomplished Halsey's intent.

During VMF-221's second tour, Halsey's intent was to seize New Georgia and its airfield on Munda. The damage inflicted by the Eleventh Air Fleet from 30 June to 4 July failed to slow the buildup of U.S. combat power on Rendova. The seizure of Rendova enabled American artillery to support the infantry on New Georgia and provided a safe base for the radars and fighter direction center of the New Georgia Air Force. Due to the fighter protection afforded by VMF-221 and the hundreds of fighters supporting the New Georgia Air Force, the Southeast Area Fleet failed to prevent the seizure of New Georgia.

In the third combat tour, Halsey's intent was to establish a beachhead at Cape Torokina on Bougainville and build an airfield there within fighter range of Rabaul. VMF-221 protected the ships and vessels at Bougainville. The squadron escorted bombers on strikes against Japanese airfields and surface vessels. It also covered the carrier task forces while they raided Rabaul. These operations were intended to limit Japan's reinforcement and resupply of its Bougainville garrison and to limit air strikes and naval action against the amphibious force. The Eleventh Air Fleet and warships of Kusaka's Southeast Area Fleet inflicted almost no damage on the Third Fleet's amphibious force at Bougainville during daylight.

Moreover, Halsey's offensive had a second purpose equally important to neutralizing Rabaul. In its directive, the Joint Chiefs had included "to inflict losses on Japanese forces" among the reasons for the Solomons campaign. AirSols broke the back of Japanese naval aviation. The U.S. Strategic Bombing Survey assessed that Japan lost 752 aircraft in the Solomons and at Rabaul between August 1942 and March 1944. These figures, which the survey characterized as "conservative," included an irreplaceable number of carrier aircraft and their pilots. These numbers do not include aircraft destroyed over New Guinea in the Southwest Pacific Area.[4]

According to Commander Ryosuke Nomura, who served with the Eleventh Air Fleet from November 1942 to July 1943, "The naval land-based aircraft losses in the Rabaul–Solomons–New Guinea areas were extremely high and finally resulted in the destruction of the cream of the [Japanese] Naval Air Forces."[5] Other officers interrogated during the survey revealed that the Imperial Japanese Navy could not replace these losses because its training pipeline was restricted beginning in 1943. One of the same officers stated, "The loss of the Solomon Islands was not too important, but the losses in ships and pilots trying to hold them was vital."[6]

The intent of the U.S. Joint Chiefs and the Third Fleet commander was to inflict heavy losses in a grinding battle of attrition in the Solomons. VMF-221 claimed seventy-six aircraft destroyed and another twenty on the surface. Even adjusting for mistaken claims, it is clear the squadron was effective at destroying enemy aircraft and killing Japanese naval aviators.

This attrition enabled both Halsey's advance up the Solomons and Nimitz's drive across the Central Pacific that began in November 1943. Captain Takashi Miyazaki, a naval aviator who served at Rabaul from September 1942 to April 1944, told his postwar interrogator,

> During the campaign, our aircraft and pilot losses became too great to make it practical to continue to hold the Solomons. Without aircraft cover and support we were unable to supply our garrisons without a useless expenditure of surface shipping. When our attempt to hold the Solomons was at its greatest in the last part of 1943, your advance through the Gilberts made it impracticable to hold the Solomons any longer. At that time our Naval Air Force had become too weak to assist in the defense of the Gilberts.[7]

Factors Contributing to VMF-221's Success

VMF-221's performance and effectiveness in the Solomons can be attributed to the capabilities and limitations of the aircraft the squadron flew, the tactics the squadron employed, the proficiency and health of its aviators, the time the squadron had to prepare, command and control, logistics and maintenance, early warning and fighter direction, aircrew survivability, and Japanese capabilities.

Aircraft

The F4U-1 clearly outperformed the F4F-4. VMF-221 lost 4 F4U-1s in aerial combat while claiming 51 aerial victories, a better than 12-to-1 claim-to-loss ratio. The squadron lost 7 F4F-4s in combat while claiming 25 victories, achieving a respectable, but inferior, 3.5-to-1 claim-to-loss ratio. The F4U-1's greater range also enabled the squadron to escort bombers to targets on Bougainville that F4F-4s could not reach. After the F4U-1 and the F6F came on the scene, Japanese aviators "had a horror of American fighters," according to Commander Nomura. "The pilots continually discussed the relative merits of the Japanese and American aircraft and were convinced in their own mind that they were flying greatly inferior aircraft."[8]

However, the F4U-1 proved more difficult to maintain than the F4F-4. The squadron suffered far more aborts, and divisions flew understrength far more often with the F4U-1 than with the F4F-4.

Neither aircraft had the range of the P-38, so both were unsuitable escorts for heavy bombers on long-range missions. And neither the F4F-4 nor the F4U-1 could fight at night, leaving vessels such as the high-speed transport *McKean* unprotected from Japanese night strikes.

Doctrine and Tactics

Improved tactics appear to have directly contributed to the squadron's superior performance and effectiveness in the Solomons. A preponderance of the enemy aircraft destroyed on 1 April fell to aircraft with an altitude advantage conducting overhead gunnery passes.[9] The pilots themselves attributed their survivability to the defensive power of the beam defense tactic (the weave) and the ease with which they could escape a tight situation by executing a diving right-hand turn in the Corsair. The aggressive fighter sweeps and bait-and-ambush tactics pushed by Major Boyington proved particularly effective at drawing enemy fighters into a disadvantageous battle.

Pilot Training, Experience, and Health

The pilots who flew with VMF-221 in the Solomons were better trained than the ones who had fought at Midway. Though in the second half of 1942 the Marine Corps had filled and emptied the squadron roster in a bewildering series of transfers, the pilots who landed on Guadalcanal in March 1943 had spent at least three months with the squadron. These months included several weeks of intense, dedicated training at Ewa and Espiritu Santo. As all but one of these aviators survived their first combat tour, the squadron's collective proficiency only heightened with each succeeding combat tour. When VMF-221 returned for its third combat tour, several of its replacement pilots were veterans as well. When combined with the superior F4U-1, the squadron's combat edge was sharper than ever.

The squadron benefited from the experience of preceding squadrons that had exhausted their pilots and lost aviators and mechanics to tropical disease. The aviators consistently spent at least seven weeks resting and training between combat tours, and never more than seven weeks in combat. The trips to Sydney restored morale and enabled the pilots to recover from stress, disease, and exhaustion. The improved living conditions and sanitation enforced by commanders and the rigorous Atabrine protocols resulted in very few evacuations for malaria after the first combat tour.[10]

Time

VMF-221 had sufficient time to prepare for each combat tour in the Solomons and used that time efficiently. Though the squadron enjoyed just two months at Ewa with most of its aviators, Major Mitchener led the squadron through a rigorous, systematic training syllabus. At Espiritu Santo, Captain Burns utilized the final month prior to combat to continue the squadron's training. In between combat tours, Marine Aircraft Wings South Pacific afforded the squadron sufficient time to qualify with the Corsair and sharpen its pilots' skills.

Command and Control

Effective command and control was certainly a factor in VMF-221's performance and effectiveness. Halsey integrated army air force, marine, navy, and New Zealand squadrons under AirSols, enabling Mitscher and Twining to fight a single air battle. AirSols likewise consolidated all fighting squadrons under Fighter Command, enabling Pugh to mass fighters against the Eleventh Air Fleet raids in April. As Third Fleet pushed north, the New Georgia Air Force and Air Command North Solomons co-located local fighter direction in the forward area with early-warning radar, facilitating timely interception.

The confusing organization of aviation logistics contributed to the squadron's poor aircraft readiness. Aircraft South Pacific and Marine

Aircraft Wings South Pacific treated pilots, ground echelons, and aircraft as interchangeable cogs. While this practice economized on theater air and sea transportation, it obscured lines of authority and accountability, fostering neglect and waste.

Logistics and Maintenance

The logistics and maintenance troubles Commander Spangler reported in April appear to have become worse by October. On 30 November, Major Post typed out some observations on the difficulties the squadron encountered on its third combat tour. He noted that none of the twenty F4U-1s the squadron inherited came with maintenance logs. The ground echelon on Vella Lavella was from VMF-222, so the pilots and their ground support were strangers to each other as well as the aircraft. Post and the engineering officer of VMF-222 agreed that the 20 Corsairs could have been put in good condition by completing a standard 180-hour check or overhaul, but there were no facilities at Barakoma to do such work. Oxygen, carbon dioxide, and spare parts were in short supply. Post directly attributed the nine aborted missions and one ditching on this tour to the sorry condition of the aircraft. He also noted that the pilots frequently flew at lower altitudes than planned because of oxygen problems.[11]

Shortly after VMF-221 departed Barakoma, Lt. John J. Hospers, in navy uniform but representing Chance Vought, the Corsair's manufacturer, inspected the condition of F4U-1s at the base. He found many Corsairs with over 350 hours of operation without an engine change. He also learned that some aircraft had been handed over from one squadron to the next four, five, and even six times after being used as training aircraft stateside. The navy Carrier Aircraft Service Unit at Barakoma—the unit whose efficiency and motivation Major Williamson had criticized—was not equipped to make engine changes or even to repair accessories. Throughout the Solomons, but particularly at Barakoma, Hospers saw an alarming accumulation of corrosion and rust on exposed metal, not only on aircraft but on spare parts, rendering them useless. He reported that any bare metal surface not coated with oil or grease quickly rusted in the tropics.[12]

Intelligence, Early Warning, and Fighter Direction

On 1 and 7 April, Fighter Command had demonstrated that it held a very distinct advantage: its coast watchers and radar enabled its fighter direction to see every aircraft in the sky—friendly and enemy. Once aloft, Japanese flight leaders could only be sure of the location of aircraft they could see. Throughout the three combat tours, VMF-221 benefited from excellent aerial reconnaissance, early warning, and fighter direction. The lapse in radar coverage on 2 July and Mitscher's untimely withdrawal of fighter coverage stand as a terrible exception.

Search and Rescue

VMF-221 lost twenty-three aircraft in the Solomons in combat and mishaps but only four pilots. The exceptional survival rate of the squadron's aviators can be attributed to the priority AirSols placed on their recovery. Dedicated PBYs and rescue boats pulled aviators from shark-infested waters. Friendly islanders hid pilots who came ashore. These aspects of the air war in the Solomons not only returned experienced pilots to the fight but also boosted their morale. In contrast, Japanese aviators knew their country would not risk aircraft and aviators on rescue missions. Not only were downed Japanese aviators lost to the force, but the morale of surviving aviators plummeted as the campaign progressed.[13]

Japanese Capabilities

This plummeting morale corresponded with a deterioration in the efficiency of Japanese naval aviation. As the Pacific Fleet and Kenney's Fifth Air Force strangled Rabaul, the shortage of spare parts and basic supplies devastated Eleventh Air Fleet's readiness. Even worse, according to Captain Miyazaki, was the skill of the mechanics and the quality of the parts.

> In 1943, at any one time, only 50 percent of the planes were ever available and the next day following an all-out operation only 30 percent would be available. By the end of 1943, only 40 percent at any one time would be

> serviceable. In 1942, the low availability was due to lack of supply; from 1943 on, it was due to lack of skill on the part of maintenance personnel and faulty manufacturing methods. Inspection of the aircraft and spare parts, prior to their delivery to Rabaul, was inadequate, and there were many poorly constructed and weak parts discovered. The Japanese tried to increase production figures so fast that proper examination was impossible.[14]

As the Japanese lost pilots, they shortened their training pipeline to remedy the deficit. Pilot training dropped from two hundred hours and two years to sixty hours and six months. This put Japanese naval aviation in a death spiral: the worse the pilots, the sooner they died; the higher the casualties, the more urgent became the need for replacements, no matter how unready.[15]

VMF-221's effectiveness in the Solomons indicates that land-based marine aviation supported the Third Fleet extremely well. Marine aviation was on the ascendance, with superior aircraft, better pilots, superb early warning and fighter direction, and effective command and control. That ascendance was hindered by inefficient logistics and inadequate maintenance, but the mass production of American industry overshadowed the shortcomings of aviation logistics in the South Pacific. As the strength and proficiency of marine aviation blossomed, the numbers and ability of Japanese naval aviation dropped precipitously, creating opportunities for the Pacific Fleet to exploit in 1944.

PART THREE

★ ★ ★

ABOARD USS *BUNKER HILL*, JANUARY–MAY 1945

11

★ ★ ★

Redeployment to California and Reconstitution, 1944

Return to the United States

VMF-221 sailed under the Golden Gate bridge on the last day of 1943, more than two years after it had departed San Diego, to reorganize and retrain for another deployment. But it also came home because the Pacific Fleet had more marine squadrons than it could use. The Marine Corps had redeployed seven veteran fighting squadrons to the United States, leaving twenty-six fighting in the Pacific. Another fifteen fighting squadrons waited stateside for orders to deploy.[1]

After helping neutralize Rabaul, marine squadrons found fewer opportunities to fight. With the concurrence of Maj. Gen. Ross Rowell, then commanding Marine Aircraft Wings Pacific, Nimitz had discontinued carrier qualification for marine aviators in June 1943. This appeared to make sense at the time. Marines were taking up a third of carrier training, yet their squadrons were fighting from island airstrips rather than carriers. This decision prevented marine squadrons from supporting marine and army divisions in the central Pacific in 1944. Marine aircraft did not have the range to support amphibious assaults from advanced bases, and marine pilots could not operate from carriers. In the southwest Pacific, Kenney's Fifth Air

Force and the Royal Australian Air Force supported MacArthur's westward offensive. In the wake of both offensives, marine squadrons were relegated to patrolling rear areas and striking bypassed garrisons.[2]

Rotation and Replacements

The day after arriving in San Francisco, the marines boarded a troop train for Marine Corps Air Depot Miramar outside San Diego. Upon arrival, all but eight officers and fifty enlisted marines departed for other commands. Two weeks later, Major Post and the remaining marines moved to Marine Corps Air Station Goleta outside Santa Barbara, California. All hands then received thirty days' leave.[3]

By the end of March, another four veteran pilots had departed and forty-two new aviators had arrived. Pilots came and went throughout 1944, but all those who would deploy with VMF-221 in January 1945 had joined the squadron by June 1944. Only four pilots who had fought in the Solomons remained: Captain Baldwin, Capt. Donald Balch, Captain Snider, and Captain Swett.[4]

The ground echelon experienced similar turnover. After the leave period, 131 marines joined the 50 veterans. By the end of 1944 the squadron had a ground echelon of 2 officers, 224 enlisted marines, a navy medical officer, and 8 hospital corpsmen.[5]

Maj. Edwin S. Roberts Jr. was waiting at Goleta when the veterans returned from leave. Roberts would serve as Post's executive officer until 13 October. When Post moved up to be the group operations officer at Goleta, he turned the squadron over to Roberts, who made Swett his executive officer.[6]

Roberts had learned to fly in 1940 with the United Flying School of America while he was a student at the University of Southern California. He joined the naval aviation cadet program and earned his wings in May 1941, then spent two years at Naval Air Station Grosse Ile, Michigan, where he flew nearly two thousand hours instructing American and Allied students. After his promotion to major in May 1943, Roberts attended a command and staff course at Quantico before reporting to Marine Base Defense Aircraft Group 41 at Goleta in October 1943. Unlike most marine aviators, Roberts was a family man, with a pregnant wife and two children awaiting his return.[7]

Aircraft

The squadron received twenty-two Corsairs at Goleta: thirteen FG-1s, five F4U-1s, and four F3A-1s. All three types were the same aircraft but built by different manufacturers: the FG-1 by Goodyear, the F4U-1 by Vought, and the F3A-1 by Brewster. The Brewster F3A-1s had a reputation for inferior reliability and were often relegated to stateside training.[8]

The newer Corsairs were more suitable for carrier operations. To mitigate the perilous left-wing stall on final approach, a small spoiler had been installed on the leading edge of the starboard wing. The spoiler caused both wings to stall symmetrically, preventing a dangerous roll at low altitude. The new tail hook did not skip over arresting cables as the older ones had tended to do. A less rigid oleo strut mitigated the bouncing that Corsairs had experienced on landings. A new water injection system reduced detonations and cooled supercharged air. This feature enabled the pilot to increase carburetor inlet pressure and boost engine power to 300 horsepower for 5 minutes, giving the fighter a top speed of 415 mph.[9]

In January 1945, just prior to deployment, the squadron exchanged these aircraft for new F4U-1Ds. The F4U-1D had four rocket launchers and a bomb pylon under each wing. It could carry either eight High Velocity Aircraft Rockets (HVARs), two 500-pound or 1,000-pound bombs, or napalm canisters under its wings. These weapons enabled the F4U-1D to attack vessels and ground targets in rocket and dive-bombing attacks. Because of the weight this ordnance added, the 63-gallon wing tanks were eliminated. Instead, the twin pylons under the fuselage could each carry a 154-gallon drop tank. With this fuel load a Corsair carrying a 1,000-pound bomb could fly 1,200 miles.[10]

Flying equipment had also improved. Gravitational forces in combat pulled blood from a pilot's brain, causing disorientation and blackouts. VMF-221 received Type Z antigravitation suits. The inflatable trousers compressed the pilot's legs, preventing blood from pooling there. Corsair pilots could now endure seven times their body weight for five seconds or more without significant handicap.[11]

The Japanese had also developed new fighters. In addition to the Zero and Tony, VMF-221 would encounter four newer fighters in significant numbers.

They were faster than the Zeros they replaced, and most carried more firepower. The Kawanishi N1K2-J "George" could reach 400 mph (55 mph faster than the Zero). It had four 20-mm cannons (two more than the Zero) and two 7.7-mm machine guns (the same as the Zero). The Nakajima Ki-44 "Tojo" and Nakajima Ki-84 "Frank" carried the same twin 20-mm cannons and twin 7.7-mm machine guns as the Zero. The Tojo could reach 383 mph. Only the Frank was faster than the F4U-1D, topping out at 426 mph.[12]

Though VMF-221 would face better aircraft in 1945, it would not face better pilots. Japanese training standards continued to plummet as aviation fuel stocks dwindled and combat losses climbed. In late 1943 the Japanese Naval Air Force discontinued intermediate training. Combat squadrons took on the burden of training pilots how to fly their type and model of aircraft and how to fight, as VMF-221 had done in 1942. As a result, the adversaries VMF-221 would face in 1945 usually had far less experience than their predecessors had in 1942 and 1943.[13]

Training and Tactics

VMF-221's new training incorporated a syllabus influenced by two years of war. In contrast to the rushed and hectic training previous squadron commanders oversaw, Post and Roberts directed a systematic, unhurried process.[14]

From February to November the pilots averaged 22.7 hours each month. The aviators did not merely fly more hours; they spent those hours becoming more lethal. The war diary regularly recorded gunnery, division and squadron tactics, and instrument flying. Gunnery was the most frequent activity, at both low altitude and higher elevations on oxygen, at slow and high speeds, using both live ammunition against towed sleeves and gun camera footage. Instrument flying progressed from the Link simulator to SNJ flights to flying Corsairs on instruments alone at night. Countless times, pilots bombed and strafed a prominence known as Wilson's Rock two miles off San Miguel Island. The squadron practiced scrambles and intercepted army air force and navy bombers under radar direction. On the ground, pilots took turns working with the engineering section to learn the intricacies of their aircraft and its maintenance. They spent time in a pressure chamber to recognize the effects of thinner air, dropped from a suspended parachute harness into Santa Barbara Harbor, and quizzed each other on aircraft and vessel recognition.[15]

The squadron still had enough idle time to schedule events that marines a generation later would recognize. Wednesday morning inspections included close-order drill. Pilots participated in combat conditioning, bayonet drills, hand-to-hand fighting, and judo. The squadron sent pilots to skeet and pistol ranges to hone their marksmanship. They sat through lectures on infantry tactics and films on air combat maneuvers, survival, and the progress of the war. They played other squadrons in baseball, speedball, and water polo. They even visited the gas chamber, just in case. In step with the squadron's Fighting Falcons nickname, someone returned from leave in July with a caged falcon as the squadron's mascot. When wildfires threatened Santa Barbara, the enlisted marines fought fires for four days. In early November, 2nd Lt. Ralph O. Glendinning was tapped to deliver lectures on the history of the U.S. Marine Corps.[16]

It was a tenet of Marine Corps doctrine that marine aviation existed to support marines on the ground. For VMF-221 and most other marine squadrons in the Pacific, that had not been the case thus far. As VMF-221's experience suggests, marine squadrons primarily defended advance bases and helped the fleet achieve air superiority and sea control. The squadron's training now incorporated air support for the landing force. It conducted mock attacks against army ground units at Camp Roberts a hundred miles to the north. In one of Roberts' first operations as the commander, the squadron supported a landing at Camp Pendleton. On 26 November, the squadron sortied four divisions to San Clemente Island during an amphibious operation. Commander, Support Air, a naval aviator on the staff of the amphibious force commander, directed the Corsairs using a grid overlay. As only two pilots had the overlays, they had to lead the other fourteen on bombing and strafing runs.[17]

The navy and marines were still ironing out the wrinkles. At Saipan in June 1944, Commander, Support Air directed airstrikes by navy carrier planes with the assistance of air observers aloft and air liaison officers at the division and regimental command posts. After the landing force captured an airfield, army air force P-47s also flew support missions. The amphibious force commander characterized air support at Saipan as "not very good." Coordination was cumbersome and sluggish. Mistakes had killed American troops. Marine commanders urged Nimitz to embark marine squadrons trained in air support aboard escort carriers.[18]

As marines and soldiers wrapped up the fighting on Saipan, Brig. Gen. Louis E. Woods, the director of aviation at Headquarters, Marine Corps, realized that the F4U-1D might be a better dive-bomber than the SBD. The F4U-1D flew faster and farther than the SBD. Using the Corsair as both a fighter and a scout dive-bomber would create a number of efficiencies. Air commanders could task Corsair squadrons to gain air superiority early in an operation and then use them on strikes and close air support missions when they were no longer required on fighter sweeps and combat air patrol. Corsairs could strafe targets with six .50-caliber machine guns instead of the SBD's two. Maintenance crews would only need training, tools, and parts for one type of aircraft.[19]

Three SBD squadrons and four F4U squadrons experimented in the Marshalls and found that 50 percent of the SBD's bombs consistently landed within 175 feet of the target. For the Corsair, the distance was only marginally worse, 195 feet.[20]

The F4U-1D could also shoot rockets. Each HVAR weighed 134 pounds and had a range of 3 miles.[21] Rockets came in a general-purpose variant with 7.6 pounds of TNT, and an armor-piercing variant with 2.2 pounds of ammonium picrate. Rockets could penetrate four feet of reinforced concrete and were effective against fortifications, armored vehicles, and soft targets such as ammunition and fuel.[22]

The pilots of VMF-221 watched a film about the rockets on 17 October 1944.[23] In December they flew up to Marine Auxiliary Air Station Mojave in Kern County, California. After four days of lectures on field carrier landing procedures and the employment of the aircraft rockets, they practiced both at the remote field. However, since the squadron still flew the earlier-model Corsairs, rocket practice was limited to dummy runs.[24] In early January the squadron received its first F4U-1Ds. The marines flew to Naval Auxiliary Air Station Holtville in Imperial County, California, for three days of live rocket firing at 35- and 50-degree dives.[25]

Carrier Qualification

Marine fighting squadrons could be trained and equipped to support marines on the ground, but until they could fly off carriers they would have to wait until the landing force captured an airfield. Since becoming Commandant in January 1944, Lt. Gen. Alexander A. Vandegrift had been trying to get his squadrons aboard carriers. He did not want the squadrons relegated to the rear areas in the Pacific War. Moreover, he wanted marine squadrons to support marine landing forces during amphibious assaults. After navy and army air force squadrons had performed unspectacularly in the Marianas, Vandegrift persuaded Nimitz to recommend to Admiral King that marine aircraft groups deploy aboard six escort carriers. King agreed, and the Marine Corps began organizing escort carrier aircraft groups to provide close air support to marines ashore.[26]

VMF-221's assignment to a carrier came later in 1944. On 25 October, Japanese pilots shocked the Pacific Fleet when they conducted the first organized suicide attacks against escort carriers off Samar. Vice Adm. George D. Murray, commanding Air Force, Pacific Fleet, concluded that carriers needed more fighters for protection against these "special attack" planes. And since the Combined Fleet now had fewer ships, the carriers could get away with fewer bombers. Reducing an air group by fifteen torpedo and dive-bombers made room for nineteen fighters.[27]

The navy was short of fighter pilots, but providentially, the marines had an abundance of underemployed fighting squadrons. Moreover, the marines had Corsairs. The F4U-1Ds' superior speed would make them even deadlier interceptors than the navy's F6F Hellcats. The F4U-1D's ground attack capability would offset the reduction in bombers. On 2 December, Murray recommended that Nimitz assign ten marine fighting squadrons to five fleet carriers. Each carrier would receive two squadrons of eighteen fighters each. VMF-221 and VMF-451 were assigned to *Bunker Hill*. VMF-221 began a field carrier landing refresher course at Mojave just four days later. It is unlikely that any of the squadron's pilots had landed a plane aboard a carrier before.[28]

Carrier training began with lectures and films in August, followed by four days of practice on a grass field near Oxnard, California. Field carrier landing practice required the pilot to mimic the approach and landing he would employ at sea, including following the directions of a landing signal officer. After the training at Mojave the squadron flew down to Naval Air Station North Island in San Diego on 11 December. The following day, the pilots flew out to rendezvous with USS *Ranger* (CV 4).[29]

Landing aboard a carrier is one of the most difficult tasks any aviator can attempt, and the F4U was one of the most difficult aircraft in which to attempt it. With a stall speed at around 86 mph when configured for landing, the Corsair had to approach the carrier fast, typically at about 103 mph. Though the carrier would be sailing into the wind, which reduced the aircraft's relative airspeed over the deck by as much as a third, the ship would pitch and roll, forcing the pilot to correct in three dimensions. The landing signal officer on the port side of the fantail guided the pilot down with paddles. But the Corsair's long nose prevented the pilot from seeing the landing signal officer on a straight-in approach. Corsair pilots therefore had to approach the carrier at an angle to keep both the ship and the signal officer in sight. As the ship sailed ahead, this required the pilot to constantly turn left. The Corsair's powerful torque required the pilot to add right rudder while making this left turn. If the pilot increased power too quickly, that torque could roll the Corsair, a deadly emergency two hundred feet above the water. While following the landing signal officer's directions and managing his airspeed, rate of descent, and angle of approach, the pilot had to remember to ensure the aircraft was configured for landing: electric fuel pump on, tail wheel unlocked, fuel selector on reserve, mixture to auto rich, supercharger in neutral, propeller control between 2,300 and 2,400 rpm, cowl flaps closed, wheels down, flaps at 50 degrees, arresting hook down, and guns and rockets off and safe.[30]

When the landing signal officer waved a paddle across his throat, the pilot cut his throttle and the Corsair dropped to the deck. It took nerve and self-control to resist diving toward the flight deck and just letting the fighter fall.[31]

Landing was a perilous maneuver, but once aboard, the pilot then faced the peril of a carrier launch. The pilot first taxied to the takeoff spot facing the bow. After extending his flaps fully and raising the arresting hook, he confirmed that the fuel tank selector, mixture, supercharger, and propeller control were still properly configured. He then opened the cowl flaps two-thirds, closed the intercooler flap, and opened the oil cooler flap. The pilot adjusted the rudder tab 6 degrees to the right and the right aileron tab 6 degrees down to compensate for the radial engine's tremendous torque, which could cause the Corsair to drift to the right. Once that was done, the pilot locked the tail wheel, locked the cockpit open, and checked the manifold pressure, cylinder head temperature, and oil temperature. On a signal from the launch control officer, the pilot applied full toe brakes and held the control stick back while advancing the throttle. The brakes held the aircraft in place and the elevator control kept the tail on the deck as the engine roared and the aircraft shook. Once he was set, the pilot nodded. The launch control officer threw his arm toward the bow, the pilot released the brakes, and the Corsair surged forward. As the pilot increased rpm, he maintained right rudder, always fighting the engine's torque. When he released the back pressure on the control stick, the tail lifted, pitching the aircraft level. Now the pilot could see the bow rapidly approaching. During routine takeoffs, the aircraft lifted off before reaching the bow. The pilot had only to circle around and make seven more landings to qualify—if nothing went wrong.[32]

When aircraft crowding the deck limited the space available for takeoff, fleet carriers could also launch aircraft using large H-4 catapults. The maximum takeoff weight of a Corsair was 14,200 pounds. The H-4 could accelerate an 18,000-pound aircraft to 90 mph in 96 feet.[33]

During VMF-221's three days aboard *Ranger* twenty-seven aviators qualified, averaging fourteen landings each by the time the squadron deployed.[34] Not every pilot passed. On each of his attempts to land, 2nd Lt. Fred Briggs watched the landing signal officer wave the pilot ahead of him off and duck into the safety net on the ship's port side. Each time, Briggs had to go around while the officer moved back in position. Through no fault of his own, Briggs exhausted his fuel before getting an opportunity to attempt a landing and had to return to North Island. He pleaded with Roberts to take him anyway. Roberts relented, and Briggs made his first carrier landing when he returned from his first combat mission.[35]

Mishaps

VMF-221 had not experienced a single mishap during carrier qualification. The squadron's luck changed on the night of 12 December when Captain Swett was leading three divisions back to North Island. The marines had never landed at North Island at night, and visibility that night was restricted by rain and fog, but the station duty officer refused to illuminate the runway. When Swett continued to insist, the duty officer reluctantly turned on a single row of lights. The marines landed on the wrong side of the lights and found themselves among parked aircraft and equipment instead of on the tarmac. Lt. William Ormes' fighter collided with a bulldozer, flipped on its back, and was engulfed in flames. Ormes escaped, but his severe burns required years of hospitalization. Lt. Donald G. MacFarlane collided with a PBY. He escaped injury, but the Corsair required an overhaul.[36]

The squadron suffered twenty-eight mishaps between February and December 1944, losing nine aircraft and three pilots. On 13 May, Lt. Ewell H. Haynes Jr. collided with his section leader, Captain Baldwin, during gunnery practice. Baldy parachuted and was recovered. Another pilot saw Haynes ditch and climb onto his wing, but searchers failed to locate him.[37] On 27 November, Lt. Norman K. Sark misjudged his recovery from a gunnery run and flew into the sea. In the third fatal incident, Lt. Richard Chasserre spun into the ground after a waved-off field landing attempt at North Island on 30 December.[38]

Aside from the duty officer's negligence at North Island and seven mechanical issues, the other nineteen mishaps were caused by a replacement pilot's error. Notably, fourteen of the replacements' errors occurred between February and May. As the replacements became more familiar with the Corsair, the mishap rate declined.[39]

The squadron's experience also highlighted a distinct advantage of training new aviators in California. Repairing and replacing aircraft and pilots was far simpler there than it would be overseas.

Air Group 84

A week after completing qualification aboard *Ranger*, the squadron was divided into a flight echelon and a rear echelon. The flight echelon included twenty-eight aviators and a support echelon of three officers and sixty enlisted marines. Twenty-eight of these enlisted marines had served with the squadron in the Solomons, including all ten master technical sergeants. These marines joined *Bunker Hill*'s aircraft group, Air Group 84, at North Island in mid-December. The rear echelon moved to Marine Corps Air Station El Centro in Imperial County, California, where it remained for the rest of the war.[40]

The flight echelon immediately began training with the group's torpedo (VT-84), dive-bomber (VB-84), and other fighting squadrons (VF-84 and VMF-451). VT-84 had 15 TBM Avenger torpedo bombers. VB-84 had 15 SB2U-C Helldiver dive-bombers. VF-84 had 27 F4U-1D Corsairs, 6 F6F-5P Hellcat photo reconnaissance fighters, and 4 F6F-5N Hellcat night fighters. With the 36 F4U-1Ds of VMF-221 and VMF-451 included, Air Group 84 had 103 aircraft.[41]

The group commander, Cdr. George M. Ottinger of Memphis, Tennessee, had graduated from the Naval Academy in 1932, where he had run track. Ottinger had been a naval aviator for more than a decade when he took over the group. He had instructed fighter trainees for two years and served as a dive-bomber pilot and a landing signal officer but had not yet flown in combat. He took command of Air Group 84 shortly after it was formed in May 1944. "A swell person and so damned capable," Roberts thought.[42]

At the end of 1944, Ottinger reported that all his squadrons had completed 95 percent or more of their predeployment training.[43] On 5 and 6 January, the squadrons flew out to *Ranger*, where they practiced the difficult but essential task of taking off quickly and rendezvousing as a group. After returning to North Island, VMF-221 practiced day and night carrier landings at an outlying field.[44]

On 18 and 19 January, the squadron flew from San Diego to NAS Alameda on San Francisco Bay. On 24 January, the air group embarked *Bunker Hill* at pier side. The carrier's new commander, Capt. George A. Seitz, a naval aviator for more than two decades, wasted no time. *Bunker Hill* was under way for Pearl Harbor at 1608, taking VMF-221 back to the war.[45]

12

★ ★ ★

Aboard USS *Bunker Hill*, January–February 1945

Operational Context

The Pacific War was entering its final phase in January 1945. On 3 October 1944, with the Marianas secure and the invasion of Leyte in the Philippines weeks away, the Joint Chiefs had ordered MacArthur to invade Luzon, the northernmost of the Philippine Islands, on 20 December. Nimitz was ordered to cover and support MacArthur with the Pacific Fleet, to assault Iwo Jima in the Bonin Islands on 20 January, and to follow up with an assault on Okinawa in the Ryukyu Islands by 1 March. When *Bunker Hill* sailed under the Golden Gate Bridge on 24 January, the U.S. Sixth Army was still wrestling for control of Luzon, so Nimitz was compelled to postpone the assault on Iwo Jima until 19 February.[1]

Crossing the Pacific

Bunker Hill arrived in Pearl Harbor on 28 January. Apparently, Roberts and his marines had begun to bristle under some of *Bunker Hill*'s restrictions. The navy permitted neither gambling nor liquor aboard its warships, and the rule was strictly enforced. The marines nicknamed the carrier's executive officer "Be-No" for his admonishments: "There will be no liquor, there will be no movies, there will be no shore parties," and "there will be no mail call." *Bunker Hill*'s crew and air group were not permitted to go ashore in Hawaii. At sea, pilots often spent evenings in the ready room watching movies, playing chess, and playing poker—or drinking behind closed stateroom doors.[2]

Bunker Hill departed on 29 January as part of a task group of six carriers and seven escorts. On 31 January, Commander Ottinger pulled the squadron commanders aside and confided that their first operation would be a strike on Tokyo itself, followed by support to the marines assaulting Iwo Jima. "This naturally came as quite a blow to the assembled crowd—hitting the homeland on the first operation," Roberts wrote in his diary. "But everyone was eager, and the excitement ran high." Ottinger let Roberts inform his pilots the next day. "They received the news much the same as the squadron commanders had—that same air of intense apprehension coupled with excitement and eagerness."[3]

Bunker Hill made effective use of the time under way. The fighting squadrons flew combat air patrols, becoming more familiar with task force procedures and more comfortable with carrier landings. The mechanics installed the latest updates the Bureau of Aeronautics had approved for the F4U-1Ds.[4]

Roberts was able to leave most of his enlisted ground crew in California because *Bunker Hill*'s aviation engineering division shouldered the lion's share of maintaining the aircraft. These 180–200 sailors maintained power plants, propellers, airframes, hydraulics, oxygen systems, parachutes, radios, and weapons. They overhauled engines and machined parts. Check crews certified all aircraft before flight. Ordnance technicians loaded weapons and bombs.[5]

First Lt. Charles H. Nettles was reminded of the perils of carrier aviation two days after the squadron's first combat air patrol. On approach, Nettles dropped his belly tank without first switching to his reserve tank. His engine sputtered out, and he made a water landing. He was plucked from the water by a destroyer, which he rode the rest of the way to the western Pacific.[6]

Perils were not limited to those aloft. On 2 February, the wing guns of an aircraft secured on the hangar deck fired unintentionally, blasting rounds through both thighs of TSgt. John H. Coggins. Coggins recovered in sick bay and remained with the squadron.[7]

Fifth Fleet Organization

Nine days after departing Pearl Harbor, *Bunker Hill* dropped anchor in Ulithi and joined Vice Admiral Mitscher's Task Force 58. "Carriers, cruisers, and destroyers extended as far the eye could see," Lieutenant Glendinning recalled.[8]

Task Force 58 included eleven fleet carriers, five light carriers, eight battleships, fifteen cruisers, seventy-seven destroyers, and numerous support ships. Mitscher organized this armada into five task groups, with *Bunker Hill* under Rear Adm. Frederick C. "Ted" Sherman's Task Group 58.3, along with the carrier USS *Essex* (CV 9, Sherman's flagship) and the light carrier USS *Cowpens* (CVL 25). Mitscher boarded *Bunker Hill* in Ulithi after choosing her as his task force flagship. Task Force 58 departed Ulithi with 1,200 aircraft embarked; more than 850 of these were fighters. VMF-221's 18 F4U's constituted just 1.5 percent of Mitscher's aircraft strength.[9]

Task Force 58 was the most powerful of the nine task forces in Admiral Spruance's Fifth Fleet. Spruance accompanied Task Group 58.3, flying his flag from the cruiser USS *Indianapolis* (CA 35). Nimitz had placed Spruance in charge of Operation Detachment, the Pacific Fleet's main effort in early 1945. The purpose of Detachment was to maintain pressure against Japan and extend U.S. control over the western Pacific. To accomplish this, Nimitz assigned Spruance three tasks: reduce enemy air and naval strength and industrial facilities in the home islands, destroy Japanese air and naval forces in the Bonins, and assault and capture Iwo Jima. While accomplishing these missions Spruance would also be preparing for the invasion of Okinawa. Spruance ordered Mitscher to support the landing on Iwo Jima, twelve days off, but to strike Tokyo first.[10]

The Pacific Fleet had been fighting a carrier war for more than three years when Air Group 84 joined Task Force 58.[11] At Midway in June 1942, commanders had struggled to coordinate air operations between two carriers. Task Force 58, in contrast, could coordinate carrier operations involving more

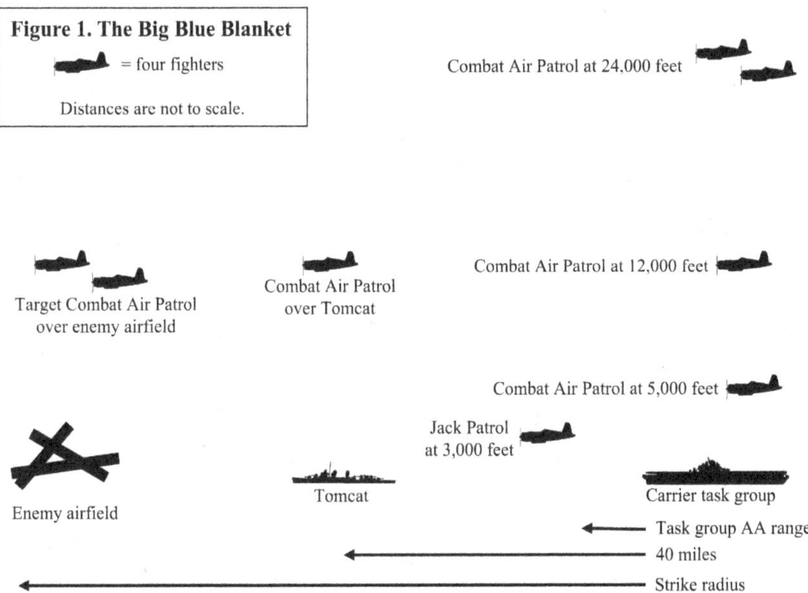

FIGURE 1. The Big Blue Blanket

than one thousand aircraft. The task force had also incorporated numerous combat-tested tactical innovations.

In opposition to the amphibious assaults on Leyte and Luzon in the Philippines, Japanese special attack (suicide) planes had struck 137 of the Pacific Fleet's vessels between 25 October 1944 and 13 January 1945, sinking 22. To combat this threat, Cdr. James Flatley, Mitscher's operations officer, implemented a tactic that his colleague Cdr. Jimmy Thach nicknamed "The Big Blue Blanket." The tactic had three components.

First, Task Force 58's fighters "blanketed" Japanese airfields within range of the carriers, particularly those suspected to be bases for special attack units. Night fighters enabled the task force to cover the bases round-the-clock.

Second, between 20 and 24 fighters patrolled above each task group: 8 at 20,000 feet, 4 at 12,000 feet, and 4 at 5,000 feet. Another 4 to 8 fighters patrolled below 3,000 feet just outside the range of the task group's antiaircraft guns. These fighters flew in two-plane "Jack Patrols" to intercept attackers attempting to sneak in under the radar. Another 8 fighters were poised on deck alert, while 20 to 24 more fighters remained in reserve.

Third, the task force positioned two or three pairs of destroyers, called "Tomcats," forty miles from the task force. The destroyers' radars gave the task force early warning of enemy aircraft. At least a division of fighters patrolled over each Tomcat pair. It took fifty-six fighters to maintain this coverage over one task group and its Tomcat. The light carriers' fighting squadrons flew the bulk of these combat air patrols, enabling the fleet carriers to concentrate their combat power in strikes.

Task Force 58 also decentralized fighter direction. Rather than employing a single task force fighter direction center, each group directed its own fighters. Moreover, any ship with fighters available and unidentified aircraft on its radar had the authority and responsibility to direct an interception.[12]

This delegation of fighter direction compensated for limitations inherent in fleet carriers like *Bunker Hill*. Though the carrier's SK radar occasionally detected large formations 140 miles or more away, individual enemy aircraft flying above 25,000 feet or at low altitudes often approached undetected to within 40 miles. Because IFF was notoriously unreliable, the combat information center could not rely on it, and individual attackers often slipped unnoticed into the busy air space above Task Force 58.[13]

At Ulithi, Task Force 58 disseminated a memorandum approved by Mitscher titled "Air Combat Notes for Pilots." The memo's tone and intent resembled a locker room talk before a football game. After stressing bombing fundamentals for the torpedo and dive-bomber pilots, it enumerated pointers for fighter pilots entering combat for the first time. The memorandum emphasized section and division integrity, the defensive weave, air speed, and recovering altitude quickly. It repeatedly stressed aggressiveness tempered with cool-headed vigilance.[14]

The Pacific Fleet issued air-sea rescue standard operating procedures in January 1945 that instilled further confidence in the aviators. Submarines, destroyers, OS2U Kingfisher seaplanes catapulted from battleships and cruisers, and long-range PBY and PBM Mariner seaplanes now supported carrier strikes. All vessels and aircraft employed common frequencies and terminology.[15]

The Big Blue Blanket, Mitscher's air combat instructions, and air-sea rescue procedures would all help protect Task Force 58's ships, aircraft, and fliers. But the purpose of Task Force 58 was not to protect itself. Mitscher could do that by steering clear of Japan. The purpose of Task Force 58 was to strike. By attacking airfields and aircraft manufacturing around Tokyo, Task Force 58 would force Japan's aviators to come out and fight or watch the Americans destroy their aircraft on the ground.[16]

In April 1942, Mitscher had taken *Hornet* 800 miles from Japan to launch 16 army air force B-25s under the command of Col. Jimmy Doolittle, then fled east before air strikes from the home islands could hit back. Three years later, Mitscher was bringing 1,200 aircraft 115 miles from Japan and staying for 3 days.

13

★ ★ ★

First Combat Cruise, 10 February–4 March 1945

Bunker Hill spent three days at Ulithi refueling and replenishing. On 9 February, Ottinger, Roberts, and the other group and squadron commanders attended a briefing on the plan of attack. Mitscher had ordered Task Group 58.3 to destroy Japanese aircraft, aircraft facilities, and naval forces in and around Tokyo from 16 to 18 February. The admiral assumed his force would be detected by air patrols and picket boats and hit with heavy air attacks and possibly submarines.

Tokyo, 16–18 February

Roberts learned that he would lead sixteen aircraft from VMF-221 as part of the first of five strikes on 16 February, a forty-plane fighter sweep led by Cdr. Frank K. Upham, *Essex*'s air group commander. After returning to *Bunker Hill*, Roberts would lead a sixteen-plane, four-hour combat air patrol at midday. Captain Swett would lead the fifth fighter sweep of the day. On day 2, Roberts would lead the second of several more sweeps. Because airmen who bailed out over Japan faced capture and interrogation, most pilots were told few specifics beyond their initial assignments. After hearing that the Japanese typically tortured officers of his rank,

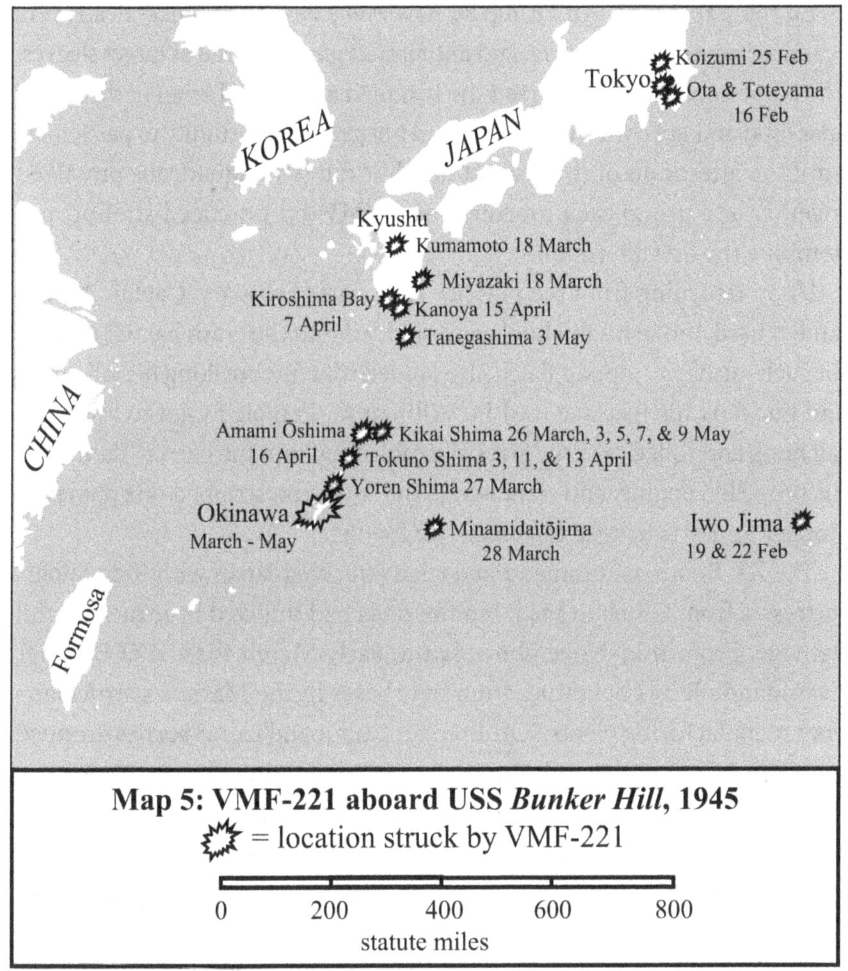

MAP 5. VMF-221 aboard USS *Bunker Hill*, 1945

Major Roberts penned in his diary, "This chicken ain't about to get himself captured—no how!"[1]

Task Group 58.3 sortied on 10 February. A day or so later, Captain Seitz assembled the crew on the flight deck and revealed to all hands that they were on their way to bomb Tokyo. "At that one word, the cheers were so loud there was concern the Japanese some 1,500 miles away might hear," Glendinning recalled.[2]

En route to Tokyo, Air Group 84 flew every day. The Tomcat destroyers practiced controlling fighters, and antiaircraft gunners fired at target sleeves. The amphibious force rehearsed the Iwo Jima assault at Tinian in the Marianas on 11 and 12 February. VMF-221 did not get an opportunity to participate until the afternoon of the second day, but the navy squadrons practiced together as a group each morning, and VMF-451 practiced strafing and bombing the first afternoon.[3]

Upon returning from the practice runs on 12 February, Captain Snider landed hard, broke his tail hook, and skidded into the crash barrier erected for such mishaps. Captain Balch also landed roughly, breaking his tail wheel and buckling his fuselage. 2nd Lt. William M. Pemble forgot to lower his tail hook and rolled over the arresting cables and into the barrier, damaging his propeller, engine, and right wing. The squadron stripped one damaged Corsair for parts to keep the other two flying.[4]

The XX Bomber Command had tried attacking Japan with B-29 Superfortresses from China in 1944, but the raids had inflicted little meaningful damage. From mid-November 1944 to early March 1945, XXI Bomber Command's B-29s operating from new bases in the Marianas struck aircraft manufacturing plants. XXI Bomber Command's 2,198 sorties dropped 5,398 tons of bombs but failed to knock out Japan's aircraft industry. Recognizing that high winds and thick cloud cover rendered daylight, high-altitude precision bombing ineffective, XXI Bomber Command switched tactics. The B-29s would fly their first nighttime, low-altitude area fire-bombing of Tokyo on 25 February.[5]

To outmaneuver the miserable weather, Task Force 58 would try daylight, low-level precision strikes by carrier aircraft. In between combat air patrols the pilots attended detailed briefings regarding the upcoming strikes against Tokyo. The target folders for the Tokyo strikes provided to *Bunker Hill*'s pilots included aerial photographs and damage assessments from B-29 raids, which greatly aided mission planning.[6]

Bunker Hill served steak and green powdered eggs to the aviators on the morning of 16 February. Roberts, about to lead fifteen of his young fighter pilots on his first combat operation, had no appetite. "My mouth was dry and everything I tried to swallow nauseated me," he remembered. He and his marines emerged onto the pitch-dark flight deck into a miserable mix of icy rain and snow. Winds were gusting to 40 mph; the sky was thoroughly overcast, and the ceiling was just 2,500 feet. Visibility was only two miles at best, and negligible during squalls. The nasty weather would hide the task force until enemy radar pickets detected it, but it would complicate rendezvous, navigation, and targeting, not to mention finding the carrier again and landing.[7]

The pilots shivered in their open cockpits as they waited for the squalls to subside. Ice covered the deck, creating a real danger that the Corsair's enormous torque might send a fighter sliding over the side into the frigid ocean. A plane captain climbed on 1st Lt. Arthur B. Imel's wing and yelled in his ear. "He told me that once I was in takeoff position, the Signal Officer would point and pass responsibility of taking off to me," Imel remembered. "That meant I would power up just enough to reach flight, but not enough to allow torque to steer me off course or just spin like a top."[8]

Roberts took off twenty minutes late at 0705. Only five of his marines found him in the rain and clouds, and they could not locate Upham and his twenty-two Hellcats. Roberts elected to attack Japan with his tiny force and flew northwest, three hundred feet above the waves.[9]

By the time he crossed the coast, Roberts had only a vague idea of where he was. He began climbing. Through a rare break in the clouds he spotted Tateyama Airfield. Roberts and his marines strafed the field, setting three twin-engine planes and a hangar on fire as well as crippling or damaging seven other aircraft. The six Corsairs then climbed to find more targets. They found four of their missing F4Us three miles offshore. This group had sunk a fishing boat on its way in. About fifteen miles southwest of Tateyama, Lieutenant Snider spotted a Betty. He and his wingman, 2nd Lt. Donald G. MacFarlane, shot it down. Roberts found a barge, which the marines strafed but did not sink, then headed back to *Bunker Hill*.[10]

Second Lt. James G. Turner had found a flight of F6Fs from *Essex* and joined them in another strafing attack on Tateyama. Two other pilots found no aircraft or targets. Three others could not find the rendezvous and joined the combat air patrol over the task force. Despite the weather and a few aircraft with homing equipment failures, all sixteen aircraft were recovered by 1100. An hour later Roberts was back in the cockpit for a combat air patrol.[11]

Task Group 58.3's next three fighter sweeps battled the weather. When breaks in the clouds revealed airfields or surface ships, they struck. The final strike of the day, launched at 1415, found fewer clouds over the Nakajima Aircraft Assembly Plant at Ota, on the northwest side of Tokyo Bay. The flight included fifteen F4U-1Ds from VF-84, thirteen SB2C-4Es from VB-84, and fourteen TBM-3s from VT-84. To assess bombing damage, a single F6F-5P was assigned to photograph the target immediately after the strike. F4U-1Ds from VMF-221 flown by 2nd Lt. George R. A. Johns and 2nd Lieutenant Pemble protected the reconnaissance fighter and its wingman, a VF-84 F4U-1D.[12]

The bombers approached the target from the northwest at 13,500 feet. VF-84 flew top cover at 18,000 feet, with the photography section and marines in between. The clearing weather enabled the Japanese to send up a large number of Oscar and Tojo fighters, which circled the formation. Five of the TBMs were equipped with electronic jamming equipment to interfere with enemy communications. The bombers' gunners tossed out sleeves of aluminum strips to confuse antiaircraft radars. When the bombers began their dives, the Japanese fighters swarmed in. None of the bombers was lost on the bombing run, but fighters took down two TBMs on the return trip.[13]

Johns and Pemble, who had volunteered at the last minute, had not been told that VF-84's fighters were going to dive with the bombers to strafe antiaircraft emplacements. The four navy and marine fighters found themselves alone, high over Ota, amid what looked to Johns like a hundred enemy aircraft. By the time the photo plane began its run across the target, Pemble was missing. Johns rolled around the F6F-5N as it snapped the precious photos, firing at fighters as they swooped by. As soon as the Hellcat had its photos, Johns yelled to its pilot, "Firewall the S.O.B. and dive!" The three fighters evaded the attackers. Pemble did not return with them; a bomber crewman reported seeing an out-of-control Corsair crash into a hillside. The photos taken by the Hellcat and others taken on 25 February confirmed the bombing accuracy claimed by the torpedo and dive-bomber pilots of Air Group 84. The plant appeared to be 90 percent destroyed.[14]

On 17 February, Air Group 84 conducted a fighter sweep at 0715 followed by a hundred-plane Task Group 58.3 strike at 0900. VMF-221 flew combat air patrol over the task group and saw no action. The strike scored multiple hits on two engine plants. One SB2C ditched within the task group, and its aircrew were recovered. As the weather worsened, Mitchener called off further strikes. Task Force 58 sailed for Iwo Jima.[15]

Close Air Support Doctrine

The Marine Corps had endeavored not only to get marine squadrons on board carriers, but to develop doctrine and units to support landing forces ashore as well. After a poor showing at Tarawa, close air support by navy and army air force squadrons had steadily improved. For the assault on Iwo Jima, carrier aircraft would check in with Commander, Support Aircraft. Once the landing force was ashore, air liaison parties embedded with each battalion, regiment, and division would request air support from Commander, Support Aircraft. The supporting aircraft would be directed to contact an air liaison party, who would confirm the target location and provide updates on friendly troop locations. Air liaison parties used several techniques to help pilots locate targets on the ground. In addition to providing map coordinates, they laid out orange panels to identify friendly units and dropped white phosphorus mortar rounds to indicate targets.[16]

The Marine Corps had developed a Landing Force Air Support Control Unit (LFASCU) that would control aircraft once it was established ashore. The LFASCU did not begin controlling aircraft on Iwo Jima until 1 March, however, long after Task Force 58 had departed.[17]

VMF-221 had practiced close air support several times in California and for an afternoon at Tinian on the way to Iwo Jima. But within Air Group 84, it appears the navy squadrons were more proficient at this mission than the marines. The navy bomber squadrons had spent weeks practicing with amphibious forces on San Clemente Island off San Diego. During the rehearsal at Tinian, it was VB-84, VT-84, and VF-84 that had participated in the practice landing.[18]

Four Days at Iwo Jima, 19–22 February

While *Bunker Hill* was at Ulithi, a LFASCU team had come aboard to review the landing and air support plans for Iwo Jima. They had explained that the

4th and 5th Marine Divisions would land side by side on D-day, with the 3rd Marine Division in floating reserve. VMF-221 and VMF-451 would fly close air support missions all afternoon. Each Corsair would be heavily loaded with .50-caliber ammunition, eight rockets, and one napalm bomb. "That's a lot of stuff to hang on a fighter," Roberts had noted. "And they will have to give us *lots* of deck to get off on."[19]

As rehearsed at Tinian, *Bunker Hill*'s three navy squadrons supported the initial landings on 19 February. With no troops yet ashore, Air Group 84 bombed, strafed, and rocketed areas on the left and right flanks of the landing beaches. Though the pilots reported they hit their assigned areas, they could not see whether they inflicted significant damage.[20] That afternoon, Roberts led Air Group 84's second support mission of the day. His strike included sixteen VMF-221 F4U-1Ds, twelve more from VMF-451, and eleven bombers each from VB-84 and VT-84. As Roberts had feared, each Corsair was heavily burdened with a napalm bomb, eight rockets, and a full load of machine-gun ammunition.[21]

Napalm was a mixture of napalm powder and gasoline. Ordnance technicians mixed the components on the flight deck, then filled bombs with the mixture and affixed fuses to the nose and tail. Each fuse had a safety pin that was removed just before the aircraft launched. Marines were told the burning napalm would not only set fire to whatever it contacted but would also asphyxiate defenders underground.[22]

Despite Roberts' fears about the weight of this ordnance, his aircraft all launched safely and rendezvoused. The marines had been tasked to attack artillery and mortar emplacements and fortified positions four hundred yards north of Iwo Jima's Airfield Number 2. These areas were far in advance of the Allied assault units. Between dodging other aircraft and the dust and smoke generated from all the bombing and naval gunfire, the fighter pilots could not make out any Japanese emplacements. They dropped their napalm on the first run, fired their rockets on the second, and strafed the area on the third. Five of VMF-221's napalm bombs failed to drop, and four of Captain Swett's rockets failed to launch. The pilots jettisoned most of these over the ocean. Captain Snider and 2nd Lt. Walter Goeggel each landed with a rocket still hanging on the wing. All of *Bunker Hill*'s aircraft returned safely, though one TBM-3 crashed into the landing barrier and had to be scrapped. None of the group's pilots could swear they had hit anything other than the right piece of the island.[23]

Bunker Hill's air group flew only combat air patrols on 20 February as the carrier refueled. VMF-221 contributed two divisions, neither of which encountered enemy aircraft. The Japanese limited air attacks to nighttime forays, which Task Group 58.3 detected on radar and evaded.[24]

On 21 February, Swett and nine VMF-221 pilots joined fifteen VMF-451 Corsairs, eleven VB-84 SB2Cs, and five VB-84 TBMs on a support mission to Iwo Jima led by Commander Ottinger. Instead of napalm, each Corsair carried a 500-pound general-purpose bomb. When Ottinger checked in with the air support control unit at 0730, he was directed to provide continuous attacks from 0820 to 0850 on an area just north of Airfield Number 2 in support of a 0810 attack by the 4th and 5th Marine Divisions.[25]

This time the marines began their attack with rockets, then dropped their bombs, followed by three strafing attacks. Lieutenant Glendinning recalled seeing "the thousands of individual Marines inching forward, firing their weapons, but on the other side we could not see a single Japanese, all of whom were holed up in their underground tunnels connecting pillboxes and fortified blockhouses." Though most of the defenders were concealed, Captain Balch spotted an artillery emplacement well north of his assigned area. He obtained clearance from the air support control unit and then led his division in a strafing attack. The three navy squadrons conducted a second air support mission that afternoon. All of Air Group 84's planes returned safely once again.[26]

That evening fifty special attack aircraft penetrated the combat air patrol over the amphibious force, Task Force 52. *Saratoga* was struck by three of the planes and one bomb. Another special attack plane hit the escort carrier USS *Bismarck Sea* (CVE 95). Uncontrollable fires resulted in a catastrophic explosion, and the escort carrier sank. Special attack planes also damaged a second escort carrier, a cargo ship, and a landing ship. The attack not only killed hundreds of sailors but also destroyed *Saratoga*'s night fighter group. As a result, Mitscher detached *Enterprise* and her night fighter group to Task Force 52, leaving Task Force 58 temporarily without a dedicated night fighter carrier.[27]

On 22 February, *Bunker Hill*'s last day at Iwo Jima, Air Group 84 launched one support mission at 1250. Roberts was assigned twenty-six fighters from the two marine squadrons, and Ottinger flew along to coordinate the entire mission. The ceiling was just three hundred feet. In the heavy rain, only sixteen fighters linked up with Roberts. He headed for Iwo Jima on instruments just two hundred feet above the waves. When Roberts was ten miles from the island, Ottinger ordered the flight back. Roberts wrote in his diary that night, "The damndest rat race developed when we arrived over the task force. They were not ready to take us aboard for almost an hour; so about 100 planes milled around in all directions, scaring the hell out of everyone. I damned near got creamed about 6 times. It was raining so hard and there was only about a 250 foot ceiling. We finally got all aboard, but why no one was killed in that melee I will never know."[28]

Tokyo Again, 25 February

After refueling on 23 February, *Bunker Hill* sailed west for Task Force 58's second strike against Japan. En route, as he was recovering from a combat air patrol, Lieutenant Nettles upended his Corsair onto its nose. He was uninjured, but his aircraft was scrapped for parts.[29]

VF-84 started 25 February by joining fighters from *Essex* in an early-morning fighter sweep. The navy pilots claimed nine enemy fighters destroyed and another four probables but lost one of their own.[30] Twenty F4U-1Ds from VMF-221 were airborne by 0845, led by Major Roberts. The marines flew top cover for VT-84 and VB-84, which each had thirteen bombers up, and a four-plane photo reconnaissance section from VF-84. The Air Group 84 strike linked up with similar groups from *Essex* and *Cowpens* and headed toward the Nakajima Musashima aircraft plant near Tokyo.[31]

The sky was overcast at three thousand feet, but visibility was good enough for the pilots to see that the ground was covered in snow. Thick clouds over Tokyo Bay forced *Bunker Hill*'s strike to divert to its secondary target, the Nakajima Koizumi factory sixty miles inland. The *Essex* and *Cowpens* groups headed for the Nakajima Ota plant, which "had been creamed earlier by our bombers on the previous trip," according to Roberts. He was unimpressed, writing, "They petered out!"[32]

Air Group 84 found clear skies when it reached its secondary target around 1030 without facing any fighters. In addition to the bombs carried by VB-84 and VT-84, each Corsair carried a 500-pound bomb. One after another, the F4Us attacked from the southeast in 50-degree dives, releasing their bombs at 2,000 feet. Antiaircraft fire failed to bring down a single *Bunker Hill* aircraft. Photographs taken by an F6F-5N confirmed the bombing accuracy was superb. Task Group 58.3 estimated 20 percent of the plant was destroyed.[33]

After the strike, a few of the marines strafed three nearby airfields. Roberts saw what looked like a hundred aircraft parked around the Koizumi airfield. Unfortunately, they had to depart to escort the bombers back and could not linger to strafe the field more deliberately.[34]

Lieutenant Glendinning joined on Captain Swett and gestured toward the flames and smoke billowing from the plant. "Look at that!" he mouthed. Swett nodded and led Glendinning down for a second strafing run. Only later did Glendinning learn Swett had thought he had said, "Let's go back!"[35]

A few Japanese fighters shadowed AG-84 to the coast but did not attack. Over the ocean, Roberts saw about twenty fishing trawlers. He ordered two divisions to strafe them, and they set five boats on fire. The after-action report postulated that the trawlers might have been picket boats headed toward the American rescue submarine stationed offshore. Roberts had mixed feelings, which he confided in his diary. "It might discourage Jap fishermen from venturing out into those waters, but other than that it did no good whatever except to ruin a few boats and maybe kill a few fishermen." The strike recovered without losing an aircraft.[36]

Okinawa, 1 March

The mild weather did not last. Mitscher canceled further Tokyo strikes and ordered Task Force 58 to head southwest to strike shipping around Nagoya the next day. En route, his ships battled gale-force winds. The heavy seas slowed the task force, and it was late to its launch point. Mitscher canceled the Nagoya operation, too, and on 27 February Task Group 58.3 headed away from Japan to refuel.[37]

A couple of mishaps occurred en route. Nettles dove at the deck during a landing and damaged his F4U. A VMF-221 pilot recovering after a combat air patrol the next day had to wave off several times. He finally made a hard landing that totaled yet another Corsair. Roberts grounded the pilot pending a review board. "Old 221 is really stealing the limelight on stinking landing performances," Roberts vented in his diary.[38]

Task Force 58's final action during this underway period consisted of strikes and reconnaissance flights at Okinawa. The landing was now scheduled for 1 April. Spruance wanted Mitscher to strike every airfield in the Ryukyus and photograph Okinawa. Task Force 58 completed its refueling and reached a position seventy miles southeast of Okinawa early on the morning of 1 March.[39]

Mitscher directed Task Group 58.3 to strike and photograph airfields and installations in the Naha area on the southern end of Okinawa and on Minamidaitōjima, a small island two hundred miles east of Okinawa. VMF-221 provided two divisions led by Captain Swett and Captain Balch to Air Group 84's first fighter sweep of the day, an escort of five fighters led by Capt. John B. Delancey for a photographic mission and combat air patrols led by Roberts, Baldwin, and Snider.[40]

Swett found no enemy aircraft aloft, so he began by strafing and rocketing Suba Harbor and an airfield on Ie Shima off Okinawa's northwest coast. After that he flew south to Yontan and did the same to its airfield. Most of the aircraft the marines found on the ground were dummies or inoperable.[41]

While Lieutenant Briggs was attacking antiaircraft positions, his plane suffered a violent hit that took out the hydraulics and flaps. Machine-gun rounds began detonating in his burning right wing. "It scared the pants off me, to be sure, because I did know what was going to happen next," recalled Briggs. He kept the aircraft flying by applying forward right stick and left rudder. He could climb, but the burning fighter would stall if he slowed below 200 mph. Landing or ditching was impossible at that speed, so Briggs bailed out when he reached the task force. A destroyer hove to and hoisted him aboard within minutes.[42]

After the F6F-5P finished taking its pictures, Delancey's division strafed Yontan airfield. Antiaircraft fire struck 2nd Lt. Richard Wasley's fighter on his third pass. Despite losing his flaps and aileron control, Wasley managed to land aboard *Bunker Hill* and crash into the barrier. He was unhurt.[43]

Task Group 58.3's pilots encountered only one enemy aircraft aloft, but destroyed or damaged forty-four on the ground and damaged the airfields on and around Okinawa. All of the photographic flights completed their missions. The group lost eleven aircraft to combat and mishaps, but only three aircrewmen.[44]

Ulithi Refitting and Replacements, 4–13 March

On 4 March, after three weeks underway, Task Group 58.3 anchored at Ulithi. For the next ten days *Bunker Hill* and Air Group 84 restocked supplies, repaired aircraft, and rested. The sailors and marines rode landing craft across the lagoon to Mog Mog Atoll, where they played softball, swam, drank beer, and enjoyed fresh food.[45]

Four veterans from VMF-213 joined VMF-221 at this time. Their squadron had been one of the first marine squadrons to deploy aboard a carrier. Navy Corsair squadrons were replacing these marine units, but the four marine pilots had elected to stay and fight rather than rotate back to California. Roberts was happy to see the squadron's air combat intelligence officer, 2nd Lt. Leo B. Pambrum, arrive from California. When *Bunker Hill* hoisted anchor on 14 March, the squadron had thirty aviators and all its aircraft were ready to fly.[46]

While Ulithi offered a respite from combat, one sobering incident warned of what loomed ahead. On the night of 11–12 March, twenty-four long-range Kugisho P1Y1 "Frances" twin-engine bombers made a suicide attack against the Ulithi anchorage. One struck USS *Randolph* (CV 15), setting her on fire, killing twenty-six of her crew, wounding a hundred more, and forcing her to undertake repairs for the next eighteen days.[47]

The following morning, on *Bunker Hill*'s last full day at anchor, Roberts attended a task group briefing led by Admiral Sherman. For the first time, Roberts and the other squadron commanders learned the details of Operation Iceberg, the invasion of Okinawa.[48]

14

★ ★ ★

Second Combat Cruise, 14 March–11 May 1945

The importance of Okinawa, just three hundred miles south of Kyushu, was obvious to both American and Japanese planners. So long as Japan held Okinawa, Japanese aircraft based there could interfere with American vessels en route to Kyushu. By seizing Okinawa, the United States could base medium bombers and long-range fighters there to support landings on Kyushu.

Operation Iceberg: The Invasion of Okinawa

Though the Japanese Combined Fleet no longer had the capability to challenge the U.S. Pacific Fleet, taking Okinawa would be no easy feat. American planners estimated the 32nd Army on Okinawa had between 53,000 and 56,000 soldiers whose presence would ensure a protracted and costly battle for the island. American commanders anticipated the Japanese would allocate most of their remaining aircraft to attack the American fleet from their bases in the Ryukyus, Formosa, and Kyushu.[1]

Iceberg was the largest operation of the Pacific War. Spruance allocated more than 600 ships to the operation. His Fifth Fleet included 3 large task forces. Vice Adm. Richmond K. Turner's Joint Expeditionary Force (Task

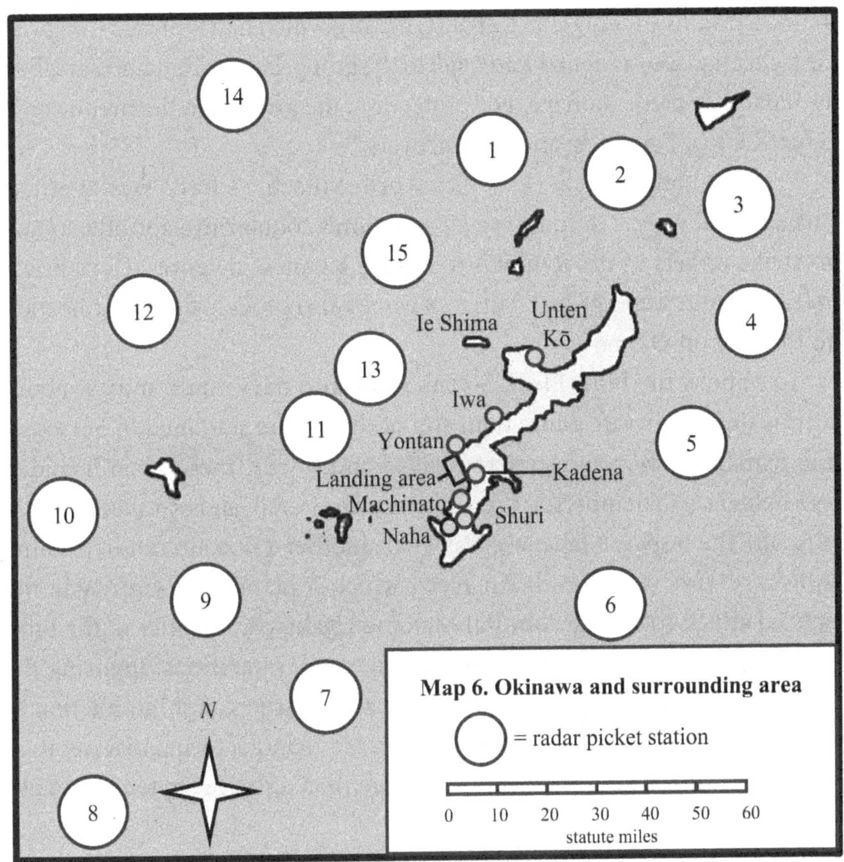

MAP 6. Okinawa and Surrounding Area

Force 51) included amphibious ships, naval gunfire support ships, a support force of 17 escort carriers, and a landing force. In addition to Task Force 58's 11 fleet carriers and 6 light carriers, Task Force 57 included 5 of the Royal Navy's smaller carriers. When the escort carriers are added, these 39 ships carried around 2,000 aircraft. Gen. Simon B. Buckner's Tenth Army, 188,000 strong, included 4 army and 2 marine divisions and was reinforced with its own air force. Once the Tenth Army was established ashore, Major General Mulcahy's Tactical Air Force Ryukyus would grow to nearly 800 aircraft.[2]

Mitscher departed Ulithi with 10 fleet carriers and 5 light carriers with more than 1,100 aircraft embarked.[3] Task Group 58.3 sailed with 3 carriers:

Bunker Hill, *Essex*, and USS *Cabot* (CVL 28), which had replaced *Cowpens*. Mitscher had also assigned *Randolph* to the group, but she remained in Ulithi to repair her battle damage. For protection, the group had the firepower of 2 battleships, 5 cruisers, and 17 destroyers.[4]

Prior to Landing day (L-day), 1 April, Mitscher's force was to attack airfields and vessels in southern Japan to limit counterinvasion attacks and to strike targets in the Ryukyus to reduce Japanese defenses. Until it was released from Iceberg, Task Force 58 would also provide fighter protection to the fleet off Okinawa.[5]

To oppose the Fifth Fleet, Japan's army and navy could muster about 2,300 combat aircraft. More than 500 of these were stationed in Formosa; the remainder were spread across Japan and Korea. These 2,300 included 950 fighters, 560 bombers, 155 reconnaissance aircraft, and 650 special attack aircraft. The Imperial Japanese Navy had another 2,000 aircraft in training and in reserve in its Tenth Air Fleet, which it planned to employ in the special attack role. Vice Admiral Matome Ugaki, commander of the Fifth Air Fleet, would direct both army and navy air operations opposing the invasion. American strategic bombing, carrier strikes, and interdiction of Japan's sea lanes had reduced Japanese aircraft manufacturing to fewer than 1,400 aircraft per month, down from more than 2,500 in September 1944.[6]

Kyushu and the Inland Sea, 18–19 March

"Today was one of those bad days for 221," Roberts wrote in his diary on 15 March. After the squadron had bungled a practice escort, 1st Lt. Robert J. Murray "wrinkled [bent] another fuselage making about 4 for him and Goeggel blew out both tires landing. Then in the afternoon Baldwin's flight had CAP and Baldwin wrinkled one. Quite a nice day's work!"[7]

Task Force 58's first operation after departing Ulithi was a series of strikes against airfields on southern Kyushu to destroy aircraft and aviation infrastructure that could contest the landing on Okinawa. Ugaki was aware that Mitscher's task force had sortied and anticipated the American strike on 18 March. On the night of 17–18 March, Japanese scouts located the American fleet, and Ugaki ordered counterstrikes against Task Force 58.[8]

VMF-221's day started early with reveille at 0340. At 0638, Commander Ottinger led the first strike of sixteen VMF-221 Corsairs, fourteen VB-84 dive-bombers, and thirteen VT-84 torpedo bombers against Miyazaki airfield. They encountered no fighters. Ottinger circled the airfield and struck from the northwest so that his force would be headed out to sea after their attack runs. The bombs and rockets damaged hangars and fuel tanks and destroyed or damaged at least six Bettys on the ground. Ottinger led his own division and Captain Delancey's on a second strafing attack to destroy more Bettys. During this run antiaircraft fire hit Lieutenant Glendinning's plane. He nursed his Corsair out to sea, survived ditching, and bobbed in an inflatable raft for six cold, wet hours before an OS2U from USS *New Jersey* (BB 62) retrieved him. Glendinning was returned to *Bunker Hill* that evening.[9]

Around the time Glendinning ditched, a single Judy attacked *Bunker Hill* from out of the sun. Antiaircraft guns from *Bunker Hill* and *Essex* did not hit the dive-bomber until after it released its bomb, which detonated off *Bunker Hill*'s starboard quarter, splashing seawater all the way up to the flight deck. The burning Judy crashed 1,500 yards off the port beam. Elsewhere in Task Force 58, bombs damaged the carriers *Enterprise* and USS *Intrepid* (CV 11).[10]

That afternoon, Captain Snider led a three-division sweep over southern Kyushu. One fighter suffered an oil leak and aborted along with its wingman, leaving Snider with ten Corsairs. After rocketing the Kumamoto Airframe Plant, Sider led his flight up to 13,000 feet. Near Tomitaka Airfield the marines encountered about twenty-five Zeros and Franks. Snider's flight attacked immediately. First Lt. Wesley S. Todd, one of the volunteer replacements from VMF-213, described the encounter:

> The closure rate was incredible as a Zero dived headlong toward me. I opened up with my guns and observed strikes on the now rolling Zero. As we passed, I still had full control of my airplane, but my foe did not. He cart-wheeled downward. Airplanes were everywhere, turning, rolling, and fighting one another.
>
> I had temporarily lost sight of my wingman [1st Lt. John McManus] and found him in trouble. His engine was cutting in and out, and he was

> going down. Frantically making throttle and mixture corrections, he got it going again, just as he found himself behind a fleeing Zero. Suddenly, my wingman's engine cut out again; his Corsair was like a rock, no forward speed, only downward!
>
> I dived from above, and my Corsair picked up speed as I shoved my throttle forward while the Zero pilot believed "all was well" now that his tail was clear. He never knew what hit him. The combination of .50-caliber incendiary, armor-piercing, and tracer rounds from my plane tore into the lightly armored Zero. Smoke turned into flame as the Zero disintegrated.
>
> A shower of oil and debris soon covered my windscreen and I skidded right to avoid the burning carnage. I was able to pull alongside the Zero and noted that the entire cockpit was engulfed in flames. No one could survive that.[11]

When Todd reviewed his gun camera's footage, he was surprised to see the pilot of the Zero "as if in no hurry at all, exiting his stricken mount and falling back to mother earth."[12] After debriefing the pilots and reviewing their footage, Roberts concluded his marines had destroyed eleven enemy fighters. Roberts awarded Todd credit for one Zero and gave Snider and 2nd Lt. Dean Caswell credit for three each. Only one VMF-221 fighter had suffered damage, returning with a single hole in its vertical stabilizer. During the debrief, the marines noted that the Japanese pilots did not exploit their superior maneuverability. "Their turns were wide and sloppy. Their speed and dives were inferior, and their only maneuver seemed to be the split-S."[13]

Throughout the night Japanese bombers searched for Task Group 58.3 as it steamed northeast. The bombers dropped flares frequently. Two of these floated down within ten thousand yards of the task group, but the ships escaped detection.[14]

At 0540, *Bunker Hill* launched eight VMF-221 Corsairs under Captain Snider for the group's combat air patrol. At 0825 the fighter direction officer vectored Snider's patrol to intercept several unidentified aircraft. Lieutenant Turner spotted a single Zero low over the water, heading toward the task force. He pushed his nose down and dove full throttle in pursuit. His faster Corsair closed from behind. Turner fired from eight hundred feet astern of the Zero, which exploded. The powerful blast knocked Turner's aircraft out of control, and he hit the waves, disappearing immediately. His body was not recovered.[15]

Turner's Zero was one of many special and bombing attacks against Task Force 58 that day. *Essex* narrowly evaded two aircraft shot down by antiaircraft fire. A fighter from another squadron shot down a Judy just short of *Bunker Hill*. Bombs struck USS *Wasp* (CV 7), USS *Yorktown* (CV 10), and USS *Franklin* (CV 13). Although she survived the attack, *Franklin* burned spectacularly. Her crew saved the ship, but she required major repairs, and 724 of her crew perished in the explosions and flames. Aboard *Bunker Hill*, Air Group 84 temporarily moved its pilots out of their vulnerable ready rooms, which were situated just beneath the flight deck, and into the wardroom below the hanger deck.[16]

Snider and his patrol had protected the task group while other squadrons made a fighter sweep over the naval base at Kure that encountered no enemy aircraft. A follow-up strike from *Bunker Hill* and *Essex* damaged the aircraft carrier *Katsuragi*, the light carriers *Ryujo* and *Kaiyō*, the battleships *Haruna* and *Yamato*, and a cruiser. The Japanese antiaircraft barrage downed five Helldivers and one Avenger.[17]

At 1015, Major Roberts led a second fighter sweep of fourteen VMF-221 F4Us over the airfields on Shokaku. They encountered no aircraft aloft but destroyed at least ten on the ground and damaged another forty in rocket and strafing attacks.[18] Task Force 58 then retired to the south on 20 March to lend its weight against the Japanese defenses on Okinawa.

Okinawa, 23–27 March

With *Enterprise*, *Franklin*, and *Wasp* out of action, Mitscher reorganized Task Force 58 into three task groups. USS *Hancock* (CV 19), USS *Bataan* (CVL 29), USS *Washington* (BB 56), and a cruiser joined Task Group 58.3 on 22 March, while the battleship *New Jersey* departed the task group. Though Mitscher still wielded a powerful air force, the 3 wounded carriers departed with more than 250 aircraft, leaving Task Force 58 with fewer than 900 planes.[19]

The task force refueled from oilers and replenished their ammunition from supply ships while steaming toward Okinawa that morning. This underway replenishment, one of the many innovative techniques developed during the war, enabled the Pacific Fleet to keep Task Force 58 at sea and in combat without returning to Ulithi.[20]

As Task Force 58 sailed toward Okinawa, Japanese scouts, bombers, and special attack planes shadowed and jabbed at Mitscher's ships. VMF-221 flew combat air patrols to protect the group. During the morning of 21 March, 2nd Lt. William L. Bailey and 1st Lt. Jarvis H. Carpenter each shot down interlopers. They reported that neither Japanese pilot maneuvered effectively.[21]

On the morning of 23 March, in *Bunker Hill*'s first strike against Okinawa, Commander Ottinger led fifteen VMF-221 Corsairs, nine Helldivers, and thirteen Avengers to hit a midget submarine base at Unten Kō on the Motobu Peninsula. Major Roberts destroyed one small submarine with rockets, but the damage inflicted by the remainder of the strike was inconsequential. Six aircraft carried rockets that failed to launch, and three napalm bombs failed to explode.[22]

The following morning Roberts led twenty-one Corsairs from his squadron on a fighter sweep to Yontan Airfield. Though they counted twenty-five aircraft parked around the field, the marines claimed only one definitely destroyed and eleven probably destroyed or damaged. Antiaircraft fire peppered the fighters as they bombed, strafed, and rocketed the airfield. Lieutenant Wasley's engine caught fire on the first pass. He bailed out a hundred feet over the water, too low for his parachute to open. Captain Delancey searched the waves where Wasley hit but could find no trace of him. The squadron had fewer problems with its ordnance on this strike but nonetheless could only guess at the damage it had inflicted on the airfield's defenses and infrastructure.[23]

In a subsequent strike, antiaircraft hits forced Ottinger to make a water landing. He escaped from the wreckage, but when a rescue seaplane arrived, the aircrew discovered only his floating corpse. Returning from the same strike, Maj. Emerson H. Dedrick of VMF-451 made a water landing within the task force. Dedrick's Corsair broke apart on impact, and he too perished. Lt. Cdr. Roger R. Hedrick, the commander of VF-84, took command of the air group. Hedrick had shot down nine aircraft in the Solomons as the executive officer of VF-17, the legendary "Jolly Rogers" Corsair squadron.[24]

That afternoon, two divisions from VMF-221 under Captain Balch provided fighter cover for twelve dive-bombers and thirteen torpedo bombers headed back to Yontan Airfield. After the bombers struck the airfield, Balch's fighters strafed defensive positions and minor craft along the coast. First Lt. John E. Jorgensen's aircraft caught fire after the second strafing run, and he ditched fifteen miles offshore. Despite the heavy seas, an OS2U rescued Jorgensen a brief time later.[25]

VMF-221 did not fly on 25 March while *Bunker Hill* replenished ammunition and refueled. For the last six days of March, VMF-221 flew combat air patrols and escorted strikes and photoreconnaissance missions. Task Group 58.3 directed most of Air Group 84's strikes against airfields, small vessels, and infrastructure on Okinawa and Minamidaitōjima. VMF-221 encountered no enemy aircraft on any of these strikes, so the fighters rocketed, strafed, and bombed antiaircraft positions at will. *Bunker Hill* lost only two aircraft to enemy fire with no loss of aircrew, but there is little evidence that Air Group 84 accomplished much to pave the way for the coming amphibious assault. Except for active antiaircraft positions, the defenders were largely invisible to aircraft overhead. In its action reports for the ten missions to Okinawa and Minamidaitōjima, VMF-221's pilots could not attest to destroying much aside from structures and small boats of questionable importance.[26]

Task Group 58.3 and Task Group 58.4 struck Kyushu on 29 March, hoping to find Japanese naval vessels. When they found no warships, they struck airfields and small coastal vessels. A combat air patrol led by Captain Balch intercepted a special attack plane off Kyushu, which 1st Lt. Earl W. Langston shot down without difficulty.[27]

The Japanese failed to damage any of Task Group 58.3's ships during the last week of March, and Japanese antiaircraft fire shot down only two of the group's aircraft, whose aircrew survived. Nonetheless, Air Group 84 and VMF-221 suffered several fatal mishaps. During the 29 March strike against Kyushu, Air Group 84's torpedo and dive-bomber squadrons entered thick clouds. Three Avengers and two Helldivers collided and were lost, along with five of the thirteen aircrew.[28]

The next day, 1st Lt. Gerald D. Scott of VMF-221 returned early from a combat air patrol over Okinawa in a damaged plane. In Roberts' account,

"Scotty was rapidly losing oil pressure. He dived out of formation and came down from 20,000 feet, like a shot to try to get aboard before his engine quit. He didn't make it though as his prop froze." Scott ditched violently, breaking off one of the Corsair's wings. Three squadronmates circled, watching the plane's tail section float for a full minute, but Scott did not emerge. Glendinning suspected the canopy had snapped shut and Scott was unable to open it before the heavy Corsair sank. Roberts presumed the same, or that Scott was knocked unconscious when his aircraft struck the water.[29]

The following day, two hours into a combat air patrol, divisions led by Roberts and Capt. Mitchell L. Parks, a replacement from VMF-213, began practicing aerial combat maneuvers. As Roberts executed a mock gunnery pass, Parks responded too abruptly. The maneuver sent his fighter into a flat spin at ten thousand feet. He did not recover or bail out and was lost.[30]

To keep *Bunker Hill*'s air group at maximum strength, the Pacific Fleet dispatched replacement aircraft and pilots, ferrying them there aboard escort carriers from advance bases such as Guam. Once Iwo Jima was secured, Corsairs would fly there from the Marianas and then on to Task Force 58 and Okinawa. *Bunker Hill* received replacement aircraft on 16, 22, 25, and 28 March. VMF-221 received seven replacement aircraft for the seven it had lost during March. Though none of the replacement aviators joined VMF-221, presumably because they were navy pilots, the squadron had 31 pilots and 17 fighters on 31 March, or 1.8 aviators per aircraft.[31]

Protecting the Fleet and Supporting the Landing Force, 1–5 April

L-day on Okinawa was 1 April 1945. *Bunker Hill* and her air group provided close air support to the troops ashore and protected the ships of the amphibious force from Japanese aircraft and warships. Task Force 51, the amphibious force commanded by Vice Admiral Turner, controlled all aircraft over and around Okinawa. When bombing the island or protecting the landing ships, Task Force 58's aircraft reported to Commander, Air Support Control Unit aboard Turner's flagship, the amphibious force command ship USS *Eldorado* (AGC 11).[32]

Mitscher's Big Blue Blanket relied on radar picket vessels to provide early warning and direct fighters to intercept incoming aircraft. The pickets consisted of a destroyer or two and at least one smaller Landing Craft Support (Large) vessel, or LCS(L), posted as far as seventy-five miles from Okinawa. Commander, Air Support Control Unit farmed out at least a division of fighters to each picket.[33]

VMF-221's first mission on L-day was to napalm the beaches forty-five minutes ahead of the assault waves of the 1st and 6th Marine Divisions. Major Roberts led twelve Corsairs from VMF-451 and sixteen from his own squadron. To improve bombing accuracy, the ordnance officer had affixed fins to the troublesome napalm bombs.[34]

It was still dark as Lieutenant Johns and Lieutenant Imel warmed up their engines. They watched the first few aircraft catapult off and the plane captains position a Corsair piloted by 1st Lt. Roger F. Marble from VMF-451 abreast of the island. Marble's heavily laden fighter cleared the bow, stalled—and plunged into the sea. "Yellow flames erupted at the bow of the flight deck and exploded into the sky," Imel later wrote. "The carrier rolled to starboard; and in seconds we were passing the flames on the port side of the ship. It was obvious the first aircraft didn't make it. Even though I was 100 feet above the water line, the flames and heat made me turn my face."[35]

Despite the tragic beginning, *Bunker Hill* had a strike to launch. The flight deck crew rolled 2nd Lt. John E. Mercer's VMF-451 Corsair into position. Mercer's F4U accelerated down the flight deck, stalled, plummeted into the sea, and burst into flames, this time on the starboard side of the ship.[36]

Johns, next in line, frantically waved for the deck crew to check under his plane for a problem, thinking, "It was unlikely I could make a successful take-off with the same napalm and bomb load." *Bunker Hill* paused the launch while the plane captains investigated. They quickly determined that the new fins on the napalm canisters were obstructing the flaps, preventing them from extending to 40 degrees and locking. As the Corsairs had accelerated, the airflow under the wings had pushed the unlocked flaps level, reducing lift and causing the heavy fighters to stall. The deck crew hastily remedied the problem. Some plane captains bent the new fins out of the way. Others directed pilots to take off with just 20 degrees of flaps. Johns and Imel took off without difficulty, though Imel "was praying mightily as I was pushing the throttle forward."[37]

No more Corsairs crashed, but four of VMF-221's fighters aborted before launching. A fifth returned to *Bunker Hill* with engine trouble, leaving Roberts with twenty-one aircraft instead of twenty-eight. Once over the beach, his Corsairs dropped their napalm canisters in a good pattern. Most exploded. The fighters then commenced a series of strafing runs, beginning at the water's edge. As the landing craft neared the beach, the Corsairs strafed slightly farther inland with each pass. The assault troops landed against light opposition at 0830, and the fighters returned to *Bunker Hill* fifteen minutes later.[38]

Roberts and his marines did not support troops ashore again for the next eighteen days. During the first five days of April, VMF-221 flew combat air patrols but encountered no enemy aircraft. The squadron also flew target combat air patrols, so named because they were flown over a target such as Okinawa, a radar picket, or an enemy airfield. Target combat air patrols typically consisted of eight fighters. They had an additional mission of attacking targets of opportunity.[39]

VMF-221's patrols encountered no air opposition on 1 and 2 April. One patrol attacked some 30-foot boats on the northwest coast of the island. The squadron also provided escorts to two Air Group 84 strikes, which destroyed some coastal vessels, a few buildings, and some antiaircraft positions. During recovery on 2 April, Lieutenant Murray crash-landed but walked away uninjured.[40]

In a more significant action, on 4 April, Major Roberts led eight Corsairs on a predawn fighter sweep of a group of islands halfway between Okinawa and Kyushu. Intelligence officers estimated that seventy-five enemy aircraft had been flown down to an airfield on Tokuno Shima. From Tokuno Shima, aircraft could strike the American warships off Okinawa. The intelligence officers appear to have overestimated the number of aircraft there. The marines found and destroyed just four parked aircraft and damaged several others.[41]

The fighter sweep to Tokuno Shima was exceptional in that the marines found targets. The battle for Okinawa was underway, but the Japanese army and navy seemed curiously absent. Japan still had more than four thousand aircraft that could strike against the Fifth Fleet off Okinawa, but very few of them appeared. VMF-221 had not been directed to strike significant targets on Okinawa because the marines and soldiers of the Tenth Army had not yet encountered serious opposition. The marines of VMF-221, growing exhausted after three weeks of combat, began to speculate that *Bunker Hill* might retire to Ulithi soon for a much-needed rest and refit.[42]

"A Very Exciting and Interesting Day": Operation Ten, 6–7 April

Task Force 58's strikes against Kyushu and airfields throughout the Ryukyus had forced the Japanese to keep the bulk of their aircraft farther north, beyond the reach of the American carrier planes but also too distant to strike the American fleet off Okinawa. Vice Admiral Ugaki began staging aircraft to take advantage of clear weather forecast for 6 April. He succeeded in assembling more than seven hundred aircraft for the strike, dubbed Operation Ten, including more than three hundred special attack planes.[43]

Ugaki did not catch Spruance by surprise. Codebreakers at Nimitz's Joint Intelligence Center and in Washington had decrypted diplomatic and naval traffic that revealed Ugaki's intentions. In addition to the heads-up about the air strikes, Spruance received warning that the Japanese Combined Fleet would sortie a task force built around the battleship *Yamato*.[44]

On the evening of 5 April, Roberts wrote in his diary, "We got word tonight that the Japs are going to make the all-out effort to get the fleet tomorrow. They are supposed to be mustering every pilot and every plane in the homeland to send down here tomorrow. Should be a very exciting and interesting day if this is true."[45]

Spruance canceled all air support missions for the Tenth Army. A few strikes would hit airfields to disrupt aircraft concentrations. Carriers would stow the remaining torpedo and dive-bombers below on their hangar decks, keeping flight decks free to cycle fighters.[46]

One of the squadron's master technical sergeants had begun standing next to the launch officer during takeoffs. He would listen to the revolutions increase and give the pilot a thumb up or down based on how the engine sounded to him. On this morning's launch, just as Lieutenant Glendinning hurtled toward the bow, he was horrified to see the thumb flip from up to down. Seconds later, Glendinning heard his engine sputter. He retracted his wheels and avoided ditching, then climbed to eight thousand feet. The engine continued running rough. Swett, Glendinning's division leader, advised him to abort. Glendinning obtained permission to drop his bombs and fire his rockets. After doing so, he asked permission to land. "Negative," replied *Bunker Hill*. "Land in the water. We expect an enemy attack."[47]

Glendinning picked out a destroyer and began his water landing preparations. He pulled the canopy safety pins and then the emergency jettison handles. Instead of flying off into space, the canopy jumped its track and refused to budge. Terrified that he might be trapped in a sinking Corsair, Glendinning decided to bail out. He undid his restraints, stood on his seat, and attempted to shoulder his canopy off. It wouldn't move.[48]

Glendinning radioed *Bunker Hill*, "Ahhh—I can't get my hatch open." He had dropped to 1,500 feet by now, and the engine was coughing and belching black smoke. Glendinning looked down at the flight deck and was relieved to see crewmen respotting aircraft and the carrier turning into the wind. With only seconds until his engine seized, he began his approach, even though the landing signal officer (LSO) was running down the flight deck waving him off. Glendinning ignored the LSO and caught the second wire. He sat numbly in his cockpit while sailors doused the smoking engine with fire extinguishers and a plane handler cut open the cockpit with wire cutters.[49]

Glendinning later asked the plane handler why the canopy would not release. "That wire to the canopy kept breaking," the handler explained, "so I replaced it with some heavy cable." Glendinning was sickened to realize that Scott may have been trapped in his cockpit by the same error. Glendinning notified 1st Lt. Norman D. Smith, the squadron engineering officer, who found several other Corsairs with cable installed in the same "fix."[50]

Roberts led two divisions of Corsairs on a combat air patrol. At 1030 the fighter director aboard *Cabot* vectored the marines west of the task group, where they intercepted a Dinah twin-engine reconnaissance plane. After ten minutes of hide-and-seek among the clouds, 2nd Lt. Eugene D. Cameron spotted the Dinah diving away. "I was successful at getting a tail-on approach at full speed, water injection and all," reported Cameron. He set the Dinah on fire at seven thousand feet, and it floated lazily into the sea.[51]

At 1135 the fighter director vectored Roberts' two divisions fifty miles north of the task group. They intercepted two Zeros at 18,000 feet and another nine or ten at 20,000 feet. Roberts ordered Lieutenant Murray to attack the lower pair with his division while he attacked the larger flight with his own division. Murray's division chased down the two lower fighters and shot them down. The leader of the higher Japanese flight turned abruptly toward Roberts. The two groups missed each other in the head-on pass, then engaged in a general melee. Roberts pursued one Zero in a series of split-S turns but lost it in the clouds. He was particularly impressed with his antigravity suit, as he pulled eight Gs in this action and suffered no ill effects. Cameron shot down a Zero on the tail of Roberts' wingman, 1st Lt. Charles B. Quick Jr. But afterward Cameron could not find his own wingman, Lieutenant Carpenter. No one saw Carpenter go down, but he failed to return. His loss hit Roberts hard. "I don't know what to tell his wife," Roberts penned in his diary. "They were really in love."[52]

When Roberts returned to the task group after noon, the ships were under attack. Roberts received the command "Salvo," warning him to stand clear. The fighters circled, burning their fuel reserve. Antiaircraft gunners shot down three attackers, including two Judys whose bombs narrowly missed *Cabot*. All seven Corsairs then recovered. Cameron's fuel was so low he ignored a wave-off. As he began to taxi free of the arresting cables, his engine sputtered and died.[53]

That afternoon the task group sent eighteen fighters from VMF-221 three hundred miles north to search for *Yamato* and the other surface ships that had sortied from Kyushu. The distance was so great that two divisions under Captain Bailey and Captain Snider orbited at the halfway point to relay communications from the other three divisions. While there, Snider spotted eight enemy aircraft. Snider led his division in a single gunnery pass, claiming one Tony.[54]

Later in the flight, Lieutenant Johns heard the controller recall Captain Baldwin's division from the search and provide them targets to intercept. When Baldwin did not respond, Johns realized Baldwin's radio was out. He came alongside Baldwin, pointed toward his earphone, and then signaled he would lead. As Johns eased ahead and started to turn, he spotted a dozen enemy aircraft in a large vee to his left and slightly below them. Johns began a gunnery run from above and behind the formation, assuming the other three knew what was happening and were right behind him.[55]

Unaware of Johns' intentions, Imel had spotted two Zeros of his own. Imel had yet to shoot down a plane and was eager. He charged and test-fired his guns, then scanned for his targets. He spotted one a thousand feet below and off his port wing making a gentle turn. "I slowed the Corsair down a bit and lined up from a ninety-degree deflection shot just like we did on those tow sleeves in training and pulled the trigger." Imel had his first "meatball."[56]

As Imel and his wingman sped to catch up to Johns, Imel found himself behind and two hundred feet below a Jill. "I doubted if the pilot saw me, but his rear gunner soon did." Imel attacked from below, so the Jill's tail masked the rear gun, and sent the dive-bomber down in flames.[57]

Johns had started his run before he realized he was alone but continued anyway. He shot down two Jills and a Zero before the defenders began to turn the tables. The rest of the division finally showed up, shooting down five and scaring away the rest. "I think I got out of this by the skin of my teeth," Johns admitted.[58]

All eighteen Corsairs from the search mission recovered aboard *Bunker Hill* by 1804. The squadron claimed twelve victories for the day.[59]

The Japanese lost about three hundred aircraft on 6 April, though admittedly many were special attack planes not expected to return. Mitscher's Big Blue Blanket was covering the fleet, but its protection was not absolute. Operation Ten's attackers sank three of Task Force 51's picket destroyers, two ammunition ships, and an LST (Landing Ship, Tank); and severely damaged another eight destroyers, a destroyer escort, and a minelayer.[60]

Task Group 58.3 launched searches at dawn on 7 April to find *Yamato* and her task force. Roberts led a search with twenty-three F4U-1Ds from VMF-221. He and his divisions separated, some searching the southern tip of Kyushu and others flying farther south relaying communications. The ceiling was a low two thousand feet, forcing the marines to fly under it. Roberts found no ships offshore and thought the elusive warships could be hiding somewhere in Kagoshima Bay, a twenty-mile-wide inlet surrounded by enemy gun emplacements and airfields. After weighing the considerable risks against the imperative of finding the Japanese task force—"I had to do a lot of arguing with myself"—Roberts led his division up Kagoshima Bay. The marines spotted hundreds of small coastal vessels and a seaplane base, but no warships. On his return flight, having encountered no fighters, Roberts exploited the chance to attack the seaplane base. After strafing the hangers, he spotted several Kawanishi N1K "Rex" floatplanes "screaming across the bay at about 10 feet." In quick succession Cameron shot one down, 1st Lt. Clay D. Haggard Jr. shot two down, and Roberts downed two—his first aerial victories. Out over the South China Sea, Captain Delancey shot down a Jill dive-bomber.[61]

As he exited Kagoshima Bay, Roberts heard that *Essex*'s air group had located *Yamato* at 0815. Mitscher launched a 280-plane strike at 1000; *Bunker Hill* contributed 15 fighters, 13 torpedo-bombers, and 10 dive-bombers. VT-84's Avengers scored at least two torpedo hits and possibly as many as nine, losing one bomber to antiaircraft fire. A fighter from VF-84 was also lost. *Yamato* exploded spectacularly at 1442. A light cruiser and four of her eight destroyer escorts also sank.[62]

Roberts' flight recovered shortly after *Bunker Hill* had launched her strike. For the remainder of the day, *Bunker Hill* cycled marine fighters from VMF-221 and VMF-451 aloft to protect the task group. Though the marines intercepted no aircraft, other fighters shot down two Frances bombers, and antiaircraft gunners shot down two Jills. The second Jill released its bomb just before crashing into the flight deck of *Hancock*, 2,700 yards astern of *Bunker Hill*. Both the bomb and the aircraft set off ferocious fires that killed forty-three of *Hancock*'s crew, wounded more than fifty, and took the carrier and her air group out of the fight for three months.[63]

With the day's action over, Task Force 58 recovered its strike and patrol aircraft and sailed south, back to Okinawa.

Protecting the Fleet, 8–18 April

From 8 to 10 April VMF-221 flew combat air patrols while also keeping an eye out for enemy vessels and downed aviators. Roberts pulled his enlisted marines up to the ready room on 9 April "to hear bitches and inform them of our progress to date. They are just like kids when it comes to wanting to hear about your experiences," Roberts wrote. "You can see they take a lot of pride in the pilots of their squadron outdoing the other pilots." On the evening of 10 April, *Enterprise* rejoined Task Group 58.3, replacing *Hancock* and bringing the group's strength to four carriers: *Bunker Hill, Enterprise, Essex*, and the light carrier *Bataan*, which had replaced *Cabot*.[64]

Over the next six days the task group fended off attacks and struck enemy airfields to limit their use. On 11 April Captain Snider escorted another Air Group 84 morning strike to Tokuno Shima. The group's bombs cratered the runways once more and the Corsairs shot some more rounds through the sixty or so hulks.[65]

From 1352 on, Task Group 58.3 was under continuous attack by special attack planes, which used the scattered cumulus clouds to conceal their approach. Fortunately for the antiaircraft gunners, the attackers dove at the ships one at a time, enabling the gunners to destroy ten aircraft one after another. One Zero hit *Enterprise*, hurting her badly enough that she departed three days later for Ulithi. *Essex* and several destroyers also suffered damage. During the action an eight-plane combat air patrol led by Captain Swett intercepted a Jill making a torpedo attack against a picket destroyer. Between the damage inflicted by Captain Baldwin's division and the destroyer's antiaircraft fire, the bomber's torpedo missed, and the Jill crashed in flames. Swett's division later helped three F6F's knock down a Judy skimming the surface.[66]

Task Force 58 was forewarned that 12 April would bring heavy strikes. Ugaki had postponed his second major attack while he waited for skies to clear. Japan's army and navy amassed 478 aircraft for the operation, including 185 in the special attack role. VMF-221 would mount three missions: an early-morning combat air patrol above the task force led by Captain Swett, an escort mission for a photoreconnaissance flight over Tokuno Shima, and a twelve-plane combat air patrol over Okinawa led by Roberts. Roberts looked forward to another big action, reasoning that the sooner the Japanese ran out of aircraft, the sooner the fleet could sail unchallenged around Japan's home islands and invade them.[67]

Swett's patrol was uneventful. After the F6F-Ps photographed Tokuno Shima, Delancey led his division forty miles northeast to Kikai Shima where Hellcats from USS *Bennington* (CV 20) were engaged. Delancey destroyed a Zero at one thousand feet with a 20-degree deflection shot. First Lt. Joseph Brocia Jr. shot a Zero down from astern. Lieutenant McManus pursued a

Frank over Kikai Shima, ignoring antiaircraft fire that drove off some *Bennington* fighters, and fired several long bursts to bring it down.[68]

Lieutenant Caswell recalled this action clearly decades later.

> The twisting, turning and high-G pullouts were thrilling and scary as we chased our opponents at low altitude. I finally used my head and pulled in behind a Zero and was able to get a good lead on his tight turn. All six .50-caliber machine guns were working and blowing bits and pieces off the Zero. His canopy came back and he attempted to bail out. He did not succeed.
>
> One of the awful sights of combat now took place. I am now 50 feet behind him, seeing his ill-fated attempt when he sagged into his cockpit, minus his head. A sight I have never forgotten as his plane exploded into many fragments, which I flew through.[69]

Roberts checked in with a fighter director aboard one of the picket destroyers, who assigned each of Roberts' three divisions a position to orbit. A destroyer vectored Captain Baldwin's division to intercept a section of three Vals attacking one of the pickets. Jorgensen, Imel, and Baldwin each shot down one of the slow dive-bombers. Baldwin's Val released its bomb first but missed.[70]

Captain Balch's division was ordered to protect USS *Purdy* (DD 734). *Purdy*'s gunners had shot down four Vals, but a fifth crashed close alongside her. The Val's bomb had ricocheted off the water and exploded inside the destroyer. *Purdy* ordered Balch to "keep the Japs away as we cannot fire." Nettles hung on Balch's wing as Balch pursued a dive-bomber and then downed a Zero. Abruptly, Nettles "found a Zero almost colliding with me and it scared the devil out of me. I got him in my sights, pulled the trigger on my six .50 cal. Guns, and hit him in the cockpit and wing roots. The Jap fighter went into a dive with many pieces flying off the aircraft and dove straight into the water. It looked like he was trying to hit one of the destroyers as he went in. The geyser of water, where it hit, washed over the destroyer deck. It was one heck of a fight."[71] *Purdy* survived the attack, though she lost thirteen sailors and had to withdraw.[72]

Purdy had been at the epicenter of the day's action at Radar Picket Number 1, due north of Okinawa. Ugaki had adjusted his tactics and was targeting the vulnerable pickets instead of the carriers and landing ships. By the end of the day, Ugaki's aircraft had sunk one destroyer and one support vessel while hitting another three destroyers and four support vessels.[73]

To limit the enemy's ability to stage attacks from Tokunoshima, Roberts and Snider led target combat air patrols there on 13 April. They found no aircraft aloft, but strafed and rocketed the airfield, destroying what appeared to be three single-engine aircraft. Captain Swett led eight Corsairs in an uneventful combat air patrol.[74]

The following day, Task Group 58.3 refueled and took on ammunition two hundred miles southeast of Okinawa, well outside the range of enemy aircraft. VMF-221 gained four replacement pilots, all marines, the first since the four veterans had joined from VMF-213 in early March. Three veterans joined from marine fighting squadrons aboard *Essex* and *Wasp*. Roberts was dismayed to see the fourth replacement: an unsteady pilot he had sent away at Ulithi. Roberts did not relent. That lieutenant did not fly with VMF-221 and was sent back to California.[75]

On 15 April, VMF-221 reinforced ten VF-84 Corsairs with two divisions under Captain Baldwin and Captain Delancey to sweep Kanoya East Airfield on Kyushu. Lieutenant Brocia's engine froze up just after takeoff, but he ditched safely and was rescued by a destroyer. The fighters dropped 500-pound bombs over the target and rocketed and machine-gunned several aircraft but could not set them afire. The marines suspected the Japanese had defueled them to prevent their destruction.[76]

VMF-221's sweep helped spoil a third large Japanese strike that Ugaki had originally planned for that morning. Poor weather delayed Ugaki's attack until the afternoon, and VMF-221's raid disrupted his ability to pull together an afternoon attack. At dawn on 16 April, with more favorable weather, Ugaki launched eight bombers to strike the U.S. airfields on Okinawa and sent fifty-eight Zeros to engage the American fighters covering the fleet. Forty-five dive-bombers, sixty-five army fighters and special attack aircraft, and a dozen twin-engine Frances bombers followed. Six of the Frances bombers carried a Kugisho MXY7 Ohka 11 "Baka Bomb," a manned special attack rocket. The plane had to drop the Baka Bomb within about twenty miles of its target because its rocket would only burn for ten seconds, but it could reach 615 mph and carried a 2,646-pound warhead.[77]

VMF-221 flew three missions this day. At 0938, *Bunker Hill* scrambled two divisions led by Major Roberts and two from VMF-451. Neither made contact with enemy aircraft. A second combat air patrol of two divisions under Swett and Snider took off at noon. The flight orbited at 15,000 feet 30 miles north of Task Group 58.3. Snider's division spotted three Tojos 5,000 feet below them headed toward the task group. Snider attacked from the eight o'clock position. The Tojos split up. Snider caught the leader in a climb and fired a very short burst into the cowling from three hundred yards. The Tojo exploded. The squadron action report stated, "The pilot bailed out, but was hit by stray bullets and killed."[78]

Bailey caught a second Tojo in a diving turn to starboard. Bailey's first burst hit the wing roots from three hundred yards. His second burst from one hundred yards set the Tojo on fire. The plane exploded, and the pilot was hurled free of the wreckage. The pilot deployed his parachute and "was observed floating down for a time, then seen to leap from his harness at 6000 [feet] and plunge seaward."[79]

Murray's Tojo dove for sea level, but Murray steadily closed the distance. At 3,000 feet he scored hits with a 10-degree deflection shot from 250 yards astern, then missed from 1,000 feet and closed to 75 yards at sea level. His final, long burst knocked large pieces off the Tojo. Some of the debris punctured Murray's wing. The third Tojo crashed without exploding.[80]

The flight returned to the task group on schedule at 1530, only to find the ships under attack. As they waited out the action, Snider spotted a Zero on the surface headed away from the task group. Snider pursued until the Zero filled his gun ring and then pulled the trigger. Nothing happened. He had forgotten to turn on his gun switches. Snider flipped them on and made a second run. Again, nothing happened. Snider had failed to charge his guns. Embarrassed, he methodically cocked his six charging handles, reengaged, and shot the Zero down on his third pass.[81]

In the squadron's third mission, divisions led by Delancey and Glendinning along with a third from VMF-451 orbited Amami Ōshima. Glendinning narrowly averted disaster when he mistook a B-24 for a Betty. The marines turned away, but the B-24's turret gunner fired a few long-range bursts in their direction for emphasis. Before returning to *Bunker Hill*, the marines strafed a naval installation on Amami Ōshima.[82]

Task Group 58.3 escaped damage, but elsewhere in the task force, a special attack plane connected with *Intrepid*'s flight deck. Her crew extinguished the fire, and the ship resumed flight operations three hours later. The pickets took another beating, with one destroyer sunk and six warships damaged. The crew of the destroyer USS *Laffey* (DD 724) shot down eight attackers and kept her afloat despite suffering hits by six special attack planes and four bombs. In addition to the aircraft shot down by the fleet's gunners, aviators claimed 192 aerial victories.[83]

After this violent eleven-day stretch, VMF-221 encountered no enemy aircraft for the following eleven days. During replenishment on 18 April, *Bunker Hill* took on eleven new F4U-1Cs armed with 20-mm cannons instead of machine guns.[84] As Ugaki husbanded his dwindling air fleet, Task Force 58 used the respite to turn its combat power back against Okinawa.

Strikes and Supporting the Landing Force, 19–27 April

From 19 to 27 April, VMF-221 flew nine combat air patrols of four to eight fighters over Task Force 58 and another five target combat air patrols over Okinawa. The marines strafed targets of opportunity in a couple of the patrols but could not attest to inflicting much damage. On 19 and 20 April, VMF-221 escorted Air Group 84 strikes against Okinawa. The fighters strafed the towns of Iwa and Naha, where they destroyed some buildings and docks but otherwise observed no results. On 21 April, VMF-221 sent three two-division target combat air patrols over Kikai airfield that set eight parked aircraft on fire.[85]

As the fighting ashore intensified, VMF-221 began to support troops directly more often. The U.S. Army's XXIV Corps had hit stiff opposition in its drive south. The Japanese 32nd Army had fortified the rugged hills on the southern third of Okinawa with tunnels and caves. After a week of vicious fighting, American soldiers had forced the Japanese to withdraw from their first defensive line on the night of 23–24 April. But these defenders now occupied a second line of prepared fortifications running the width of the narrow island.[86]

Air support to the Tenth Army ashore had matured since L-day. The Tactical Air Force, which included MAG-31 and MAG-33, operated from Kadena and Yontan. The marine LFASCU, co-located with the Tenth Army command post, coordinated requests from the divisions for air support missions. As on Iwo Jima, air liaison parties attached to frontline units directed aircraft when they reported overhead. Air coordinators aloft also directed attacks.[87]

However, pre-mission coordination between the landing force and Task Force 58 still challenged carrier squadrons and limited their effectiveness in the ground support role. Air groups usually received air support requests late at night for the next day. This limited the time planners had to analyze targets and design missions. Support requests specified the time to show, the number and type of aircraft needed, and the type of ordnance desired, but they seldom identified targets. Reports of friendly troop locations were often a week out of date. Once a flight checked in with a controller, the aircraft often loitered while controllers on the ground and aloft figured out which targets to assign to them.[88]

On 25 April, Air Group 84 began close air support missions. Captain Swett's division accompanied twelve Helldivers and eleven Avengers on a morning mission. Each Corsair took off with a full load of machine-gun ammunition, eight rockets, and a 500-pound bomb. A controller directed Swett's division to attack caves and defensive emplacements east of Shuri in the zone of the U.S. Army's 96th Infantry Division. With a heavy cloud layer at 3,500 feet, Swett opted for a glide-bombing attack. After the bombs and rockets hit home, the Corsairs returned to strafe defenders fleeing their positions.[89]

Major Roberts led his division on a nearly identical mission the following morning, but instead of rockets and a 500-pound bomb, each Corsair carried a 1,000-pound bomb. Roberts' flight struck caves, pillboxes, and trenches on the north slope of Conical Hill, slightly southeast of the positions attacked the day before. The weather was "stinking," according to Roberts, with the cloud layer at just 1,200 feet. To hit his target, Roberts led his division in a level bombing run directly over the target. The marines flew so low that the concussions of their bombs rattled the F4Us. "I thought my plane was falling apart the way it lurched and jumped around," Roberts wrote in his diary. "So I guess we were close enough to kill any Japs in the area." Roberts worried he had overshot his target, but the controller on the ground reported good effects.[90]

During replenishment on 27 April, Roberts opened a letter from MAG-42 at El Centro and discovered that the squadron's entire allocation of enlisted promotions had gone to the marines he had left with the rear echelon. Roberts fumed, "The way it stands now the boys are being penalized for their combat duty while the home front boys grab the promotions, and it's damned unfair." Roberts resolved to appeal.

Ugaki's Fourth Attack, 28 April

Air Group 84 resumed its support missions the next day. Captain Snider's division, armed with rockets and 500-pound bombs, joined eight Avengers and eight Helldivers in support of the 96th Division. The cloud cover was light, and the marines' bombs and rockets plastered artillery emplacements and caves east of Shuri.[91]

As these close support missions were underway, Ugaki attempted his fourth large attack. B-29 Superfortress bombers in the Marianas had severely damaged airfields on Kyushu and Shokaku on 26 and 27 April. As a result, the Japanese were forced to retain more fighters for home island defense, curtailing the size of Ugaki's next attack. On 28 April he could muster just 165 aircraft—only 59 of them special attack planes—to strike the radar pickets.[92]

At 1430 Major Roberts took sixteen Corsairs over Radar Picket Number 2. Captain Delancey had to abort, leaving Lieutenant Brocia leading Delancey's division. Roberts took his division and Swett's sixty miles northwest of Okinawa, where VF-84 had recently shot down eighteen enemy planes. Balch and Brocia orbited with their divisions over the picket about twenty miles southeast of Roberts, west of the island of Izenajima.[93]

Shortly after the aircraft arrived, the fighter director calmly informed Balch and Brocia, "Many bogeys, north, thirty miles out and high." Balch and Brocia climbed to intercept the formation. Lieutenant McManus, who had straggled during the climb due to a blower issue, dove after a Zero and shot it down, then rejoined Lieutenant Caswell at ten thousand feet. In his postwar account, Caswell described the encounter:

> Those big Corsair propellers bit hard as we changed to "high boost," all 2,000 horsepower with water injection doing the job for the engines. As we reached 20,000 feet, visibility was rotten with a bad high-level haze delaying our sighting of the Jap fighters until they were right on us.
>
> I was frantic to see that I was in a head-on collision with a "Tony" fighter, coming straight at me and filling my sights. As I am firing all six fifty-caliber machine guns at my head-on attacker, McManus is yelling over the radio, "Break right there is a Zero on your tail." By now the Tony is filling my sights, I'm squeezing the trigger to death, there are tracers flying by both sides of my Corsair coming from front and rear and I clearly wished my whole body could be small, small, small. In far less time than it takes to tell it, the Tony exploded in front of me. I'm flying through pieces and parts and McManus is yelling, "I got the Zero on your tail."
>
> There seemed to be a hundred fighters in the sky wheeling, climbing, and diving in a frantic effort to latch on to three Corsairs.[94]

McManus and Caswell began weaving. Caswell remembered, "I am feeling so scared that I could throw up and have already wet my pants thoroughly."[95] Despite the odds, McManus and Caswell each shot two down in the swirling battle. Brocia chased one Zero from 25,000 feet down to 3,000 feet before destroying it.[96]

In Balch's division, Lieutenant Langston found himself alone with three Zeros. He managed to shoot down two of them. The third Zero disabled Langston's Corsair in a pass from below, and he bailed out at ten thousand feet. The Japanese pilot machine-gunned Langston three times as he floated down but did not hit him. An LCS pulled Langston from his raft ninety minutes later. During the next strike an attacker crashed close alongside the LCS. Debris hurtled around Langston, and the splashes soaked the dry clothes the crew had loaned him.[97]

Balch and his wingman, Bailey, each shot down two fighters. Bailey downed his second by unintentionally colliding with it after his guns jammed. Bailey recovered from his spin, but his adversary could not. The seven marines claimed fourteen Zeros and lost just Langston's Corsair.[98]

Now low on fuel, the marines departed. Shortly afterward a flight of eight to ten Vals attacked Picket Number 2. The picket had no fighter protection, but the antiaircraft gunners aboard the destroyers USS *Daly* (DD 519) and USS *Twiggs* (DD 591) knocked special attack planes down one after another. Near misses inflicted only minor damage.[99]

More Strikes and Support to the Landing Force, 29 April–10 May

On 29 and 30 April, VMF-221 provided a division each day to Air Group 84 support missions to Okinawa. The *Bunker Hill* pilots dropped their ordnance in front of the 27th and 96th Infantry Divisions' troops assaulting the Japanese second line of defense east of Naha. The supported unit on 29 April reported Captain Baldwin's division delivered "the best damn bombing they'd ever seen." On 30 April, Captain Delancey first made a dummy run to confirm he had identified the correct caves, which were close to friendly troops, before his four Corsairs each dropped a 500-pound bomb and fired eight rockets into the caves.[100]

By the end of April the squadron had flown more than a thousand sorties since first departing Ulithi ten weeks earlier. The pilots, mechanics, and ship's crew were bushed—"tired and edgy," in Lieutenant Imel's words.[101]

The aviators rested while *Bunker Hill* refueled and replenished on 1 May. The ship's executive officer, "Be-No," took the opportunity to investigate singing coming from one of VMF-221's staterooms, where he found pilots "drinking and having a harmless community sing," in Roberts' words. The executive officer took their names and expanded his censorship to officers' mail—not to protect operational secrets but to detect officer misconduct. Roberts' diary revealed his exasperation: "That S.O.B. is the most disliked man I have ever heard of. There isn't a single person on the ship who even faintly respects that man. He is just a complete bastard of the first order."[102]

After a second no-flying day of harsh weather, Captain Swett led a fourteen-plane fighter sweep on 3 May to Kikai and Tanegashima, two islands just twenty miles off the southern tip of Kyushu, to disrupt Ugaki's fifth large offensive. Ugaki had assembled 449 aircraft, including 160 special attack planes. The marines cratered Kikai's runway with 500-pound bombs and destroyed three aircraft in revetments on Tanegashima. On his run Captain Delancey spotted additional aircraft in revetments and led his division back to get them. The heavy antiaircraft defenses hit Delancey's aircraft. He ditched offshore but was likely knocked unconscious on impact. He did not escape the aircraft. Bullets also riddled Lieutenant Goeggel's engine. He nursed his Corsair nearly all the way to the task force before ditching. An OS2U from a cruiser picked him up. Despite damage from a 40-mm shell, 1st Lt. Edward K. Nicolaides landed safely, but his aircraft had so many holes that the crew rolled it over the side.[103]

That evening, Ugaki's preliminary strikes sank a picket destroyer and a support vessel and damaged two other vessels. The following day, Ugaki unleashed the bulk of his aircraft. In one of the costlier attacks for the pickets, the attackers sank two destroyers and two support vessels and damaged seven other warships. Just before noon, special attack aircraft struck the Royal Navy carriers HMS *Formidable* and HMS *Indomitable* in Task Force 57. Unlike American carriers, these British ships had steel flight decks, which protected them from catastrophic damage.[104]

Though Mitscher had warning of Ugaki's fifth offensive, he did not curtail support to the Tenth Army or concentrate all his fighters against the attacks. Ugaki's attack coincided with a Japanese ground counterattack supported by an amphibious landing of infantry in barges against the 1st Marine Division and the 7th Infantry Division in front of the Shuri line. Instead of intercepting special attacks and bombers, two divisions from VMF-221 dropped bombs and fired rockets to suppress antiaircraft guns east of Naha, enabling twenty-three torpedo and dive-bombers to attack gun emplacements in front of the 1st Marine Division. No *Bunker Hill* aircraft were lost, and the marines and soldiers soundly repulsed the Japanese counterattacks.[105]

The following afternoon Major Roberts led twelve Corsairs back to Amami Ōshima. This was *Bunker Hill*'s fifth strike against that island and the second that day. The Corsairs carried napalm canisters to ensure that parked aircraft would burn, dry tanks or not. The marines bombed a wooded area suspected of concealing aircraft and supplies. Despite antiaircraft fire that shot away Roberts' left flap, the marines achieved good hits. One fighter's canister failed to drop, so the pilot diverted to Yontan to have it removed rather than risk damaging the carrier. Without flaps it took Roberts three attempts to recover aboard *Bunker Hill*, but he landed safely, an impressive piece of airmanship.[106]

After Task Group 58.3 replenished on 6 May, Mitscher assigned returning warships to the group. *Bunker Hill* was now accompanied by *Essex*, *Enterprise*, *Randolph*, and the light carrier *Bataan*. The battleships *Washington* and USS *South Dakota* (BB 57) and five light cruisers encircled the carriers with a ring of antiaircraft guns.[107]

On the morning of 7 May, Captain Snider's division accompanied an Air Group 84 support mission to Okinawa. The marines blasted gun positions and troop concentrations facing the 1st Marine Division at Shuri with 500-pound bombs. That afternoon, Major Roberts led eight VMF-221 fighters and four from VF-84 back to Kikai, where he had the satisfaction of placing a 500-pound bomb dead center of the antiaircraft emplacement that had shot away his flap two days earlier. In addition to hitting the antiaircraft positions the fighters strafed small craft but found nothing more consequential.[108]

Continuous rain and a low overcast interrupted flight operations on 8 May, but visibility was unrestricted the following day. Captain Swett led a division along with an Air Group 84 strike back to Kikai in the afternoon, where they dropped napalm canisters on the docks. All aircraft returned safely. Task Group 58.3 replenished and conducted antiaircraft target practice on 10 May. The light carrier USS *Langley* (CVL 27) joined the task group.[109]

15

★ ★ ★

Attack on USS *Bunker Hill*, 11 May 1945

Ugaki's Sixth Offensive

Vice Admiral Ugaki assembled 217 aircraft—a mixture of dive-bombers, fighters, and 104 special attack planes—for his attack on 11 May. The attack would begin with an early-morning strike on the marine aircraft groups at Yontan to limit their ability to intercept subsequent strikes. In addition to pummeling the radar pickets again, Ugaki tasked some special attack units to strike the aircraft carriers of Task Force 58.[1] The picket destroyers and radars on Okinawa detected the aircraft attacking Yontan. Fighters from Okinawa and Task Force 58 intercepted them all, and the marines at Yontan escaped injury.[2]

The Battle at Picket 15

The attackers next concentrated against Radar Picket No. 15, thirty-eight miles northwest of Okinawa, where Captain Swett waited with seven Corsairs. By 0800 the flight was on station at 15,000 feet, under the fighter direction of USS *Hugh W. Hadley* (DD 774). Swett and Glendinning flew F4U-1Cs armed with 20-mm cannon. This was the first mission on which VMF-221's pilots had the opportunity to fly them.[3]

The seven marines were entering a great air clash that had begun twenty minutes earlier. Almost immediately, Lieutenant Jorgensen spotted a lone Frances three thousand feet below him. Swett attacked it, only to discover that his 20-mm guns had frozen at high altitude and would not all fire. Lieutenant Goeggel in a F4U-1D blasted the bomber to bits with .50-caliber machine guns.[4]

By 0830, *Hadley* was directing five squadrons against waves of attackers. Her gunners downed thirteen aircraft during these first raids. So many pilots were talking over each other that transmissions became indecipherable, and *Hadley* told the fighters they "were on their own."[5]

Swett spotted a single Judy dive-bomber. With his cannons now working, he quickly torched it. But the lack of fighter direction from *Hadley* incensed him. There were clearly bandits around, but he did not know where. After nearly an hour, his division spotted a Betty carrying a Baka Bomb. All four pilots scored hits before Glendinning's 20-mm cannon ripped into the Betty's right engine, causing the bomber to burn and explode. At 0915, the VMF-221 pilots headed back toward *Bunker Hill* while the battle raged on.[6]

A few minutes later, over a dozen more attackers swarmed over *Hadley*. The embattled destroyer shot down the first ten, but then a bomb, a Baka Bomb, and two special attack planes struck her in quick succession. Twenty-eight of her crew perished, and sixty-seven were wounded. The survivors kept her afloat. Her fighter direction officer counted 156 aircraft that had attacked in 5 waves. Fighters claimed 68 of these; the destroyers claimed many more. In addition to hurting *Hadley*, the attackers had damaged the other destroyer and a support vessel.[7]

Bunker Hill, Midmorning

After securing from general quarters earlier, *Bunker Hill* had set Condition Able Modified. The "modified" condition permitted the scuttles of watertight hatches between decks to be left open above the third deck to enable the crew to transit between their living and work spaces.[8]

Air Group 84's squadrons, no longer sheltered in the wardroom, had reoccupied their ready rooms on the gallery deck. With most of the squadron aloft, only Captain Balch, Lieutenant Imel, Lieutenant Nettles, and Lieutenant Pambrum were in VMF-221's ready room. One door in the ready room exited directly onto the port catwalk, and a second door exited into a fore-and-aft passageway. Imel stepped out on the catwalk for some air and noted the high solid overcast. Many marines and sailors were jumpy after so many air attacks; all were exhausted. "There's something wrong," one sergeant said to Imel. "Something terrible is going to happen."[9]

Swett's flight arrived over *Bunker Hill* around 1000 and found that aircraft still obstructed her deck. The Corsairs circled off the carrier's starboard quarter at one thousand feet while the deck crew respotted aircraft. Cumulus clouds covered eight-tenths of the sky two thousand feet above the task group.[10]

At 1005, lookouts and gunners spotted a Zero approaching *Bunker Hill* from astern at high speed, one hundred feet above the waves and only a thousand yards away—seven seconds from impact. Swett yelled a warning into his radio. The ship's gunners were not poised to fire. One 20-mm gunner got off a short burst before the Zero crashed into a parked Corsair, skidded across the deck, and plunged over the port side, carrying a section of the catwalk with it. The fighter's 500-pound armor-piercing bomb punched through the wooden flight deck, exited the port side of the hull, and detonated thirty feet beyond. The Corsair topside and several aircraft on the hanger deck burst into flames. The impact and explosion severed a fire main, disabling fire suppression in that section of the hangar deck.[11]

Less than a minute later, a Judy emerged from the low-lying clouds diving steeply at the carrier. Lieutenant Glendinning's section tried to intercept the dive-bomber, but they were too far away. The gun crews were alert now. Four 5-inch guns, two 40-mm quad-mounts, and twenty 20-mm guns peppered the dive-bomber for twelve seconds, hitting it several times but failing to knock it down. The Japanese pilot released his 500-pound high-explosive bomb seconds before crashing into the base of the island. The detonation blasted a forty-foot hole in the flight deck. Fires engulfed the hangar deck and raged through the gallery deck between the flight and hangar decks, immolating ready rooms and squadron offices.[12]

A third attacker, another Zero, approached the starboard beam in a shallow glide from one thousand feet. This time *Bunker Hill*'s gunners found their mark. Four 5-inch guns and three 40-mm quad-mounts shot the fighter down at 3,500 yards.[13]

Escape and Damage Control

Smoke from the raging fires filled the passageways and spaces, plunging VMF-221's ready room into darkness. Many aviators from VF-84 and VT-84 died from either the bomb blast or smoke inhalation. Nettles fought his way to the flight deck through passageways crowded with panicked crewmen. Balch, Imel, Pambrum, and a young navy steward who had just brought the marines some sandwiches crawled through the pitch-dark smoke the short distance toward the port catwalk. "The smoke was choking us and we were moving fast," remembered Imel. "At this point in time I do remember making my amends to the maker." The four men emerged onto the catwalk, which was already crowded with a couple dozen sailors and marines cornered there by the smoke and fire. Machine-gun rounds in a ready magazine began detonating from the heat. A locker full of rockets was also heating up from the fire on the hangar deck below. Balch organized a daisy chain, and the trapped men tossed the scorching hot rockets one by one over the rail.[14]

After what seemed like thirty minutes, the trapped men concluded their chances of survival were better in the ocean. The mess steward said he could not swim. Balch had both a Mae West and his life jacket, so he handed the life jacket to the steward. They deployed an escape ladder from its locker, but its rotten anchor ropes immediately parted, and it dropped into the sea. Pambrum attempted to rig a fire hose to slide down but concluded it wouldn't work. Imel remembered his abandon ship training from a thirty-foot tower at the North Island pool and decided to take the plunge. He covered his nose and crotch and stepped off. All four survived the seventy-five-foot drop, but the mess steward lost control of his life jacket. The pilots swam to the struggling sailor, but he disappeared before they could reach him. *Bunker Hill* sailed on, leaving the swimmers alone in the quiet sea.[15]

When the bombs hit, Lieutenant Caswell and Lieutenant McManus were in the officers' mess room below the hangar deck. Because the gasoline fire on the hangar deck had wiped out the repair section responsible for this area, the ventilator continued to run, drawing toxic smoke into the berthing and mess decks. "I was running for my life, had nowhere to go, and we were ablaze," recalled Caswell. He and McManus each still carried gas masks from general quarters. They donned them and crawled into a smoke-filled passageway. "It was full of bodies, all asphyxiated," Caswell wrote a few days later. "It was hellish, crawling over mounds of dead sailors, while blindly trying to find a ladder going up to the hanger deck." They groped in the oily darkness and located a ladder. They climbed it, only to find that it led to a hatch dogged from above. They banged frantically on the hatch. A passing shipmate heard them and opened it, and they emerged onto the burning hanger deck.[16]

Crewmen had deployed hoses on the flight deck within sixty seconds of the second aircraft strike. On the hangar deck, the blast severed fire mains and the intense heat melted sprinklers.[17] After catching their breath, the two lieutenants joined the firefighting effort. The marines had no training in firefighting and damage control. Caswell had trouble controlling the 150 psi of back-pressure of a 1.5-inch hose, but with the help of shipmates managed to direct it where it seemed most needed. Caswell admitted later that it was "debatable how much good we were doing."[18]

On the flight deck, Lieutenant Nettles had the same trouble. "The first fire hose we uncoiled was rotten and of no use. We finally found one that was usable, and I was on the nozzle end. When they turned on the water it flopped me all over the deck." A large shipmate jumped on the hose behind Nettles and helped him get it under control.[19]

McManus decided someone should check the squadron ready room. He located a silver crash fire rescue suit and figured out how to pull it on. As Caswell and others sprayed seawater on him from the hangar deck, he climbed a ladder to the gallery deck between the flight and hangar decks. The ready rooms were an inferno, but McManus searched VMF-221's ready room, departing only after he confirmed no one remained inside.[20]

By that time, *Bunker Hill*'s crew had the fire on the flight deck under control. The hanger deck continued to burn, detonating the fuel tanks of the aircraft stowed there. Captain Seitz maneuvered the ship to blow heat and smoke away from the firefighting teams and maintained a slight list to drain water, fuel, and oil over the side. Two destroyers, a submarine tender, and a light cruiser came alongside blasting seawater into the burning hangar deck. In a monumental effort, *Bunker Hill*'s boiler crew kept the ship under power and underway, enabling her firefighting crews to get the inferno under control by 1130. Able to steam but unable to fight, the smoking carrier set a course for Ulithi.[21]

"A Nauseating Hollow Feeling"

Swett's flight circled the sailors and marines who had abandoned ship or been blown over the side. The pilots dropped life preservers and dye marker to the men and continued circling overhead until USS *Porter* (DD 356) headed over. With their own ship ablaze, the seven Corsair pilots recovered aboard *Enterprise* at 1130. When *Porter* hove to near Balch's group, Imel was too tired to climb up the ladder. A crewman hauled him aboard. Only then did Imel realize he had severely injured his back when he hit the water.[22]

Major Roberts had taken off with two divisions on a fighter sweep to Kakai. His eight Corsairs were diverted to a combat air patrol off Okinawa, where they stood by but did not receive any intercepts.[23] They returned to the task group at 1215, only to find their carrier billowing smoke into the sky. "A nauseating hollow feeling ran through all of us," Roberts wrote that night. After circling *Bunker Hill* twice, appalled at the damage and flames, the two divisions landed on *Enterprise*.[24]

The End

The attack had killed 346 of *Bunker Hill*'s air group and crew. Most died from smoke inhalation.[25] Another 43 men were missing—blown over the side in the initial blast or forced to jump and never found. The explosions, fires, and smoke decimated VMF-221's ground echelon. Some died on the flight and hanger decks. Others were trapped in the messing and berthing areas below. Of the squadron's sixty enlisted marines, eleven—all Solomons veterans—perished: Master TSgt. Herman H. Delaney, Master TSgt. Kenneth W. Muthard, TSgt. Russell E. Dorniden, TSgt. Earl R. Herrman, TSgt. Perry E. Pert, TSgt. Lawrence F. Sonderman, TSgt. Oswald A. Spinetti, Sgt. Mariano A. Moscolino, Sgt. Francis Petty, Cpl. Ellis E. Lowery, and

Cpl. Edward W. Yanik.[26] Glendinning heard rumors that one of the senior plane handlers had left the flight deck to retrieve $32,000 in poker winnings and was clutching his metal cashbox when his body was found.[27]

The damage to the ship was not fatal, but she and VMF-221 were done with the war. *Bunker Hill* would need months of repairs before she could fight again. Though the aviators and surviving ground echelon marines of VMF-221 were still combat capable, and fifteen Corsairs had escaped the fire by landing on *Enterprise*, Task Force 58 could not use them. There was no room on any of the other carriers for another fighting squadron.

The aviators aboard *Enterprise* flew their Corsairs to Yontan, turned them over to the marine aircraft groups there, and rode transport aircraft to Ulithi, where they rejoined *Bunker Hill* for the voyage to the shipyard in Bremerton, Washington.[28] En route, the few typewriters available clacked around the clock. The April and May squadron war diary and aircraft combat action reports had burned in the squadron office, so the officers reconstructed them from the surviving master log and their logbooks.[29]

16

★ ★ ★

VMF-221's Effectiveness Aboard USS *Bunker Hill*

Several factors contributed to the effectiveness of VMF-221 while the squadron was aboard *Bunker Hill*: the number of aircraft the squadron sortied; the number of enemy aircraft, vessels, and ground targets the squadron destroyed; the number of aircraft and personnel the squadron lost; and the number of aircraft lost and vessels damaged while protected by the squadron. These factors must then be considered in the context of the role the squadron was assigned within the fleet commander's intent.

Sorties

The squadron's sorties were to some extent determined by the number of aircraft on hand and capable of flying in combat. *Bunker Hill*'s action reports provide the air group's daily availability, but they are not broken down by squadron. This is because the three fighting squadrons—VF-84, VMF-221, and VMF-451—swapped F4Us among themselves to meet mission requirements. *Bunker Hill* left San Diego with fifty-three Corsairs aboard. She departed Ulithi on 10 February with sixty-two Corsairs available. She averaged fifty-seven available during her first combat cruise and fifty-four

TABLE 3. VMF-221 Days of Combat and Sorties, 1945

Combat cruise	Days underway	Sorties	Average sorties per day underway	Days of combat	Sorties on combat days	Average sorties per combat day
First cruise 10 February–4 March	23	226	9.8	8	124	15.5
Second cruise 14 March–11 May	59	1,009	17.1	39	919	23.6
Total	82	1,235	15.1	47	1,043	22.2

Sources: "CV-17 Action Report, 10 February–5 March 1945," 27; "CV-17 Action Report, 14 March–14 May 1945," 199–200; VMF-221 war diaries, March–May 1945, passim.

during her second. Her lowest strength of forty-one available Corsairs occurred the day after the landing on Okinawa.[1]

Table 3 summarizes the sorties flown by VMF-221 during *Bunker Hill*'s two 1945 combat cruises. During eighty-two days underway, from her first sortie from Ulithi until her last day of combat, *Bunker Hill*'s air group flew combat missions on forty-seven days. On noncombat days while underway, the carrier launched combat air patrols, but these involved only a fraction of her fighter complement.

VMF-221's sortie rate on combat days is slightly higher than its combat sortie rate flying Wildcats in 1943, and 74 percent higher than its combat sortie rate flying the Corsair that year (see Table 1). Though the squadron's sortie rate was lower during its first 1945 combat cruise than during its second, aircraft availability was higher during the first cruise. The lower sortie rate during the first cruise was not due to aircraft availability, but because fewer sorties were required.

Table 4 tabulates the times a four-plane division launched short an aircraft, the times an aircraft aborted a mission, the mishaps attributed to mechanical

TABLE 4. VMF-221 Air Strength Shortfalls in Combat, 1945

Month	Days in combat	Divisions sortied understrength	Aborts	Mishaps (mechanical)	Aircraft losses from mishaps	Mishap fatalities
First combat cruise, 16 February–4 March						
February	6	5				
March	2		1			
Second combat cruise, 14 March–11 May						
March	12		2			
April	21	2	2	3	3	2
May	6	2	1			

Source: VMF-221 war diaries, March–May 1945; passim.

issues, and the aircraft and aviators lost in mishaps. When compared with similar measures in 1943, the data suggest that the squadron suffered fewer air strength shortfalls in 1945 (see Table 2).

Enemy Aircraft, Vessels, and Ground Targets Destroyed

As the aviators' frequent miscounting of aerial victories noted earlier suggests, pilots engaged in combat experienced tremendous difficulty determining whether an enemy aircraft had actually gone down. On 5 March 1944, Admiral Nimitz had adopted uniform criteria for reporting enemy aircraft destroyed: "Aircraft in flight were considered destroyed when: (1) seen to crash, (2) seen to disintegrate or be enveloped in flames, (3) seen to descend on friendly territory and be captured, or (4) pilot and entire crew seen to bail out."[2]

While the criteria appear unequivocal, implementing them proved difficult. The advent of gun cameras helped fighting squadrons apply Nimitz's criteria with greater certainty by 1945. According to Lieutenant Caswell, Major Roberts relied on these films and awarded credit guardedly.[3] The squadron awarded credit for fifty-one aerial victories to its pilots during 1945. Caswell was the Marine Corps' leading carrier ace with seven victories.[4]

Assessing the damage the squadron inflicted on targets on the ground and at sea is less precise. Gun cameras could verify the destruction of parked aircraft. Aerial photography enabled interpreters to assess damage to factories and airfields. Aviators' eyewitness statements of vessels sunk or damaged were credible. By such methods, VMF-221 assessed that it destroyed thirty aircraft, twenty-five small craft, and a midget submarine during 1945.[5]

In contrast, damage inflicted on enemy troops and fortifications was often speculative. As Air Group 84's action report noted, "The efficiency of many of these missions was exceedingly difficult to evaluate, since many of the targets assigned were gun positions, trenches, and caves, on which damage assessment is next to impossible."[6] The LFASCU concluded that carrier aviation was ineffective prior to the landing at Iwo Jima due to enemy concealment and dispersion.[7] Once the squadron began flying close air support for frontline units on Okinawa, air controllers provided more reliable damage assessments. Ground controllers appear to have assessed that VMF-221 inflicted significant damage to defenders when the controllers could pinpoint targets.

Aircraft and Personnel Lost

VMF-221 suffered few losses in aircraft and personnel prior to 11 May. The squadron lost twenty-five aircraft and seventeen marines while embarked aboard *Bunker Hill*: three aviators and four aircraft in air-to-air combat, one aviator and five aircraft to antiaircraft fire, and two aviators and six aircraft in mishaps. Eleven marines died and ten aircraft were burned aboard *Bunker Hill* on 11 May.[8]

Had it not been for the loss of ten aircraft on *Bunker Hill* that day, VMF-221's aircraft losses would have been markedly lower in 1945 than they had been in the Solomons. When 11 May losses are included, the numbers for 1943 and 1945 are equivalent. Fatalities for 1943 and 1945 are comparable when 11 May casualties are excluded.

The squadron claimed more than a dozen aerial victories for every air-to-air loss in 1945. While a precise examination of claims amid the gigantic air clashes off Okinawa and Japan is problematic, it appears the squadron won aerial combats more often and lost them less often in 1945 than it had in 1943.

Though the improved kill-to-loss ratio in aerial combat is remarkable, those figures do not capture an important consideration. The United States could replace VMF-221's aircraft, but Japan's aircraft industry was failing by mid-1945. VMF-221 had lost only six aviators, and the Marine Corps swiftly replaced its losses, but the squadron usually killed every Japanese pilot it shot down. Squadrons like VMF-221 were breaking Japanese air power.

Aircraft Lost and Vessels Damaged while Protected by the Squadron

Air Group 84 lost only two bombers to enemy fighters, both on the Tokyo strike on 16 February. The group lost only five fighters in aerial combat; four of those were lost by VMF-221. The fifth, a VF-84 fighter, was lost to an exploding enemy aircraft, as had happened to the unfortunate Lieutenant Turner.[9]

Attributing damage to vessels that were under VMF-221's protection is more complicated. It is easy to identify warships sunk or damaged while VMF-221 was providing them with a combat air patrol, but that is only part of the story. In addition to defending vessels with combat air patrols, VMF-221 also protected the vessels of the Fifth Fleet through strikes against enemy airfields and fighter sweeps. But as VMF-221 never constituted more than 2 percent of Task Force 58's fighter strength, Fifth Fleet's aggregate warship losses cannot be taken as a helpful indicator of VMF-221's performance.

In 1945, Japanese aircraft damaged six vessels under VMF-221's direct protection. On 7 April, the carrier *Hancock* suffered a bomb hit while a VMF-221 combat air patrol was over Task Group 58.3. In this instance, the fighter director sent another squadron's fighters to intercept the attackers. On 12 April, a crashing Judy damaged the destroyer *Purdy* shortly before VMF-221's fighters arrived overhead. On 28 April, near misses by special attack units damaged the destroyers *Daly* and *Twiggs* after VMF-221's fighters had exhausted their fuel in aerial combat and departed. The same happened to *Hadley* on 11 May. When two dive-bombers struck *Bunker Hill* later that morning, seven fighters from VMF-221 were waiting to recover, not assigned to combat air patrol but certainly in a position to intercept the attack had any ship detected and identified the attackers.

VMF-221 and the Fleet Commander's Intent

Among the factors determining VMF-221's effectiveness aboard *Bunker Hill* were the tasks assigned to the squadron in the context of the fleet commander's intent.

The Fifth Fleet commander's intent for Task Force 58 during the February strikes around Tokyo was to reduce enemy air and naval strength as well as industrial facilities in the home islands. The Japanese aircraft industry was manufacturing just 1,391 airframes and 1,695 engines per month by February 1945, about half the airframes and a third of the engines it had produced at its peak in 1944. VMF-221's role was to fly fighter sweeps and combat air patrols and to escort strikes and photoreconnaissance missions gathering information to protect the fleet and enable its bombers to strike aircraft factories.

After the war, the U.S. Strategic Bombing Survey attempted to assess the effectiveness of American bombing during the war. Though its conclusions seem to have been influenced by partisan service interests, the survey's method of assessing the effectiveness of individual American bombing raids against the Japanese aircraft industry appears rigorously objective. Three of Task Force 58's strikes inflicted "heavy" damage on Japan's aircraft industry.[10] During the strike on the Nakajima Aircraft Assembly plant in Ota on 16 February, Major Roberts led the first fighter sweep, two Corsairs escorted the photoreconnaissance aircraft, and other divisions protected the task force. During the strike on the Nakajima Musashi plant in Tokyo the next day, the squadron flew combat air patrol above the task force. For the 25 February strike against the Nakajima plant at Koizumi, VMF-221 escorted the strike, dropped bombs, and rocketed the target. The squadron fulfilled its role on each mission, helping Task Force 58 to accomplish the fleet commander's intent.

VMF-221 contributed little to the seizure of Iwo Jima in February, and likewise inflicted little significant damage to Japanese air and naval strength in the Ryukyus in March. Nonetheless, Task Force 58's Big Blue Blanket forced Vice Admiral Ugaki to cede control of the skies over the Ryukyus until the mass attacks of 6–7 April. Until then, the offensive fighter sweeps and powerful combat air patrols by VMF-221 and the other fighting squadrons prevented Ugaki from interfering with the Fifth Fleet's pre-landing operations and the amphibious assault.

After the landing, Task Force 58 continued to prevent the Japanese Combined Fleet from repelling Operation Iceberg, but not from severely hurting the Fifth Fleet. The U.S. Tenth Army finally declared Okinawa secure on 21 June. By then the Fifth Fleet had lost 36 ships and 642 aircraft. Another 368 ships had suffered damage. Some, like *Bunker Hill*, required months of repair before they would be ready for action again. The Joint Chiefs had ordered MacArthur and Nimitz to invade Kyushu on 1 November, giving both commanders time to reconstitute and reinforce their bloodied commands.[11]

The protection that squadrons like VMF-221 provided the Fifth Fleet was not perfect, but it was good enough. The Fifth Fleet captured Iwo Jima and Okinawa with sufficient naval power preserved to meet the requirements identified for an invasion of Kyushu later that year.

Contributing Factors

The factors that contributed to VMF-221's effectiveness aboard *Bunker Hill* include the capabilities and limitations of the aircraft the squadron flew; the tactics the squadron employed; the ordnance the squadron employed; the proficiency of its aviators; the time it had to prepare; command and control; logistics and maintenance; intelligence and early warning; weather; aircrew survivability; and Japanese capabilities.

Aircraft

The F4U-1D outclassed its adversaries, particularly aircraft flown by less experienced pilots. The Corsair had the speed, maneuverability, and firepower to dominate Japanese fighters. Its 1,200-mile range increased its utility as a scout. With its abilities as a stable bomber, strafer, and rocket-firing platform, the F4U-1D also turned out to be highly versatile. Perhaps as important to VMF-221, the F4U-1D as modified from earlier models could fly off carriers more safely.

Safer it was, but the F4U-1D still challenged carrier pilots. VMF-221's pilots destroyed at least eight Corsairs in botched landings. Captain Seitz, *Bunker Hill*'s captain, noted that an excessively high number of Corsairs had to be scrapped when their fuselage buckled during hard landings. He considered this to be a pilot-training problem.[12] Lieutenant Commander Hedrick, the air group commander, agreed. "When the pilots of this group got over diving for the deck after a cut, wrinkled fuselages were eliminated."[13]

The Corsair had other troublesome drawbacks. The drop tanks caused the aircraft to buffet at low speeds and in dive-bombing runs, which contributed to the mishaps VMF-221 experienced and hindered bombing accuracy.[14] And for all its advantages, the Corsair was neither a night fighter nor an all-weather fighter. Nonetheless, the F4U-1D's superiority as a daytime fighter continued to contribute to the squadron's high kill ratio.

Tactics

Fighter tactics had not changed much since 1943, but fleet tactics had evolved significantly. The Fifth Fleet's ability to fight its more than six hundred ships and two thousand aircraft as a single team in multiple dimensions created conditions that set VMF-221 up for success, placing its fighters in the right place at the right time to fight and win. Task Force 58's Big Blue Blanket was not an ironclad tactic, but it proved sufficient to protect the fleet from Japanese aircraft. Refinements in air support control enabled squadrons like VMF-221 to inflict meaningful damage on Japanese defenders.

Ordnance

The F4U-1D's rockets added an effective ground-attack weapon to the squadron's arsenal, though pilot reports rarely attributed damage specifically to rockets. Rockets seldom malfunctioned, while *Bunker Hill*'s pilots estimated that napalm canisters detonated only 75 percent of the time. The canister's fins not only prevented the Corsair's flaps from fully extending but did little to improve the canister's dismal accuracy. "Damned worthless," Roberts concluded.[15] Notwithstanding Jimmy Swett's experience on 11 May, the 20-mm cannons of the F4U-1Cs did not suffer stoppages more often than .50-caliber machine guns once ordnance crews learned to belt ammunition properly.[16]

Aviators

VMF-221 brought no novice pilots aboard *Bunker Hill*. Though only four were Solomons veterans, the squadron's most inexperienced aviator had joined the squadron seven months before the deployment. All had completed a systematic and progressive training syllabus in California. All had qualified to land aboard carriers (except for Briggs, who proved capable). The replacements were combat veterans and experienced carrier pilots. When Roberts decided a pilot was unsafe, he was able to transfer him. VMF-221's aviators were meticulously trained and thoroughly outclassed their opponents.

Time

VMF-221 had not squandered the extended period at Goleta. Major Post and Major Roberts led the squadron through a progressive, well-rounded syllabus. When the Pacific Fleet directed the squadron to qualify aboard carriers two months before deploying, the squadron was already so proficient that this additional requirement did not interfere with other essential training. The fleet allocated enough days on *Ranger* to provide VMF-221 and the other squadrons time to qualify.

Command and Control

Though part of a vast fleet, VMF-221 benefited from a mature command-and-control system that leveraged technology, processes, and communications to put the squadron's fighters in the right place at the right time to fight and win. The squadron's fighters frequently participated in air group–sized strikes, protected their task group, flew under the fighter direction of a picket destroyer, and dropped bombs under the control of an air liaison party attached to an infantry unit, all within the same week or even the same day.

The command-and-control system was a force multiplier when it worked, but it did not always work. Premission coordination between the landing force and carrier air groups left much to be desired. Targets were assigned so late that aircrews had insufficient time to plan how they would approach, acquire, and attack the target. Task Force 58 often ordered its aviators to target aircraft and warships. When the pilots could not find any, they expended their ordnance on ground targets of dubious value. Aviators often had to guess at the damage they inflicted when they were instructed to hit targets of opportunity and those not identified by controllers in close proximity to a target.

These difficulties so vexed Admiral Sherman, Task Group 58.3's commander, that he advocated limiting fleet carriers to two days of high-tempo support missions for the landing force and then unleashing the carriers to focus on offensive strikes against enemy air power. By lingering off Okinawa for such a long time, the carriers sacrificed mobility and exposed themselves to enemy attacks, in Sherman's words, like "a worm on a hook."[17]

Tactical communications also hindered command and control, even between aircraft of the same squadron. *Bunker Hill* noted that replacement aircraft often arrived with the AN ARC-5 radio, which was incompatible with the AN ARC-1 in use. One hundred man-hours were required to swap it out—if an AN ARC-1 was available.[18] The task force did not have enough voice channels to direct intercepts. Captain Swett was particularly chagrined at the crowded fighter direction net at Radar Picket No. 15 on 11 May, which prevented *Hadley* from vectoring its fighters effectively.

Logistics and Maintenance

VMF-221 and *Bunker Hill* were underway and fighting from 10 February to 11 May, with only one ten-day break at anchor in Ulithi. Replacement aircraft flew aboard from escort carriers and, later, from Iwo Jima. The Pacific Fleet supplied all the carrier's fuel, ammunition, food, and spare parts at sea, 1,000 miles from Ulithi and 6,500 miles from California. The oilers also restocked drop tanks, which were often in short supply. The oilers became so efficient that many captains preferred to replenish at sea rather than in port.[19]

The squadron's high sortie rate reflects the effectiveness of the fleet's supply chain. It also indicates that it was easier to maintain aircraft on a carrier than on a jungle island. Working conditions on a carrier at war were hardly pleasant, but they far surpassed the disease, oppressive heat, tropical downpours, and spoiled food that plagued marines on land. The tools, parts, and supplies the mechanics needed were usually at hand. Further, Roberts had hand-picked the sixty marines of VMF-221's ground echelon aboard *Bunker Hill.* This group included twenty-eight Solomons veterans, who ensured that a highly experienced team maintained the squadron's fighters.

Nonetheless, combat and the sea took a toll on men and their machines. The Fifth Fleet could not have continued its operational tempo indefinitely. After Okinawa, Admiral Sherman expressed his great pride in the stamina of Task Group 58.3's ships and their crews but thought that both needed thirty days' rest and repair followed by ten to twelve days of training before they would be ready for another such combat cruise. That would have kept the group out of action until early August 1945.[20]

As helpful as having the supply chain and working conditions at sea was, logistics were the single greatest inhibitor to VMF-221's sortie rate. On her two combat cruises, *Bunker Hill* replenished on sixteen of her eighty-two days underway. On only one of these replenishment days did she fly combat operations aside from combat air patrols. The requirement to spend every fifth day off the line gave her aviators a rest but limited the number of punches she was throwing.[21]

Intelligence and Early Warning

Intelligence could be spotty. VMF-221 benefited from excellent intelligence at times, but there were frustrating gaps at others. Intelligence regarding Japanese dispositions and intentions kept the Fifth Fleet one step ahead of the Combined Fleet. Intelligence regarding strike targets was inconsistent. The target folders for the Tokyo strikes provided to *Bunker Hill*'s pilots included aerial photographs and damage assessments from B-29 raids, which greatly enhanced mission planning. Photographs of the airfields on Kyushu often revealed hundreds of camouflaged aircraft protected within revetments. Pilots could get in, hit known aircraft locations, and leave instead of orbiting the airfield looking for targets, which exposed them to responding fighters and antiaircraft guns. Aerial photographs also revealed the location of midget submarines on Okinawa. But that type of information was often absent when it came to the entrenched defenders on Okinawa, as it had been on Iwo Jima. Information about the battle on Okinawa was so sporadic that pilots relied on *Bunker Hill*'s internal newspaper for updates.[22]

Early warning of enemy air attacks was usually good but occasionally failed. With no equivalent to the coast watchers, Task Force 58 depended on radar operators aboard pickets, on Okinawa, and aboard its own vessels. All of those radars detected aircraft inconsistently. IFF systems failed so often that their value was limited. U.S. radars could not detect aircraft above 25,000 feet beyond 30 miles, or accurately track them once detected, greatly inhibiting fighter interception. The radars in the task group's flagship, *Essex*, were performing poorly and were in need of repair or replacement when the attack on 11 April destroyed one of the ship's radar antennas. From then on, Admiral Sherman relied on other ships in his task group to pass him radar information. Sherman concluded that the aircraft that struck *Bunker Hill* on 11 May likely evaded radar detection by approaching at a very low altitude, then climbed into the heavy, low-lying clouds where they could not be spotted and radar operators had trouble distinguishing them from friendly aircraft over the task group.[23]

Weather

The harsh winter weather in the western Pacific impaired VMF-221's effectiveness. During *Bunker Hill*'s two combat cruises, on ten of her eighty-two days underway, weather forced Admiral Mitscher to cancel or curtail operations. On several other occasions, such as during both Tokyo strikes, bad weather hamstrung VMF-221's effectiveness in the air.

Aircrew Survivability

More than a few aviators owed their lives to the robust search-and-rescue capabilities the Pacific Fleet had arranged. Five VMF-221 pilots ditched or parachuted over water and were subsequently rescued. Task Force 58's pilots had other options when they ran into difficulties. One VMF-221 pilot landed on the Yontan airfield when his napalm canister would not release. Another landed aboard *Randolph* when he could not make it to *Bunker Hill*. On 11 May, *Enterprise* recovered fifteen aviators while *Bunker Hill* burned.

Flying with Task Force 58 added a margin of safety to aircrew survival but also added new perils. Eleven of the squadron's ground crew perished in the 11 May fire. Many of the squadron's pilots escaped because they were aloft. To increase survivability for the ship and her crew, Captain Seitz urged the fleet to train air group personnel to use a rescue breathing apparatus and to fight fires.[24]

Japanese Capabilities

The damage to *Bunker Hill* illustrates how Japan's air forces adapted to their eclipse by American air power. As aircraft production diminished, aircraft performance lagged, and pilot training deteriorated, Japan resorted to suicide attacks. While these special attacks did not threaten VMF-221 in the air, they could destroy aircraft aboard ships they struck and could eliminate the squadron from the battle by forcing its carrier to withdraw for repair.

In the air, improved Japanese fighters do not appear to have given their inexperienced pilots a significant edge. Japanese fighters shot down only three VMF-221 fighters. One was likely brought down by a newer Oscar or Tojo; the other two by Zeros.

On the ground, the Japanese used camouflage to limit VMF-221's effectiveness in its ground attack role. The marines rarely inflicted significant damage on Japanese defenders until American troops uncovered their locations. VMF-221 enjoyed greater success attacking parked aircraft. The Japanese tactic of defueling aircraft to improve survivability was much less effective after the marines switched to napalm.

On an operational level, Vice Admiral Ugaki's careful management of the air war enabled him to mass aircraft against the Fifth Fleet. Ashore, the 32nd Army's prolonged defense forced Task Force 58 to linger off Okinawa for more than two months, the "worm on a hook" described by Admiral Sherman. Though Ugaki never overmatched the Fifth Fleet's air forces, and the 32nd Army eventually succumbed to the Tenth Army, Japanese commanders made the battle for Okinawa longer and bloodier than American commanders had foreseen.

★

An analysis of VMF-221's combat cruises aboard *Bunker Hill* reveals a highly effective carrier fighting squadron. Its aircraft and its pilots did the job they were tasked to do: fly off a carrier, intercept enemy aircraft, and attack enemy ground targets. There were shortcomings in their performance. The squadron's sortie rate would have been much higher had logistics and foul weather not prevented *Bunker Hill* from launching combat missions on 30 percent of her underway days. Enemy aircraft slipped past the squadron's fighters and struck warships of the fleet, either because the fleet did not detect them, the fighter director did not task the fighters to intercept them, or the fighters were off station. In the ground attack role, the aviators had tremendous difficulty identifying concealed defenders without the aid of frontline controllers.

VMF-221's successful conversion to a carrier squadron is as much a testament to the organizational efficiency of naval aviation as it is to the proficiency of the squadron's aviators. Because the marines were trained as naval aviators, equipped with carrier aircraft, and allotted the time and opportunity to qualify for carrier operations, VMF-221 was able to integrate into Task Force 58 and perform effectively.

★ ★ ★

Conclusion

This work has examined the effectiveness of marine aviation in support of the Pacific Fleet in World War II. VMF-221's experience indicates that marine aviation achieved mixed success, particularly in 1942.

Early in the war, VMF-221 suffered heavy losses at Midway while contributing modestly to the Pacific Fleet's victory there. The squadron was outnumbered, and its aircraft were inferior. MAG-22 employed the squadron in defense of the base, leaving VMSB-241 to attack without fighter protection. Most significant, too many marine aviators were inexperienced and inferior to their adversaries—"half-baked pilots," as General Rowell characterized them. Because marine aviation was expanding so rapidly, the Pacific Fleet and the Fleet Marine Force had to employ their forward squadrons as training commands. Training flight hours competed with the requirement to defend the atoll. As the battle approached, fuel shortages limited training when it mattered most for the squadron's newest pilots. As a result, VMF-221 was not ready to fight on 4 June, despite its aviators' willingness to try, the squadron's ability to get its planes in the air, and MAG-22's ability to detect the incoming strike and direct the squadron to a favorable interception point.

In striking contrast, the squadron proved highly effective in the Solomons, claiming seven aerial victories for every aerial loss. Even when flying the F4F-4 Wildcat on its first combat tour, the squadron claimed twenty-five victories. Once the squadron had transitioned to the F4U Corsair, its victory claims climbed as its losses plummeted. The protection VMF-221 and Fighter Command extended to the fleet's ships and landing forces was not airtight, as Japanese strikes occasionally sank and damaged ships and bombed forces ashore, but it was unquestionably good enough. VMF-221's performance achieved the fleet commander's intent and contributed to the Third Fleet's neutralization of Rabaul along with the attrition of Japanese naval aviation.

VMF-221's aviators were far more prepared for combat in the Solomons in 1943 than they had been at Midway. This was primarily due to a focused two-month training regimen, but their assimilation of doctrine and tactics developed by other navy and marine squadrons during 1942 added to their success. Intelligence, early warning, and fighter direction consistently placed the squadron in the right place at the right time to fight and win. The transition to the F4U Corsair measurably improved the squadron's performance in the Solomons, even though the squadron's difficulty maintaining the Corsair limited its sortie rate. The difficulty the Pacific Fleet experienced sustaining Air Command, Solomons at the end of a transoceanic supply chain constrained the squadron's ability to keep its aircraft flying. The tropical environment accelerated corrosion and other mechanical issues while requiring marines and sailors working on the aircraft to labor under miserable conditions.

The practice of separating aviators, aircraft, and ground echelons from each other while employing these components as interchangeable cogs exacerbated aircraft maintenance challenges. The squadron had better success keeping its aviators and ground echelons healthy than had earlier units, as environmental health measures and unit discipline retarded tropical diseases, and rest periods in Australia gave pilots much-needed respites. Search-and-rescue boats and aircraft improved pilot morale as well as survivability.

The squadron's operational effectiveness continued when it deployed aboard *Bunker Hill*. Its pilots benefited from a prolonged, systematic training syllabus. They claimed a better than twelve-to-one kill-to-loss ratio in air-to-air combat. When they could locate targets on the ground or at sea, they inflicted significant damage. No aircraft the squadron escorted were lost to enemy fighters. Enemy suicide attacks often penetrated Task Force 58's Big Blue Blanket and struck warships of the Fifth Fleet, but never due to the inefficiency of VMF-221.

The squadron's deployment aboard *Bunker Hill* revealed advantages and limitations of carrier aviation. The carrier's mobility enabled its air group to strike targets throughout the theater of operations, mitigating the limited operational radius of its aircraft. Aircraft were easier to maintain and supply at sea than in the Solomon Islands. However, replenishment requirements and rough weather interrupted flight operations nearly a third of the time, curtailing the number of days the carrier could sustain offensive operations. Most important, the carrier and her air group were vulnerable to enemy strikes in a way that land-based squadrons were not. As the 11 May attack demonstrated, when attacking aircraft could locate the carrier and penetrate the fleet's defenses, they could sink or damage the carrier and remove her and her aircraft from the fight.

One recurring theme across all three campaigns still evokes a measure of awe and respect. No matter the odds or the peril, when the marines of VMF-221 encountered the enemy, they attacked. Sometimes they paid dearly for their aggressiveness. Far more often, their enemies paid. One cannot read the accounts of these aviators' consistent aggressiveness without wondering where the Marine Corps got such men.

Implications

A. A. Cunningham's 1919 assertion that "the only excuse for aviation in any service is its usefulness in assisting the troops on the ground" was shortsighted, even regarding marine aviation. The experience of VMF-221 demonstrated that aviation could be an integral component of a fleet, and that its usefulness went well beyond supporting the fleet's landing force. The Pacific Fleet employed aviation to achieve air superiority, achieved air superiority to establish sea control, and established sea control to seize advance bases. Advance bases then enabled land-based aviation to help the fleet extend air superiority, and the cycle repeated.

Though VMF-221 was a marine squadron, its experience in the Pacific War more closely aligns with naval aviation than with the Fleet Marine Force. Regarding the integration of marine squadrons into naval aviation, Allan Millett noted in his seminal history of the Marine Corps, "[T]he wonder is not that Marine pilots learned the air superiority and fleet-destroying doctrines of the Navy but that they retained any Marine Corps character at all."[1]

The primary mission of Marine Corps aviation was to support the Fleet Marine Force in landing operations, and its secondary mission was to provide replacement squadrons for carriers, but few marine squadrons fulfilled either of those roles in World War II. Most who served in those roles did not do so until 1945. As VMF-221's story demonstrates, the fleet employed marine squadrons to meet its requirements and within marine aviation's capabilities.

VMF-221's experience is best understood when viewed against the larger progression of the Pacific War. For the first year, competing requirements to rapidly expand marine aviation while concurrently defending advance bases contributed to the disaster at Midway. As marine and navy aviators gained experience, naval fighting squadrons innovated and proved capable of defeating Japanese aircraft while flying the F4F Wildcat. Once marine squadrons received the F4U Corsair, their combat edge widened. The rate of attrition of Japanese aviation increased as America's industrial mobilization accelerated production. By 1945, the Pacific Fleet could exploit its superiority in numbers, logistics, technology, and experience to seize advance bases close to Japan and bring the fight to the home islands.

VMF-221's story has implications for American naval planners in the twenty-first century, but there are limitations to its relevance. In 2018, Gen. David H. Berger, then Commandant of the U.S. Marine Corps, instructed his marines, "We should ask ourselves—what do the Fleet Commanders want from the Marine Corps, and what does the Navy need from the Marine Corps?" In 1942, the fleet commander wanted marine squadrons to defend advance bases. In 1943, the fleet commander wanted marine squadrons to help the fleet achieve air superiority and sea control and attrite Japanese aviation as naval aviation's land-based component. In 1945, the fleet commander wanted marine fighting squadrons aboard carriers to protect the fleet from special attack aircraft and to support landing forces ashore.

In 2020, the U.S. naval services adopted a unifying naval doctrine that integrated the Fleet Marine Force into the fleet to "combine the effects of sea-based and land-based fires, enabling our forces to mass combat power at times and places of our choosing."[2] The Marine Corps' underlying doctrinal publication, the *Tentative Manual for Expeditionary Advanced Base Operations*, directs marine aviation to help the fleet locate the enemy while protecting the fleet from enemy scouts, to digitally communicate with air force and army elements as well as marine and navy ones, and to quickly reach across the battlespace to strike enemy forces. The *Manual* further indicates that marine and navy aviation should integrate under a single commander.[3] These roles resemble some of the functions marine aviation performed for the fleet from 1941 to 1945, when marine squadrons scouted, intercepted enemy scouts and strikes, integrated with army air force and navy squadrons, and helped the fleet commander mass combat power across the battlespace. The primary differences between the past and the present lie in the degrees to which each of these can be accomplished.

Many of the factors contributing to VMF-221's performance will be relevant to the Pacific Fleet in the twenty-first century. Aircraft numbers and capabilities as well as aircrew proficiency will likely give the side possessing them an advantage in future conflicts. The Pacific Ocean is still vast, and Pacific islands still present a harsh climate that will confound logisticians. Carriers still give the fleet mobility and simplify aircraft maintenance and supply; they also still consolidate aviation combat power aboard a warship vulnerable to enemy strikes.

Modern American naval doctrine also emphasizes maintaining combat-ready forces forward to deter aggression and prevail in conflict.[4] Naval experts have cautioned the naval services against trying to keep so large a fraction of their now smaller fleet deployed forward. The operational tempo of U.S. naval forces overseas has challenged the navy's ability to maintain readiness for combat and still operate safely.[5] In a manner that echoes VMF-221's tribulations on Midway, America's commitment to maintain a heavy forward naval presence in the western Pacific will compete with the fleet's ability to keep its people, aircraft, and warships ready to fight.

In these instances, VMF-221's experience in World War II offers historical examples that may be relevant for today's naval professionals. However, application of VMF-221's experiences should acknowledge the context in which this squadron operated. The rapid expansion of marine aviation that began in 1941 is unlikely to be duplicated in the foreseeable future, even in a conflict with a near-peer competitor. Likewise, the United States cannot mobilize its shipbuilding industry today as it did in the 1930s to build the fleet that defeated Japan in the 1940s. Nor is it likely to be able to replace its principal combat aircraft in the first couple years of a major war. The U.S. naval services' next fight will likely be a come-as-you-are affair. Transformation on the scale of the backdrop to VMF-221's war is implausible.

As the U.S. Navy and Marine Corps seek to answer General Berger's questions—what do the fleet commanders want from the Marine Corps, and what does the Navy need from the Marine Corps?—they would be well served to reflect upon the role of marine aviation in World War II. As VMF-221's story suggests, the answers to these questions could be well informed by a careful understanding of marine aviation's effectiveness in support of the Pacific Fleet and the factors that made it effective.

★NOTES★

Introduction

1. Sherrod, *History of Marine Corps Aviation*, 31–32; Owen, "The Marine Corps' Air War over the Pacific."
2. Berger, *Commandant's Planning Guidance*, 4.
3. ONI, *Japanese Aircraft Manual* ONI-249.

Chapter 1. VMF-221 and Marine Aviation prior to World War II

1. RG 127 A1 1052 Box 30, VMF-221 unit history. [Hereafter VMF-221 unit history].
2. Shaw, Ludwig, and Hough, *Pearl Harbor to Guadalcanal*, 47.
3. Johnson, *Marine Corps Aviation: The Early Years*, 68, 72.
4. Spector, *Eagle against the Sun*, 1.
5. Sherrod, *History of Marine Corps Aviation*, 32–33.
6. Naval Expansion Act, 19 July 1940, *United States Statutes at Large, 1939–41*, vol. 54, pt. 1, 394–96, 779–80.
7. U.S. Marine Corps, *Marine Corps Reserve: A History*, 59.
8. Sherrod, *History of Marine Corps Aviation*, 33; RG 127 A1 1052 Box 29, VMF-221 war diary, November 1941–March 1942; VMF-221 muster roll, January 1942.
9. Carl, *Pushing the Envelope*, 18–19; Larkins, *U.S. Navy and Marine Corps Aircraft*, 92; RG 38 NAID 77686449, USS *Saratoga* war history, 1.
10. Sherrod, *History of Marine Corps Aviation*, 463.
11. VMF-221 unit history, 2; VMF-221 muster roll, April 1942; Prange, "Miracle at Midway," Prange Papers, Box 3, Folder 3.0, Lt. Gen. Verne J. McCaul, USMC (Ret.), interview by Robert Barde, 1 June 1966, 1.
12. Maj. Gen. Marion Carl, USMC (Ret.), interview by Benis M. Frank and Major Gary W. Parker, USMC, USMC HD OHC, 117; Carl, *Pushing the Envelope*, 18–19.
13. Brown, "'Indian Joe' Bauer"; Brown, ed., "War Diary of Harold W. Bauer," " [hereafter Bauer diary].
14. Carl interview by Frank and Parker, 89; Carl, *Pushing the Envelope*, 18.
15. VMF-221 unit history, 3; VMF-221 muster roll, April 1942; *Saratoga* war history, 2; Bauer diary.
16. Miller, *War Plan Orange*, 269–71.
17. Millett, *Semper Fidelis*, 328.

18. U.S. Navy, *F.T.P. 167*, 151–58.
19. Sherrod, *History of Marine Corps Aviation*, 32–33.
20. Miller, *War Plan Orange*, 184, 191, 194–202.
21. MCPPC, Roy S. Geiger Collection (COLL/2349), Geiger to Vice Adm. F. J. Horne, 26 March 1937, cited by Peterson in "Transformation between the World Wars."
22. Bureau of Aeronautics, vol. 20, *Marine Corps Aviation*, 2.
23. BuAer, vol. 20, *Marine Corps Aviation*, 10–11.
24. Maj. F. D. Weir, "The Organization of Aviation Units," 1941, MCPPC, Lectures, Collection 3983, Box 10, Marine Corps Schools, 1940–41, Folder 23; Johnson, *Marine Corps Aviation: The Early Years*, 72; Sherrod, *History of Marine Corps Aviation*, 33; Shaw et al., *Pearl Harbor to Guadalcanal*, 68.
25. Weir, "Organization of Aviation Units" (1941).
26. MCPPC, James L. Neefus Papers, Collection 2376, Box 1, "CO VMF-221 to CO MAG-22," 7 May 1942.
27. Maas, *F2A Buffalo*, 37; VMF-221 unit history, 4, 37.
28. Tillman, *Wildcat*, 11–14.
29. Lundstrom, *The First Team*, 11–15, 139, 467–68; Tillman, *Wildcat*, 15–17; Maas, *F2A Buffalo*, 37–41; Dunn, *Exploding Fuel Tanks*, 44.
30. Carl interview, Frank and Parker, 97.
31. Larkins, *U.S. Navy and Marine Corps Aircraft*, 92.
32. This section draws primarily from two sources: Maj. William J. Wallace, "Fighting Aviation," MCPPC, Lectures, Collection 3983, Box 10, Marine Corps Schools, 1940–41, Folder 20; and Commander, Aircraft Battle Force, *USF-74, Current Tactical Orders and Doctrine U.S. Fleet Aircraft*, vol. 1, *Carrier Aircraft*, 106–19.
33. Naval Air Operational Training Command, *Fundamental Fixed Gunnery Approaches* (motion picture); Lundstrom, *The First Team*, 458–68.
34. *Fundamental Fixed Gunnery Approaches*; Lundstrom, *The First Team*, 458–68.
35. Nalty and Moody, *Officer Procurement*, 7–10.
36. BuAer, vol. 20, *Marine Corps Aviation*, 67–69, 76; BuAer, vol. 22, *Aviation Personnel, 1939–1945*, 68–70.
37. Owen, "U.S. Marine Corps Aviation in the Second World War," 57.
38. BuAer, vol. 20, *Marine Corps Aviation*, 68, 76, 112.
39. "NATC Pensacola, Florida U.S. Naval Intermediate Flight Training."
40. BuAer, vol. 20, *Marine Corps Aviation*, 68.
41. *USF-74*, 106.
42. Johnson, *Marine Corps Aviation: The Early Years*, 72–76.
43. Carl, *Pushing the Envelope*, 18–19.
44. VMF-221 muster rolls, July 1941, October 1941, January 1942.
45. James Law, interview by Maria Carrillo, 26 June 2007, MCAS El Toro OHP, 3–4, 7; Public Affairs Unit 4-1, *Marine Corps Reserve* (1966), 59.
46. VMF-221 muster rolls, July 1941, October 1941, January 1942.

47. Office of the Deputy Chief of Naval Operations (Air), vol. 13, *Aviation Training*, 317, vol. 14, pp. 74, 76, 86. Hereafter DCNO (Air).
48. Fisher, *Sustaining the Carrier War*, 69, 92, 223; MarBks [Marine Barracks], NAS Jacksonville muster rolls, April, July 1941; MarBks, NAS Pensacola muster rolls, April, July, and October 1941; VMF-221 muster roll, January 1942.
49. *Jane's Fighting Aircraft*, 184–85, 187–88, 191.
50. Lundstrom, *The First Team*, 480.
51. Dunn, "Mitsubishi Zero 21—A Question of Speed."
52. *Jane's Fighting Aircraft*; 187–88; Parshall and Tully, *Shattered Sword*, 78–80.
53. Lundstrom, *The First Team*, 480.
54. *Jane's Fighting Aircraft*, 191; Bicheno, *Midway*, 56.
55. *Jane's Fighting Aircraft*, 184–85; Bicheno, *Midway*, 57.
56. *Jane's Fighting Aircraft*, 185.
57. Parshall and Tully, *Shattered Sword*, 80–82; Dull, *Battle History of the IJN*, 14–15.
58. Lundstrom, *The First Team*, 187, 454–57, 486–89.

Chapter 2. December 1941–May 1942

1. Spector, *Eagle against the Sun*, 147.
2. OPNAV to CINCPAC, CINCAF, 9 December 1941, 0120, Nimitz, *Graybook*, 1:6.
3. Shaw et al., *Pearl Harbor to Guadalcanal*, 66–68, 100–102.
4. Sherrod, *History of Marine Corps Aviation*, 1, 33, 38; Shaw et al., *Pearl Harbor to Guadalcanal*, 71–73.
5. Lundstrom, *The First Team*, 26–27.
6. William Hall, Oral History, part 3, "Wake Island," National World War II Museum.
7. Urwin, *Facing Fearful Odds*, 412; VMF-221 unit history, 3–4.
8. Nimitz, *Graybook*, 1:49; Lundstrom, *The First Team*, 34–35; Urwin, *Facing Fearful Odds*, 413, 418.
9. Bauer diary.
10. Urwin, *Facing Fearful Odds*, 417–18, 518.
11. Lundstrom, *The First Team*, 36–40, 44.
12. Nimitz, *Graybook*, 1:71–72; Lundstrom, *The First Team*, 44; Urwin, *Facing Fearful Odds*, 518.
13. Bauer diary.
14. VMF-221 war diary, November 1941–March 1942, 3–4.
15. Bauer diary; VMF-221 war diary, November 1941–March 1942, 3–5; RG 38 NAID 77629368, BuAer interview with Lt. Col. Ira Kimes, 31 August 1942, 12.
16. VMF-221 war diary, November 1941–March 1942, 4–5.
17. VMF-221 war diary, November 1941–March 1942, 4–5, 8.
18. COMINCH TO CINCPAC, 30 December 1941, 1740, Nimitz, *Graybook*, 1:125.
19. CINCPAC estimate 2 January 1942, "Employment of Carrier Forces in January," Nimitz, *Graybook*, 1:5, 7.

20. Heinl, *Marines at Midway*, 7, 16, 17; ONI, *Battle of Midway*, 6.
21. Heinl, *Marines at Midway*, 48, 51; "The SCR-268 Radar," *Electronics* (September 1945), 100; Matt, "SCR-270/SCR-271 Radar," 36.
22. McCaul interview, Barde, 1.
23. Kimes interview, BuAer, 9, 12–13; McCaul interview, Barde, 2.
24. Heinl, *Marines at Midway*, 12–15.
25. Lundstrom, *The First Team*, 12; National Naval Aviation Museum, "SB2U Vindicator."
26. Heinl, *Marines at Midway*, 17–18.
27. VMF-221 unit history, 11.
28. RG 127 A1 1052 Box 29, CO, VMF-221 to CO, MAG-21, "Enemy Submarine Contact, Report of," 11 February 1942; Heinl, *Marines at Midway*, 18; Allison, "Out in Front at Midway."
29. VMF-221 war diaries, November 1941–March 1942, 16–17; Box 30, VMF-221 unit history, 16–17; RG 38 NAID 133892566, NAS Midway Island war diary, March 1942, 2–3; Dickey obituary.
30. Sherrod, *History of Marine Corps Aviation*, 434–35.
31. Rowell to Halsey, cited in Sherrod, *History of Marine Corps Aviation*, 54.
32. VMF-221 unit history, 7–24.
33. Bauer diary, undated entry.
34. VMF-221 war diaries, 30 November 1941–31 March, April, and May 1942. Figures do not include VMF-222.
35. Kimes interview, BuAer, 14; VMF-221 war diary, April and May 1942.
36. COMAMPHORPAC to CINCPAC, 21 May 1942, 1805, Nimitz, *Graybook*, 1:526.
37. VMF-221 war diary, 30 November 1941–31 March 1942.
38. RG 127 A1 Box 10, MAG-22 Midway Action Report, Executive Officer's Report, 7 June 1942, 2 [hereafter MAG-22 XO's report].
39. VMF-221 war diary, May 1942.
40. *USF-74*, 120.
41. Wallace, "Fighting Aviation," 12.
42. VMF-221 unit history, 15, 19; RG 38 NAID 133901293, VMSB-241 war diary, April 1942, 3–4; RG 38 NAID 77630627, VMSB-231 war history, 8.
43. VMF-221 unit history, 15, 20; Heinl, *Marines at Midway*, 19; VMSB-241 war diary, April 1942, 3–4.
44. VMSB-241 war diary, April 1942, 5.
45. VMF-221 unit history, 7–24.
46. Heinl, *Marines at Midway*, 19.
47. VMF-221 unit history, 23; "Floyd B. Parks, Maj, USMC," *USNA Virtual Memorial Hall*.
48. Carl, *Pushing the Envelope*, 22.
49. Smithsonian Institute, "ZB-1 Radio Homing Adapter and Security Cover"; Klase, "Aircraft-to-Carrier Homing"; Kern, "Striking Eagles," 19.
50. *USF-74*, 49, 52.

51. Allison, "Out in Front at Midway."
52. Shaw et al., *Pearl Harbor to Guadalcanal*, 219; Heinl, *Marines at Midway*, 24.
53. Shaw et al., *Pearl Harbor to Guadalcanal*, 220.
54. RG 313-58-3397 Box 01 Folder 013, U.S. NAS Midway Island, War Diary, 16. Retrieved 1 January 2023 from http://www.midway42.org/Midway_AAR/NavalAirStationMidway.aspx.
55. Heinl, *Marines at Midway*, 24–25; McCaul interview, Barde, 1; 6th Defense Battalion muster roll, January 1942. Some accounts ascribe the detonation to a sailor connecting the firing circuit. McCaul's account seems more credible. The official rank in 1942 was "marine gunner." This was changed to warrant officer in October 1943.
56. MAG-22 XO's report, 1–4.

Chapter 3. Battle of Midway, June 1942

1. VMF-221 unit history, 22.
2. Lundstrom, quoted by Russell, *No Right to Win*, 186–87.
3. Symonds, *Midway*, 182.
4. NHHC, "*Kitty Hawk* I (APV-1), 1941–1946" (28 July 2015).
5. COM-14 to NAS MIDWAY 20 0650, Nimitz, *Graybook*, 1:499–500.
6. 20 0359 CINCPAC TO COMINCH, Nimitz, *Graybook*, 1:487.
7. Nimitz to Capt. Milo F. Draemel, 23 May 1942, cited in Heinl, *Marines at Midway*, 23.
8. Nimitz to Capt. Arthur C. Davis, undated, cited in Heinl, *Marines at Midway*, 23.
9. CinCPacFlt Operation Plan no. 29-42, 27 May 1942, 6.
10. Op-Plan 29-42, 7–8.
11. Shaw et al., *Pearl Harbor to Guadalcanal*, 219; Horan et al., "Orders of Battle, Midway and Aleutians"; Nimitz, *Graybook*, 1:547; Symonds, *Midway*, 211; ONI, *Battle of Midway*, 6.
12. McCaul interview, Barde, 1.
13. Kimes interview, BuAer, 4–8.
14. Symonds, *Midway*, 188.
15. Heinl, *Marines at Midway*, 23.
16. NAS Midway war diary, 15, 27–28; Annex C to MAG-22 XO's report, 1; Symonds, *Midway*, 215–16.
17. RG 127 A1 1054 Box 10, MAG-22 Midway action report, CO MAG-22 "Battle of Midway Islands, Report of," 7 June 1942, 2.
18. RG 127 A1 Box 29, CO VMF-221, "Enemy Contact, Report on," 6 June 1942.
19. Aerology Section, *Aerology and Naval Warfare*, 3; Parshall and Tully, *Shattered Sword*, 109.
20. Annex C to MAG-22 XO's report, 5–9; Allison, "Out in Front at Midway;" RG 127 A1 Box 29, 2nd Lt. Roy A. Corry, USMCR, statement, 6 June 1942. All USMC Midway pilot statements are from this source unless indicated otherwise.

21. Annex C to MAG-22 XO's report, 5–9; UMD Prange papers, "Miracle at Midway," Box 2, Folder 9.0, Box 2, Folder 10.0, Colonel John F. Carey, USMC (ret.), interview by Robert Barde, 1 July 1966, 1.
22. Carl, *Pushing the Envelope*, 2.
23. Allison, "Out in Front at Midway"; Capt. Kirk A. Armistead, statement, 4 June 1942; and 2nd Lt. Charles M. Kunz, USMCR, statement, 4 June 1942; Carl, *Pushing the Envelope*, 2.
24. CO VMF-221, "Enemy Contact, Report on," 6 June 1942; 2nd Lt. Charles S. Hughes, USMCR, statement, 4 June 1942; 2nd Lt. William V. Brooks, USMCR, statement, 4 June 1942.
25. Annex C to MAG-22 XO's report, 5–9.
26. Carl, *Pushing the Envelope*, 3.
27. Corry statement; Annex C to MAG-22 XO's report, 5–9.
28. Allison, "Out in Front at Midway."
29. Parshall and Tully, *Shattered Sword*, 80–82, 125–26, 200–201; Dull, *Battle History of the IJN*, 14–15; Allison, "Out in Front at Midway"; Carey interview, Barde, 1.
30. Allison, "Out in Front at Midway"; 2nd Lt. Clayton Melbourne Canfield, USMCR, statement, 6 June 1942; "Statement of Captain John Frank Carey, USMC," from Horan, "Midway Combat Reports"; Carey interview, Barde, 1–2.
31. Carl, *Pushing the Envelope*, 3, 23–25; Capt. Marion Carl statement, 6 June 1942; Carl interview, Frank and Parker, 94–96.
32. Carl, *Pushing the Envelope*, 3, 23–25; Carl statement, 6 June 1942; Carl interview, Frank and Parker, 94–96.
33. Carl, *Pushing the Envelope*, 3, 23–25; Carl statement, 6 June 1942; Carl interview, Frank and Parker, 94–96.
34. 2nd Lt. Darrel D. Irwin, USMCR, statement, 6 June 1942.
35. Parshall and Tully, *Shattered Sword*, 200.
36. Irwin statement.
37. Annex C to MAG-22 XO's report, 5–9.
38. Capt. Philip R. White, USMC, statement, 6 June 1942; Armistead statement.
39. White statement.
40. "Statement of Captain Herbert Thompson Merrill, USMC," from Horan, "Midway Combat Reports."
41. White statement.
42. Armistead statement.
43. Capt. William C. Humberd, USMC, statement, 4 June 1942.
44. 2nd Lt. Charles M. Kunz, USMCR, statement, 4 June 1942.
45. Brooks statement.
46. Armistead statement.
47. Humberd statement.
48. Kunz statement.

49. Brooks statement.
50. Annex C to MAG-22 XO's report, 5–9.
51. Corry statement.
52. Parshall and Tully, *Shattered Sword*, 202.
53. Annex C to MAG-22 XO's report, 2; RG 38 NAID 133911503, Capt. Logan C. Ramsey, USN, "Air Operations of Midway Defense Forces during Battle of Midway 30 May 1942 to 6 June 1942," 15 June 1942, 5; VMF-221 unit history, 26.
54. Brooks statement.
55. Armistead statement.
56. Humberd statement.
57. Kunz statement.
58. Corry statement.
59. Canfield statement.
60. Carl, *Pushing the Envelope*, 25; White statement.
61. Carl, *Pushing the Envelope*, 26.
62. Pedroncelli, "The Lone Avenger."
63. Symonds, *Midway*, 236; "Battle of Midway: Army Air Forces."
64. *Jane's Fighting Aircraft*, 234, 246.
65. RG 127 A1 1054 Box 10, 2nd Lt. Emmer P. Thompson, USMCR, statement 7 June 1942; RG 38 NAID 133933925, VMSB-241 war diary, June 1942, 3–4; Kimes interview, BuAer, 1.
66. Parshall and Tully, *Shattered Sword*, 154, 177; Symonds, *Midway*, 233–36.
67. Parshall and Tully, *Shattered Sword*, 154.
68. RG 127 1054 Box 10, statement of Capt. Elmer G. Glidden, Jr., USMCR(V), 7 June 1942; 2nd Lt. Jesse D. Rollow, USMCR, statement, 7 June 1942; Parshall and Tully, *Shattered Sword*, 156, 176, 178.
69. "Battle of Midway: Army Air Forces"; Parshall and Tully, *Shattered Sword*, 156, 179–80.
70. RG 127 A1 1054 Box 10, VMSB-241 statements 7 June 1942.
71. RG 127 A1 1052 Box 10, Lt. Col. Ira L. Kimes, USMC, "Preliminary Report of Marine Aircraft Group Twenty-Two of Battle of Midway June 4, 5, 6, 1942," 8 June 1942, 4.
72. Symonds, *Midway*, 245, 276–308.
73. Ramsey, "Air Operations," 5–6.
74. Parshall and Tully, *Shattered Sword*, 269, 290, 292, 311, 316.
75. Symonds, *Midway*, 334–35.
76. Ramsey, "Air Operations," 6.
77. Kimes, "Preliminary Report, MAG-22," 4.
78. RG 38 NAID 77629368, Marine Aircraft Group 22 war history, 26 December 1944, 57.
79. Symonds, *Midway*, 341–42.
80. VMSB-241 war diary, June 1942, 8; VMSB-241 statements, 7 June 1942; Parshall and Tully, *Shattered Sword*, 362–63.
81. Symonds, *Midway*, 352–55; Parshall and Tully, *Shattered Sword*, 369–71.

Chapter 4. VMF-221's Effectiveness at Midway

1. CO VMF-221, "Enemy Contact, Report on," 2.
2. CO VMF-221, "Enemy Contact, Report on," 1.
3. RG 127 A1 1052 Box 10, Lt. Col. Ira L. Kimes, USMC, "Battle of Midway Island, Report of," 7 June 1942, 2–3.
4. Parshall and Tully, *Shattered Sword*, 204.
5. Nimitz to Davis.
6. Op-Plan 29-42, 7–8.
7. Parshall and Tully, *Shattered Sword*, 154–55, 186–89, 205, 210, 215–16.
8. Sherrod, *History of Marine Corps Aviation*, 444–45, 463–64.
9. Armistead statement.
10. CO VMF-221, "Enemy Contact, Report on," 2.
11. Carey statement.
12. Corry statement.
13. Humberd statement.
14. Kunz statement.
15. RG 127 1052 Box 29, statement of 2ndLt. J. C. Musselman, USMCR, 6 June 1942.
16. 2nd Lt. Hyde Phillips, USMCR, statement, 6 June 1942.
17. White statement.
18. CINCPACFLT to COMINCH, Subj: Battle of Midway, CincPac A16/(90) Ser. 01693 of 6/15/42, published 20 March 2018, NHHC Action Reports, WWII, Battle of Midway.
19. Maas, *F2A Buffalo*, 10–12.
20. Wallace, "Fighting Aviation," 6–8.
21. VMF-221 unit history, 23–24; Heinl, *Marines at Midway*, 53; Kimes, "Preliminary Report, MAG-22," 5–6.
22. CO MAG-22, "Battle of Midway Islands, Report of," 4.
23. Kimes interview, BuAer, 9; Annex C to MAG-22 XO's report, 1.
24. 20 0359 CINCPAC TO COMINCH, Nimitz, *Graybook*, 1:487.
25. Kimes interview, BuAer, 2.
26. MAG-22 XO's Report, 2–3.
27. Lundstrom, *The First Team*, 12; NNAM, "SB2U Vindicator"; *Jane's Fighting Aircraft*, 218, 226, 234.
28. Symonds, *Midway*, 212.
29. Lundstrom, *The First Team*, 480.
30. Musselman statement; Phillips statement.
31. Lundstrom, *The First Team*, 187, 454–57, 486–89.
32. Armistead statement.
33. Corry statement.

Chapter 5. Refitting, Rearming, and Redeploying, June 1942–February 1943

1. Sherrod, *History of Marine Corps Aviation*, 434.
2. VMF-221 muster rolls, July and October 1942; VMF 221 unit history, Appendix: "Schedule of Commissioned Personnel Changes, July 1941–December 1944," 1–7; and "Schedule of Monthly Changes in Enlisted Personnel," 4–5.
3. RG 127 A1 237-H, 2nd MAW Correspondence 1940–1946, Box 1, "Organization of Marine Corps Aircraft Units," 10 June 1942.
4. RG 127 A1 1054 Box 11, MAG-21, Senior Naval Aviator Present, 2nd MAW Hawaii, to CG, 2nd MAW, 10 July 1942.
5. "Commissioned Personnel Changes," 6–7; and "Monthly Changes in Enlisted Personnel," 5.
6. RG 38 NAID 133988362, VMF-221 war diary, September 1942, 2–3, 22, October 1942, 2–3; November 1942, 2–4, December 1942, 2–3; VMF-221 muster rolls, October 1942 and January 1943; "Commissioned Personnel Changes," 10.
7. VMF-221 war diary August 1942, 2.
8. James Swett, "Combat in the Solomon Islands," in Caswell, *Fighting Falcons*, 69.
9. Burns, Biography submitted by graduating students; Naval Aviator no. 6199 certificate, 2nd Lt. Robert R. Burns. Courtesy Jim Burns.
10. VMF-221 unit history, 4; VMF-221 muster rolls, October 1941, January and April 1942.
11. VMF-221 unit history, 28; and "Commissioned Personnel Changes," 6; Kimes, "Preparations of MAG-22 for Battle," in Heinl, *Marines at Midway*, 51–52; HqSq-21, MAG-21, 2nd MAW, FMF, C/O FPO, San Francisco, California, muster roll, July 1942.
12. VMF-221 unit history, "Commissioned Personnel Changes," 7; VMF-221 war diary, August 1942, 13, 18; VMF-211 muster roll, July 1942.
13. MCAA, *Chronolog*, 116.
14. VMF-221 muster roll, February 1943.
15. VMF-221 unit history; "Commissioned Personnel Changes," 9–10.
16. VMF-221 muster rolls, July 1942, October 1942, and February 1943; HqSq, 2nd MAW, FMF, NAS San Diego muster roll, July 1942; MarBks, NAS Corpus Christi muster roll, July 1942; MarBks, NAS Miami muster rolls, July and October 1942; BuAer, vol. 20, *Marine Aviation*, 81; BuAer, vol. 22, *Aviation Personnel, 1939–1945*, 68–70.
17. Museum of Flight. The American Fighter Aces Association Oral Interviews. "James E. Swett Oral History Interview." Interview by Eric M. Hammel, circa 1980–90, part 2, 4.
18. National Museum of the United States Air Force, "Civilian Pilot Training Program."
19. Swett interview, Hammel, pt. 2, p. 4.
20. "Colonel James Elms Swett, USMCR (Deceased)," Marine Corps History Division, Marine Corps Medal of Honor Recipients.
21. MCAS Quantico muster roll, July 1942.

22. Swett interview, Hammel, pt. 2, p. 5; HqSq, MCAS Quantico muster roll, April 1942, and Air Reg. Squadron 2 muster rolls, July and October 1942.
23. Lundstrom, *The First Team*, 453–54.
24. RG 38 NAID 133992732, ComFltAir West Coast, War Diary of Aircraft Southern Sector, Western Sea Frontier Force TG 94.1, October 1941, 1; NAID 133953491 August 1942; NAID 133978649 September 1942.
25. DeBlanc, *Guadalcanal Air War*, 35–41.
26. Grossnick, *United States Naval Aviation*, 414.
27. AirEngSq-21, Base Air Detachment Two, NAS San Diego muster roll, January 1942; AvDet MarBks, NAS Pensacola muster roll, April 1942; VMF-221 muster roll, October 1942; VMSB-231, MarAvDet, MAG-21, 2nd MAW, FMF muster roll, January 1942.
28. Muster rolls: Marine Corps Central Recruiting Division, Chicago, December 1939; Recruit Depot, San Diego December 1939; H&SSq-2, 2nd MAG, FMF, NAS San Diego, January and October 1940; H&SSq-21, MAG-21, 2nd MAW, FMF, Ewa, Oahu, T.H., July and October 1941; H&S Co., Force Special Trainers, MarFor, 14th Naval District, Pearl Harbor, T.H.; VMF-221, April and July 1942 and February 1943.
29. VMF-221 muster rolls, April, July, and October 1942, January and February 1943.
30. MarBks, NAS, Pensacola muster rolls, April, July, and October 1941.
31. VMF-221 muster roll, February 1943.
32. RG 38 A1 UD 351, VMF-221 war diaries, NAIDs 133945851 July 1942, 7–8; 133962535 August 1942, 4, 12; September 1942, 15–16; 134002532 October 1942, 3; 134025330 November 1942, 2; 134050660 December 1942, 2–3; 134084169 January 1943, 2; and 78417788 February 1943, 2, 4.
33. Tillman, *Wildcat*, 17.
34. Linn, *F4F Wildcat*, 22.
35. Tillman, *Wildcat*, 17, 83; Larry Dwyer, "Grumman F4F Wildcat," *The Aviation History Online Museum*, 2024; "Wildcat," *Naval Aviation News*, December 1971, 20–26.
36. CO VF-6 to ComAirBatFor, "F4F-4 Airplane—Performance of," 6 April 1942, cited by Lundstrom, *The First Team*, 140.
37. CO USS *Enterprise* to CinCPacFlt, "The Battle of Santa Cruz, October 26, 1942—Report of," 10 November 1942, retrieved from http://www.cv6.org/ship/logs/action19421026.htm.
38. RG 38 NAID 278481304, Capt. Joe J. Foss, USMC, interview by BuAer, 26 April 1943, 10.
39. CO USS *Enterprise*, Santa Cruz report, 10 November 1942.
40. RG 38 NAID 134067189, Maj. Frederick R. Payne, USMC, in BuAer interview of Payne and Maj. Robert E. Galer, USMC, 6 January 1943, 9.
41. BuAer to ComAirBatFor, 4 February 1942, cited by Lundstrom, *The First Team*, 140.
42. *Jane's Fighting Aircraft*, 189.

43. Porter, *Ace!*, 40–45; DeBlanc, *Guadalcanal Air War*, 32–33; Warner Chapman, "Solomon Island," in Caswell, *Fighting Falcons*, 67.
44. RG 38 NAID 134050698, VMF-213 war diary, December 1942, 2–4; RG 38 NAID 134084178, VMF-213 war diary, January 1943, 2–4; RG 127 A1 1052 Box 30, VMF-221 unit history, 37–38.
45. RG 38 NAID 135904639, BuAer interview, Maj. J. N. Renner, USMC, 17 July 1943, 2, 4.
46. Renner interview, BuAer, 1–2.
47. Lundstrom, *The First Team*, 477–85.
48. RG 127 A1 Box 42, MAG-12, Warfare Operations, 1942–1943: ComAirForPacFlt to AirForPacFlt, "Air Operations Memorandum 5-43," 3–4.
49. Renner interview, BuAer, 3.
50. Swett interview, Hammel, pt. 2, p. 6.
51. RG 38 NAID 134027140, MCAS Ewa, Oahu, war diary, December 1942, 6; NAID 134075956, MCAS Ewa, Oahu war diary, January 1943, 3; VMF-221 war diary, December 1942 and January 1943, passim.
52. VMF-221 war diary, September 1942, 4, and October 1942, 3; VMF-221 unit history, 36–37; VMF-221 muster roll, February 1942.
53. VMF-221 unit history, 37–38.
54. Swett interview, Hammel, pt. 2, p. 6; VMF-221 muster roll, February 1942; VMF-221 unit history, 39.
55. Burns, naval aviator certificate.
56. NHHC, "*Nassau I* (ACV-16), 1942–1959," *Sextant*, 14 March 2016; Dreadnaughtz, "*Bogue* Class (1941)," *Naval Encyclopedia*, 6 June 2020.
57. RG 38 NAID 134122561, USS *Nassau* war diary, February 1943, 8–10.
58. VMF-221 muster roll, February 1943.
59. VMF-221 unit history, 38.
60. Winnia, *Diary of a Corsair Pilot*, 7.
61. Roland W. Charles, *Troopships of World War II* (Washington, DC: The Army Transportation Association, 1947), 50.
62. Chapman, "Solomon Island," 67; USS *Nassau* war diary, February 1943, 13–15; RG 38 NAID 134140737, USS *Nassau* war diary, March 1943, 3–4.
63. Winnia, *Diary of a Corsair Pilot*, 5–12.
64. NHHC, "The Sinking of USS *Liscome Bay*," *History Up Close*, 24 November 2014.
65. USS *Nassau* war diary, March 1943, 4; Winnia, *Diary of a Corsair Pilot*, 12.
66. VMF-221 war diary, 39.
67. VMF-221 war diary, 39.
68. Morison, *Breaking the Bismarcks Barrier*, 103–6.
69. Winnia, *Diary of a Corsair Pilot*, 12–13, 18; VMF-221 war diary, 40.
70. VMF-221 war diary, 41.

Chapter 6. Air War in the South Pacific, March 1943

1. Shaw and Kane, *Isolation of Rabaul*, 8–10, 14, 28–29.
2. JCS to MacArthur, Nimitz, Halsey, 29 March 1943, in Nimitz, *Graybook*, 3:1473–74; see also Morton, *Strategy and Command*, 398–99.
3. JCS to MacArthur, Nimitz, Halsey, 29 March 1943.
4. Hirrel, *Bismarck Archipelago*, 3.
5. JCS to MacArthur, Nimitz, Halsey, 29 March 1943.
6. "Col. Edward Pugh Awarded Legion of Merit as Leader"; Carl, interview with Frank and Parker, 85.
7. VMF-221 unit history, 41.
8. RG 127 A1 1055 Box 27, "ComAir Command, Solomons Fighter Availability, Enemy Planes Shot Down, Our Losses, February through July 1943," 7 August 1943, 4.
9. Maj. Gen. John P. Condon, interview by Cargill Hall, 8 March 1989, USMC HD OHC 207.
10. Sherrod, *History of Marine Corps Aviation*, 457, 461; RG 38 NAID 78208287, 2nd Marine Aircraft Wing war diary, March 1943, 1.
11. Shaw and Kane, *Isolation of Rabaul*, 456.
12. RG 127 A1 1055 Box 8, Engineering Section memorandum to Chief of Staff, 1st Marine Aircraft Wing, 1 May 1943, 4.
13. Fisher, *Sustaining the Carrier War*, 208–9.
14. Engineering Section to Chief of Staff, 1st MAW, 1 May 1943, 1–5.
15. RG 127 A1 1055 Box 27, ComAirSols fighter availability February–July 1943, 4.
16. RG 38 NAID 278496541, BuAer interview, Cdr. Seldon B. Spangler, USN, 23 April 1943, 1.
17. Spangler interview, BuAer, 3.
18. Spangler interview, BuAer, 4–5.
19. Spangler interview, BuAer, 3.
20. Spangler interview, BuAer, 7, 9.
21. Spangler interview, BuAer, 12–13.
22. Spangler interview, BuAer, 17.
23. Spangler interview, BuAer, 8.
24. Spangler interview, BuAer, 8.
25. Renner interview, BuAer, 7.
26. Spangler interview, BuAer, 3.
27. RG 127 A1 1053 Box 1, Enclosure (A) to Medical Department memorandum to Lt. Col. Hagenah, USMC, 14 April 1943, "Table of Non-Effective Personnel, Monthly and Total Breakdown," 1.
28. RG 127 A1 1053 Box 1, CG 1st MAW, Wing General Order Number 22, 1943, 25 April 1943, 1–2.
29. Spangler interview, 10.

30. Morison, *Breaking the Bismarcks Barrier*, 100–101.
31. VMF-221 unit history, 41.
32. Winnia, *Diary of a Corsair Pilot*, 29–32.
33. "Guadalcanal Province Weather by Month, Weather Averages," *Climate-Data.org*.
34. Porter, *Ace!*, 119–20.
35. MCPPC, General Roy S. Geiger Papers, 1st MAW Intelligence Section, "Performance Data Sheets," undated.
36. 1st MAW Intel Section, "Performance Data Sheets."
37. Spangler interview, BuAer, 15.
38. Renner interview, BuAer, 11–12.
39. Dyer, *The Amphibians Came to Conquer*, 498.
40. Morison, *Breaking the Bismarcks Barrier*, 94–95.
41. Kramer J. Rohfleisch, "The Central Solomons," in Craven and Cate, eds., *Guadalcanal to Saipan*, 207.
42. RG 38 NAID 134244554, ComSoPacFor war diary, April 1943, 5–6.
43. Shaw and Kane, *Isolation of Rabaul*, 11; Prados, *Combined Fleet Decoded*, 448–56.
44. Morison, *Breaking the Bismarcks Barrier*, 118.
45. RG 38 NAID 134191951, ComAirSols war diary, April 1943, 4.
46. USMC HD, Archives Branch, PacFlt, SoPacFor, Intelligence Division, "Report on F/D Activities during Japanese Dive-Bombing Attack on Shipping in Guadalcanal-Tulagi Area, April 7, 1943," 1–2; Ross, "Despatch of No. 52 Radar Unit."
47. Payne interview, BuAer, 9.
48. Feldt, "Coastwatching in World War II"; P. A. Selth, "Read William John (Jack) (1905–1992)"; and James Griffin, "Mason, Paul Edward (1901–1972)," *Australian Dictionary of Biography*; Shaw and Kane, *Isolation of Rabaul*, 42–45.
49. Condon, interview by Hall, 208.
50. RG 127 A1 Box 42, MAG-12 Warfare Operations 1942–1943, ComAirPacFlt to AirForPacFlt, "Memorandum on Radar and Fighter Direction," 21 March 1943, 2, 5–6.
51. ComAirPacFlt, "Radar and Fighter Direction," 7–8.

Chapter 7. First Combat Tour, Guadalcanal, 16 March–3 May 1943

1. VMF-221 unit history, 42–44; RG 127 A1 Box 29, VMF-221 war diary, March 1943, 3–5.
2. VMF-221 war diary 4; VMF-221 unit history, 44.
3. Calvin J. Voelker flying log, 10–31 March 1943; "Original U.S. WWII USMC Named Enlisted Fighter Pilot VMF-211 Grouping."
4. VMF-221 war diary, March 1943, 3.
5. VMF-221 unit history, 42–44; VMF-221 war diary, March 1943, 4–5; Shaw and Kane, *Isolation of Rabaul*, 44.
6. Hammel, *Air War Pacific Chronology*, 147–52.

7. Except where indicated otherwise, this narrative is drawn from RG 38 NAID 134191951, ComAirSols war diary, April 1943, 1–2; and RG 127 A1 Box 27, ComAirSols Intelligence Reports, January–June 1943, "Interception of Enemy Fighters over the Russell Islands April 1, 1943," 1–2; GHQ FEAC, Japanese Monograph no. 122, 36.
8. RG 38 NAID 134181788, VMF-124 war diary, April 1943, 1.
9. VMF-124 war diary April 1943, 1; VMF-221 unit history, 45.
10. Swett, "Combat in the Solomon Islands," 69.
11. Hammel, *Air War Pacific Chronology*, 153; Maj. Paul Bechtel, "Riding the Lightning," in Hammel, *American Aces Speak*, 3:102–3.
12. GHQ FEAC, Japanese Monograph no. 122, 36.
13. VMF-221 unit history, 45; RG 38 NAID 134214360, VMF-221 war diary, April 1943, 1.
14. Shaw and Kane, *Isolation of Rabaul*, 467.
15. Voelker flying log, 1–18 April 1943.
16. VMF-221 unit history, 46.
17. VMF-221 unit history, 46.
18. AirSols war diary April 1943, 15; Hammel, *Air War Pacific Chronology*, 155.
19. AirSols war diary April 1943, 15.
20. RG 38 NAID 134175316, VMF-213 war diary, April 1943, 2.
21. Dunn, *South Pacific Air War*, 213.
22. AirSols war diary, April 1943, 16.
23. AirSols war diary, April 1943, 17; VMF-221 unit history, 46.
24. AirSols war diary, April 1943, 16.
25. SoPacFor Intelligence Division, "Report on F/D activities," 1.
26. SoPacFor Intelligence Division, "Report on F/D activities," 2.
27. Cox, *Dark Waters, Starry Skies*, 251.
28. Morison, *Breaking the Bismarcks Barrier*, 120–21.
29. SoPacFor Intelligence Division, "Report on F/D activities," 2; Claringbould, *Operation I-Go*, 50.
30. SoPacFor Intelligence Division, "Report on F/D activities," 2.
31. Morison, *Breaking the Bismarcks Barrier*, 120.
32. SoPacFor Intelligence Division, "Report on F/D activities," 2; Japanese Monograph no. 122, 38.
33. Morison, *Breaking the Bismarcks Barrier*, 120; Prados, *Combined Fleet Decoded*, 457.
34. SoPacFor Intelligence Division, "Report on F/D activities," 2.
35. SoPacFor Intelligence Division, "Report on F/D activities," 3.
36. SoPacFor Intelligence Division, "Report on F/D activities," 3.
37. Claringbould, *Operation I-Go*, 47.
38. Claringbould, *Operation I-Go*, 43–44; Japanese Monograph no. 122, 38.
39. SoPacFor Intelligence Division, "Report on F/D activities," 3–4; RG 38 NAID 135895315, VMF-214 war diary, April 1943, 1–2; VMF-221 unit history, 46–47; VMF-221 war diary,

April 1943, 3–4. These sources conflict. Because the Intelligence Division report relied on interviews conducted immediately after the action, that source is favored.

40. SoPacFor Intelligence Division, "Report on F/D activities," 3; Swett, "Combat in the Solomon Islands," 69.
41. VMF-214 war diary, April 1943, 2.
42. Swett interview, Hammel, pt. 2, 9–20; Swett, "Combat in the Solomon Islands," 69–70.
43. Swett interview, Hammel, 9–20; Swett, "Combat in the Solomon Islands," 69–70.
44. Swett interview, Hammel, 9–20; Swett, "Combat in the Solomon Islands," 69–70.
45. Swett interview, Hammel, 9–20; Swett, "Combat in the Solomon Islands," 69–70.
46. Swett, "Combat in the Solomon Islands," 69–70; VMF-221 unit history, 46–48; Olynyk, *USMC Credits*, 18.
47. VMF-221 war history, 46–48; Frank "Baldy" Baldwin, "Baptism by Fire: April 1943," in Caswell, *Fighting Falcons*, 71–72.
48. VMF-221 unit history, 46–48.
49. VMF-221 unit history, 46–48; Claringbould, *Operation I-Go*, 50–52; Olynyk, *USMC Credits*, 18; Chapman, "Solomon Island," 67.
50. VMF-221 unit history, 47.
51. Olynyk, *USMC Credits*, 18; VMF-213 war diary, April 1943, 3; VMF-214 war diary, April 1943, 2; VMF-221 unit history, 46–48; Rohfleisch, "Central Solomons," 213.
52. Dunn, *South Pacific Air War*, 227; Claringbould, *Operation I-Go*, 57, 134.
53. VMF-213 war diary, April 1943, 3; VMF-214 war diary, April 1943, 2; VMF-221 unit history, 46–48; Rohfleisch, "Central Solomons," 213; "70th Fighter Squadron (70th FS)," *Pacific Wrecks*; Dunn, *South Pacific Air War*, 227.
54. Dunn, *South Pacific Air War*, 228.
55. Claringbould, *Operation I-Go*, 55–56.
56. Dunn, *South Pacific Air War*, 219–223; Claringbould, *Operation I-Go*, 47–52.
57. Nimitz, *Graybook*, 3:1505.
58. Dunn, *South Pacific Air War*, 226; Morison, *Breaking the Bismarcks Barrier*, 124.
59. VMF-221 unit history, 46–50.
60. VMF-214 war diary, April 1943, 2; VMF-221 unit history, 46–48; Rohfleisch, "Central Solomons," 213; Claringbould, *Operation I-Go*, 134.
61. Rohfleisch, "Central Solomons," 213–14.
62. 1st MAW Intelligence Section, "Performance Data Sheets," 1.
63. ComAirSols war diary, April 1943, 18, 23.
64. VMF-221 muster rolls, April and June 1943; Hammel, *Air War Pacific Chronology*, 157.
65. ComAirSols war diary, April 1943, 18–35, 26.
66. VMF-221 unit history, 51–52.
67. VMF-221 unit history, 53.

Chapter 8. Second Combat Tour, Russell Islands, 26 June–13 August 1943

1. RG 127 A1 1055 Box 8, MASP Correspondence on Operations and Tactical Employment of Units January 1943–June 1944, CG 2nd MAW to CG MASP, "Deficiencies Brought Out in Combat Experience," 10 July 1943, 4–5.
2. For a revealing account of a marine aviator's rest period in Sydney, see Porter, *Ace!*, 158–66.
3. 1st MAW Intelligence Section, "Performance Data Sheets," 1.
4. AirSols, "Interception of Enemy Fighters," 1 April 1943, 6.
5. Tillman, *Corsair*, 19–20.
6. Tillman, *Corsair*, 9–13.
7. VMF-221 unit history, 55.
8. Jim Burns, interview by P. F. Owen, 6 June 2023.
9. USMC HD, Archives Branch, "Peyton, Monfurd K., Col., USMC."
10. VMF-213 muster roll, April 1943; Shaw and Kane, *Isolation of Rabaul*, 471; Livingood (surgeon), "Individual Pilot Log."
11. VMF-221 unit history, 57–58.
12. VMF-221 unit history, 55–58.
13. VMF-221 unit history, 55–58; VMF-221 muster roll, June 1943.
14. VMF-221 unit history, 55–58; VMF-221 muster roll, June 1943.
15. Except where noted, the narrative in this section is drawn from MAG-21 war diary June 1943, 6–7; VMF-221 unit history, 63–64; RG 127 A1 1055 Box 27, HQ New Georgia AF, "Special Action Report 29 June–13 August 1943," 1–2; RG 38 NAID 134271791, VMF-221, "Action Report of June 30, 1943," 1–2.
16. "Banika Field (North Field, Sunlight)," *Pacific Wrecks*, 7 December 2022; MAG-21 war diary June 1943, 4–6; Kramer J. Rohfleisch, "Bougainville," in Craven and Cate, ed., *Guadalcanal to Saipan*, 215; James Swett, "Hamburgers and Milkshakes," in Caswell, *Fighting Falcons*, 75.
17. Porter, *Ace!*, 138–39; Spangler interview, BuAer, 11.
18. Shaw and Kane, *Isolation of Rabaul*, 470–73.
19. Dunn, *South Pacific Air War*, 285–86.
20. Morison, *Breaking the Bismarcks Barrier*, 150–51.
21. Sherrod, *History of Marine Corps Aviation*, 148–49; RG 127 A1 1055 Box 27, AirCom New Georgia Daily Intelligence Summary, 2 July 1943; RG 38 NAID 134301981, VMF-221 war diary, July 1943, 2; Melson, *Up the Slot*, 15.
22. VMF-221 war diary, July 1943, 3; AirCom New Georgia Daily Intelligence Summary, 4 July 1943; Dunn, *South Pacific Air War*, 321–22; Melson, *Up the Slot*, 17.
23. AirCom New Georgia Daily Intelligence Summary, 30 June–20 July 1943.
24. Morison, *Breaking the Bismarcks Barrier*, 160–90.
25. VMF-221 war diary, July 1943, 2; Morison, *Breaking the Bismarcks Barrier*, 174.

26. RG 38 NAID 134301981, VMF-221, "Report of Action between Six Planes of VMF-221 and a Number of Zeros over Rendova 7/7/43," 1–5; Dunn, *South Pacific Air War*, 325.
27. Rohfleisch, "Central Solomons," 225; MAG-21 war diary, July 1943, 4; VMF-221 unit history, 61–62.
28. Except where noted, this narrative is drawn from RG 38 NAID 134301981, VMF-221, "Report of Action between Two Planes of VMF-221 and Fifteen Bombers with Zero Fighter Escort over Munda and Kula Gulf on July 11, 1943," 14 July 1943; and "Report of Action between Three Planes of VMF-221 and Fifteen Bombers with Zero Fighter Escort over Munda and Kula Gulf on July 11, 1943," 12 July 1943.
29. RG 38 NAID 134301981, VMF-221, "Report of Action between Eight Planes of VMF-221 and a Single Twin-Engine Japanese Fighter over Munda," 1–2.
30. AirCom New Georgia daily intelligence summary, 11 July 1943.
31. Chapman, "Combat at Guadalcanal," in Caswell, *Fighting Falcons*, 76.
32. Chapman, "Combat at Guadalcanal," 76.
33. VMF-221 unit history, 62; Dunn, *South Pacific Air War*; Claringbould, *Pacific Adversaries*, 4:63–67.
34. Except where noted, this narrative is drawn from RG 38 NAID 134301981, VMF-221, "Report of Action between Four Planes of VMF-221 and an Undetermined Number of Zeros in the Vicinity of Moila Point on July 17, 1943."
35. VMF-221 war diary, July 1943, 11.
36. Dunn, *South Pacific Air War*, 332–33.
37. AirSols intelligence summary, 17 July 1943, "TBF Operations."
38. AirCom New Georgia intelligence summary, 17 July; Shaw and Kane, *Isolation of Rabaul*, 474–75; Dunn, *South Pacific Air War*, 333.
39. VMF-221 unit history, 63–64.
40. VMF-221 war diary, July 1943, 1, 6; VMF-221 muster roll, July 1943.
41. MAG-21 war diary, July 1943, 7–8; VMF-221 war diary, July 1943, 11–12; RG 38 NAID 135937042, VMF-221 war diary, August 1943, 1–10; VMF-221 unit history, 63–64.
42. VMF-221 war diary, July 1943, 8.
43. RG 127 A1 1055 Box 24, ComAirSols intelligence reports, August 1943, "Report of Action between Four Corsairs of VMF-221 and 8 Corsairs of VMF-214 and 20–30 Zeros near Shortland Is. on August 6th," 1.
44. "Report of Action August 6th," 2–3.
45. "Report of Action August 6th," 2–3.
46. MAG-21 war diary, July 1943, 7–8; VMF-221 war diary, July 1943 11–12; RG 38 NAID 135937042, VMF-221 war diary, August 1943 1–10; VMF-221 unit history, 63–64.

Chapter 9. Third Combat Tour, Vella Lavella, 10 October–19 November 1943

1. USMC HD, Peyton.

2. USMC HD, Archives Branch, "Post, Nathan T. Colonel, USMC"; USNA, *The Lucky Bag, 1938*.
3. VMF-213 muster rolls, January, April, July 1943; VMF-221 unit history, 71; Olynyk, *USMC Credits*, 181, 184, 205.
4. VMF-221 unit history, 69–71; VMF-221 war diary, August 1943, 4; VMF-221 muster roll, October 1943.
5. RG 38 NAID 78240906, VMF-221 war diary, October 1943, 1.
6. Shaw and Kane, *Isolation of Rabaul*, 476.
7. USSBS, *Allied Campaign against Rabaul*, 11; Morison, *Breaking the Bismarcks Barrier*, 284–86.
8. Rohfleisch, "Bougainville," 251–52.
9. VMF-221 war diary, October 1943, 2–3; and VMF-221 Aircraft Combat Action report (ACA-1) no. 1, 16 October 1943, 3 (ACA-1s are in GMT in 1943); RG 127 A1 1054 Box 6, MAG-14 war diary, 16 August–21 October 1943, 13.
10. VMF-221 ACA-1 no. 1, 3; Gamble, *Black Sheep One*, 264–65.
11. VMF-221 ACA-1 no. 1, 3; MAG-14 war diary, 16 August–21 October 1943, 13.
12. VMF-221 unit history, 72; Shaw and Kane, *Isolation of Rabaul*, 154, 160; Dunn, *South Pacific Air War*, 408.
13. Chapman, "Solomon Island," 68.
14. RG 127 A1 1055 Box 8 CO, VMF-215 to ComAirSoPac, 2 December 1943, 1.
15. ComAirSoPac War History, 11.
16. VMF-221 unit history, 72; VMF-221 war diary, October 1943, 3; and ACA-1 no. 2, 18 October 1943 3–4; MAG-14 war diary 16 August–21 October 1943, 14; Gamble, *Black Sheep One*, 266–67; Dunn, *South Pacific Air War*, 409.
17. VMF-221 war diary, October 1943, ACA-1 no. 2, 4.
18. VMF-221 war diary, October 1943, 3–5.
19. VMF-221 unit history, October 1943, ACA-1 no. 2, 3; Dunn, *South Pacific Air War*, 410.
20. VMF-221 unit history, 74; VMF-221 war diary, October 1943, ACA-1 no. 5, 30 October 1943, 1–4.
21. Claringbould, *Operation Ro-Go 1943*, 33.
22. RG 38 NAID 78272034, VMF-221 war diary, November 1943, 1.
23. Claringbould, *Operation Ro-Go 1943*, 35.
24. Rohfleisch, "Bougainville," 259; Morison, *Breaking the Bismarcks Barrier*, 306–21.
25. VMF-221 war diary, November 1943, ACA-1 no. 6, 1 November 1943, 3; Dunn, *South Pacific Air War*, 455; Morison, *Breaking the Bismarcks Barrier*, 306–21.
26. VMF-221 war diary, November 1943, 2.
27. VMF-221 unit history, 75.
28. Morison, *Breaking the Bismarcks Barrier*, 324–28; Halsey, *Admiral Halsey's Story*, 181; VMF-221 unit history, 75–76.
29. VMF-221 unit history, 76; VMF-221 war diary, November 1943, 4; Rohfleisch, "Bougainville," 260–61.

30. VMF-221 war diary, November 1943, 5.
31. Lancaster, "Life and Death in the Darkness."
32. RG 38 NAID 78270763, ComSoPacFor war diary, November 1943, 46; VMF-221 unit diary November 1943, ACA-1 no. 8, 16 November 1943, 3; GHQ FEAC, Japanese Monograph no. 100, 27–28.
33. Shaw and Kane, *Isolation of Rabaul*, 489, 502; VMF-221 unit history, 78–79; VMF-221 muster rolls, November and December 1943.

Chapter 10. VMF-221's Effectiveness in the Solomons

1. Olynyk, *USMC Credits*, 104; VMF-221 war diary, November 1943, 7–11; VMF-221 unit history, 63, 67, 73–74.
2. Shaw and Kane, *Isolation of Rabaul*, 467; Claringbould, *Operation I-Go*, 70.
3. VMF-221 unit history, 42–77, passim.
4. USSBS, *Allied Campaign against Rabaul*, 24.
5. Interrogation of Commander Ryosuke Nomura, IJN (Ret.), by Cdr. Thomas H. Moorer, USN, 28 November 1945, Interrogation no. 116, in USSBS, *Interrogations of Japanese Officials*, 2:532.
6. Interrogation of Commander Tadishi Yamamoto, IJN, and Captain Toshikazu Ohmae, IJN, by Capt. C. Shands, USN, 20 November 1945, Interrogation no. 109, USSBS, *Interrogations of Japanese Officials*, 2:468, 474.
7. Interrogation of Captain Takashi Miyazaki, IJN, by Capt. C. Shands, USN, 19 November 1945, Interrogation no. 97, USSBS, *Interrogations of Japanese Officials*, 2:419.
8. Nomura interrogation, 532.
9. AirSols, "Interception of Enemy Fighters," 1 April 1943, 6.
10. VMF-221 muster rolls, March–November 1943.
11. RG 127 A1 1055 Box 8, CO VMF-221 to CG 2nd MAW 30 November 1943, 1.
12. RG 127 A1 1055 Box 8, Fleet Air Command South Pacific, "F4U Aircraft—South Pacific Notes," memorandum of conference held 4 December 1943, 9–11.
13. Shaw and Kane, *Isolation of Rabaul*, 474; Nomura interrogation, 532.
14. Miyazaki interrogation, 418.
15. Shaw and Kane, *Isolation of Rabaul*, 453–54.

Chapter 11. Redeployment to California and Reconstitution, 1944

1. Tillman, *Marine Corps Fighter Squadrons*, 87–153, passim.
2. Owen, "The Marine Corps, Air War over the Pacific," 16–18; Frank Futrell, "Hollandia," in Craven and Cate, *Guadalcanal to Saipan*, 647.
3. RG 38 A1 UD 351, VMF-221 war diary, January 1944, 2; VMF-221 unit history, 79–80.
4. VMF-221 unit history, 79–80; VMF-221 muster roll, January 1945.
5. VMF-221 muster rolls, January and October 1944, January 1945.
6. VMF-221 muster roll, January 1944; VMF-221 unit history, 92.

7. Marine Corps Reserve Aviation Unit NRAB Grosse Ile muster rolls, October 1941 and April 1943; Schools Detachment, Quantico muster roll July 1943; VMF-221 muster roll, October 1944; HqSq-41, MBDAG-41 muster roll October 1944; E. S. Roberts Jr. Aviators Flight Log Book, United Flying School of America Log Sheet, 15 July 1940, and Naval Aviator Certificate, 29 May 1941, collection of Judy Roberts; Roberts, *Tales from World War II*, 7.
8. RG 38 NAID 78569698, VMF 221 1944 war diaries, February 2, and March 3 and 5; Sullivan, *F4U Corsair*, 8.
9. Cory Graff, "How the Navy Tamed the 'Killer Corsair'" (Smithsonian, 2021); VMF-221 war diary, August 1944, 3–4; Tillman, *Corsair*, 13–15; Sullivan, *F4U Corsair*, 8; Spangler interview, BuAer, 10–11; AM O1–45HA-1, 31 [hereafter *Corsair Pilot's Handbook*].
10. RG 127 A1 1029 Box 29, VMF-221 war diary, January 1945, 5; *Corsair Pilot's Handbook*, 9, 62.
11. RG 38 NAID 139938807, C.O. CV-17 "ACA-1 Report—Air Group 84, First and Second Strikes on Tokyo and Support and Capture of Iwo, 10 February to 5 March 1945," AG-84 ACA-1, no. 9, 25 February 1945, 6. ACA-1 reports cited through 1 March are from this record.
12. *Jane's Fighting Aircraft of World War II*, 186–90.
13. Rear Admiral Katsumata, Seizo, IJN (Ret.), Interrogation no. 31 by Lt. Cdr. R. P. Aikin, USNR, 25 October 1945, USSBS, *Interrogations of Japanese Officials*, 1:135.
14. VMF-221 war diaries, February–November 1944.
15. VMF-221 war diaries, February–November 1944, passim.
16. VMF-221 war diaries, February–November 1944, passim.
17. VMF-221 1944 war diaries, 4 March, 2 August, 6–7 October, and 5–6 November.
18. RG 38 NAID 77586160 ComPhibGru 1, "Report of Operations in the Invasion of Saipan Island, Marianas, 16–26 June 1944," 21 July 1944, 8–11, 573–74; Allison, "The Black Sheep Squadron," 167–72.
19. RG 127 A1 1055 MASP Correspondence, Director Aviation HQMC to MAWP and others, 12 June 1944, 1–4.
20. Tillman, *Corsair*, 80.
21. Smithsonian Institute, "Rocket, Air-to-Surface, 5-inch, HVAR."
22. Air Force Test Center, "September 16, 1944: High Velocity Aircraft Rocket Testing."
23. VMF-221 war diary, 6.
24. VMF-221 war diaries, December 1944, 1–3, and January 1945, 6.
25. VMF-221 war diary, December 1944, 1–2, and January 1945, 1; Roberts, Flight Log Book, January 1945.
26. RG 127 A1 1055 Box 8, CMC to CG MAWP, "Carrier Operations for Marine Aviation Squadrons," 29 January 1944, 1–2; Frank and Shaw, *Victory and Occupation*, 412–13; Sherrod, *History of Marine Corps Aviation*, 326–30.
27. ComAirPac to CinCPac 02 0254, Nimitz, *Graybook*, 5:2296; Frank and Shaw, *Victory and Occupation*, 415.

28. ComAirPac to CinCPac, 02 0254, Nimitz, *Graybook*, 5:2296; Frank and Shaw, *Victory and Occupation*, 415; Sherrod, *History of Marine Corps Aviation*, 331.
29. VMF-221 1944 war diaries, August, 2–3, and December, 2–3; Fred Briggs, "My First Carrier Landing," in Caswell, *Fighting Falcons*, 88.
30. *Corsair Pilot's Handbook*, 40, 42; Blechman, "F4U Corsair Carrier Qualification."
31. Tillman, *Corsair*, 15–16.
32. *Corsair Pilot's Handbook*, 34–35; Blechman, "F4U Corsair Carrier Qualification."
33. *Corsair Pilot's Handbook*, 60; "Carrier Catapults," *Naval Aviation News*, 1 January 1946, 2.
34. VMF-221 war diary, January 1945, 2.
35. Briggs, "First Carrier Landing."
36. Ralph O. Glendinning, "The *Ranger* and the Bulldozer," in Caswell, *Fighting Falcons*, 86–87; VMF-221 war diary, December 1944, 2.
37. Blaine Imel, "Memories of Slick," in Caswell, *Fighting Falcons*, 84–85.
38. VMF-221 1944 war diaries, November, 6, and December, 5.
39. VMF-221 war diaries 1944, passim.
40. VMF-221 muster rolls, January, October, and December 1944, January 1945.
41. VMF-221 war diary, December 1944, 3–5; RG 38 NAID 139812413, AG-84 war diary, December 1944, 1.
42. "George M. Ottinger, CDR, USN," *USNA Virtual Memorial Hall*; RG 38 NAID 78483674, AG-84 war diary May–June 1944, 1; RG 38 NAID 77685029, Air Group 84 war history, 8; Roberts, diary, 44.
43. RG 38 NAID 139812413, AG-84 war diary, December 1944, 2.
44. VMF-221 war diary, January 1945, 2.
45. VMF-221 war diary, January 1945, 2; RG 38 NAID 139851648, USS *Bunker Hill* war diary, January 1945, 1–2; "COMO George Albert Seitz," *Find a Grave* (10 April 2009).

Chapter 12. Aboard USS *Bunker Hill*, January–February 1945

1. Smith, *Triumph in the Philippines*, 170; Garand and Strobridge, *Western Pacific Operations*, 465.
2. Edwin S. Roberts diary, Roberts Family collection, passim; Gene Cameron, "The USS *Bunker Hill*," in Caswell, *Fighting Falcons*, 137.
3. Roberts diary, 6, 8.
4. Roberts diary, 5–6.
5. Fisher, *Sustaining the Carrier War*, 120–22.
6. VMF-221 war diary, January 1945, 3, and February 1945, 2; VMF-221 muster roll, July 1945; Roberts diary, 8.
7. VMF-221 war diary, February 1945, 1; VMF-221 muster roll April 1945.
8. VMF-221 war diary, February 1945, 2; Ralph O. Glendinning, "Introduction to the Flight Deck," in Caswell, *Fighting Falcons*, 93.

9. *Bunker Hill* war diary, January 1945, 5–6; Moore, *Rain of Steel*, 10–11; RG 38 NAID 139932683, "TF 58 Combat Operations from 10 February to 4 March 1945," 2.
10. Garand and Strobridge, *Western Pacific Operations*, 435, 465–66.
11. This narrative draws on Tillman, *Hellcat*, 154; and TF 58 Combat Operations, 10 February to 4 March 1945, Enclosure (F), "Analysis of Availability of Aircraft for Offensive Operations."
12. Tillman, *Hellcat*, 154; TF 58 Combat Operations, 10 February to 4 March 1945, Enclosure (F).
13. RG 38 NAID 140018742, "CV-17 Action Report 18 March–11 May 1945," part VI-D-3–4.
14. TF 58 Combat Operations, 10 February to 4 March 1945, Enclosure (C), "Air Combat Notes for Pilots," 1–4.
15. RG 127 A1 1023 Box 42, CNO Warfare and Operations, CincPOA SOP-2A "Air-Sea Rescue in Combat Areas in the Pacific Ocean Areas," 15 January 1945, 1–7.
16. TF 58 Combat Operations, 10 February to 4 March 1945, Enclosure (A), "Calendar of Employment of Task Groups of Task Force 58," 1.

Chapter 13. First Combat Cruise, 10 February–4 March 1945

1. RG 38 NAID 139921842, C.O. CV-17, "Action Report, First and Second Strikes on Tokyo and Support of Capture of Iwo, 10 February to 5 March 1945," 18 March 1945, 2; Roberts diary, 14–15.
2. Glendinning, "Flight Deck," 94.
3. Roberts diary, 17; "TF 58 Combat Operations from 10 February to 4 March 1945," 20–21.
4. VMF-221 war diary, February 1945, 3–4.
5. James Lea Cate and James C. Olson, "Precision Bombardment Campaign," in Craven and Cate, eds., *Matterhorn to Nagasaki*, 547, 554, 560, 573–76.
6. TG-58.3, "Operations 14 March–1 June 1945," 29.
7. Roberts diary, 19–20; CV-17 Action Report, 10 February–5 March 1945, 6.
8. Blaine Imel, "You're on Your Own," in Caswell, *Fighting Falcons*, 99.
9. Roberts diary, 21–22; VMF-221 ACA-1, no. 1, 16 February 1945, 26–30.
10. Roberts diary, 21–22; VMF-221 ACA-1, no. 1, 16 February 1945, 26–30.
11. Roberts diary, 21–22; VMF-221 ACA-1, no. 1, 16 February 1945, 26–30.
12. VMF-221 ACA-1, no. 2, 16 February 1945, 31.
13. AG-84 ACA-1, no. 1, 16 February 1945, 2; VMF-221 ACA-1 no. 2, 16 February 1945, 29–30.
14. VMF-221 ACA-1, no. 1, 16 February 1945, 26; and *Bunker Hill* "Photo Interpretation Report," no. 5, 3; George R. A. Johns, "The USS *Bunker Hill* and Combat," in Caswell, *Fighting Falcons*, 97–98.
15. VMF-221 ACA-1 no. 1, 16 February 1945, 26; TG 58.3 Action Report, 10 February–4 March 1945, 6.
16. Hemler, *Delivering Destruction*, 70, 113.

17. HQ CominCh, "Amphibious Operations—Capture of Iwo Jima—16 February to 16 March 1945," 17 July 1945, 3–3, published online 23 October 2019, NHHC; USMC HD HAF HQ LFASCU-1, "Special Action Report—Iwo Jima Campaign," 17 March 1945, 2.
18. AG-84 ACA-1, no. 3, 19 February 1945, 96; "TF 58 Combat Operations from 10 February to 4 March 1945," 20–21.
19. Roberts diary, 13, 16.
20. AG-84 ACA-1, no. 3, 19 February 1945, 91–95.
21. AG-84 ACA-1, no. 4, 19 February 1945, 99–103; Roberts diary, 25.
22. Garand and Strobridge, *Western Pacific Operations*, 92, 284; CO CV-15 to ComAirForPacFlt, "Napalm Fire-Bombs—Experience with Use of," 26 May 1945, 1–2.
23. AG-84 ACA-1, no. 4, 19 February 1945, 99–103; Roberts diary, 25.
24. TG 58.3 Action Report, 10 February–4 March 1945, 7–8; VMF-221 war diary, February 1945, 5.
25. AG-84 ACA-1, nos. 3 and 4, 19 February 1945, 95–103.
26. AG-84 ACA-1 nos. 3 and 4, 19 February 1945, 95–103; Ralph O. Glendinning, "Attack on Koizumi," in Caswell, *Fighting Falcons*, 106.
27. Hammel, *Air War Pacific Chronology*, 578–79.
28. Roberts diary, 27; AG-84 ACA-1, no. 7, 22 February 1945, 124–26.
29. VMF-221 war diary, 6.
30. VF-84 ACA-1, no. 9, 25 February 1945, 134.
31. AG-84 ACA-1, no. 8, 25 February 1945, 140–45.
32. AG-84 ACA-1, no. 8, 25 February 1945, 140–45; Roberts diary, 28–30; TG 58.3 Action Report, 10 February–4 March 1945, 10.
33. AG-84 ACA-1, no. 8, 25 February 1945, 140–45; TG 58.3 Action Report, 10 February–4 March 1945, 10.
34. Roberts diary, 28–30.
35. Glendinning, "Attack on Koizumi," 105.
36. Roberts diary, 28–30.
37. TG 58.3 Action Report, 10 February–4 March 1945, 11; CV 17, Action Report, 10 February–5 March 1945, 2.
38. Roberts diary, 31.
39. Moore, *Rain of Steel*, 85.
40. TG 58.3 Action Report, 10 February–4 March 1945, 11; RG 127 A1 1052 Box 30, VMF-221 war diary, March 1945, 1; Roberts diary, 32.
41. VMF-221 ACA-1, no. 7, 1 March 1945, 1–5.
42. Fred Briggs, "Bail Out," in Caswell, *Fighting Falcons*, 111–13.
43. VF-84 ACA-1, no. 11, 1 March 1945, 166.
44. TG 58.3 Action Report, 10 February–4 March 1945, 10.
45. VMF-221 war diary, March 1945, 2; Moore, *Rain of Steel*, 151.
46. VMF-221 war diary, March 1945, 2; Roberts diary, 32–36.

47. Moore, *Rain of Steel*, 96–86; CV 17 war history, N-59.
48. Roberts diary, 36–37.

Chapter 14. Second Combat Cruise, 14 March–11 May 1945

1. Appleman, *Okinawa*, 1–6; Morison, *Victory in the Pacific*, 89.
2. Morison, *Victory in the Pacific*, 372–88; Appleman, *Okinawa*, 492.
3. Hammel, *Air War Pacific Chronology*, 595–96.
4. RG 38 NAID 140054760, TG-58.3 Action Report 14 March–1 June 1945, 18 June 1945, 2.
5. Moore, *Rain of Steel*, 104, 149–50; Morison, *Victory in the Pacific*, 94, 112.
6. Frank and Shaw, *Victory and Occupation*, 21–22; Rielly, *Kamikazes, Corsairs and Picket Ships*, 84–95; USSBS, Aircraft Division, *Japanese Aircraft Industry*, 111–12, 126; Interrogation of Captain Rikibei Inoguchi, IJN, by Lt. Cdr. J. A. Field Jr., USNR, and Lt. Cdr. R. P. Aikin, USNR, 15 October 1945, USSBS Naval Analysis Division, *Interrogations of Japanese Officials*, vol. 1, no. 62, 63.
7. Roberts diary, 37.
8. Moore, *Rain of Steel*, 104; "TG-58.3 Operations 14 March–1 June 1945," 7.
9. RG 127 A1 1052 Box 30, VMF-221 war diary, March 1945, VMF-221 ACA-1 no. 9, 18 March 1945, 1, 3–4 (VMF-221 ACA-1s for March–May 1945 are all from this record group); Ralph O. Glendinning, "Floating off Kyushu," in Caswell, *Fighting Falcons*, 118–21.
10. RG 38 NAID 139977172, CV-17 war diary, March 1945, 7; "TG-58.3 Operations 14 March–1 June 1945," 7.
11. Wesley S. Todd, "Kamikaze Attacks," in Caswell, *Fighting Falcons*, 125.
12. Todd, "Kamikaze Attacks," 125.
13. VMF-221 ACA-1 no. 10, 18 March 1945, 1–6; Dean Caswell, "From My Diary," in *Fighting Falcons*, 114–15.
14. VMF-221 ACA-1 no. 11, 19 March 1945, 4.
15. VMF-221 ACA-1 no. 11, 19 March 1945, 4.
16. "TG-58.3 Operations 14 March–1 June 1945," 10; Roberts diary, 40.
17. "TG-58.3 Operations 14 March–1 June 1945," 9.
18. VMF-221 ACA-1 no. 12, 19 March 1945, 1–5.
19. Hammel, *Air War Pacific Chronology*, 601–2.
20. CV-17 war diary, March 1945, 10–11.
21. VMF-221 ACA-1 no. 13, 21 March 1945, 1–4.
22. VMF-221 ACA-1 no. 14, 23 March 1945, 1–6.
23. VMF-221 ACA-1 no. 15, 24 March 1945, 1–7; Roberts diary, 43–44.
24. CV-17 war diary, March 1945, 13–14; AG-84 war history, 12.
25. VMF-221 ACA-1 no. 16, 24 March 1945, 1–4.
26. VMF-221 ACA-1, nos. 17–23, 24–27, 26–28, 30–31 March 1945, passim.
27. "TG-58.3 Operations 14 March–1 June 1945," 11–12.

28. CV-17 war diary, March 1945, 20; Roberts diary, 47–48.
29. Ralph O. Glendinning, "My Most Terrifying Flight," in Caswell, *Fighting Falcons*, 132; Roberts diary, 44.
30. VMF-221 war diary, March 1945, 6–7; Roberts diary, 47–48.
31. Moore, *Rain of Steel*, 175; NHHC, "Corsairs—Iwo Jima"; CV-17 war diary, March 1945, 6, 11, 15, 19; VMF-221 war diary, March 1945, 10; VMF-221 muster roll, April 1945.
32. Morison, *Victory in the Pacific*, 132.
33. CominCh, *Radar Pickets and Methods of Combating Suicide Attacks*, 81-1 to 81-5; Rielly, *Kamikazes, Corsairs and Picket Ships*, 3–12.
34. VMF-221 ACA-1 no. 28, 1 April 1945, 1–5.
35. Blaine Imel, "As Remembered," in Caswell, *Fighting Falcons*, 129–30.
36. RG 38 NAID 101725137, VMF-451 war diary, April 1945, 3; George R. A. Johns, "Catastrophe on the Flight Deck," in Caswell, *Fighting Falcons*, 126–27.
37. Johns, "Catastrophe on the Flight Deck," 126–27; Imel, "As Remembered," 129–30.
38. VMF-221 ACA-1 no. 28, 1 April 1945, 1–5.
39. RG 127 A1 1052 Box 30, VMF-221 forward echelon war diary, April 1945, 1; VMF-221 ACA-1 no. 31, 4 April 1945, 1–4; Roberts diary, 49–50.
40. VMF-221 war diary, April 1945, 1.
41. RG 127 A1 1052 Box 30, VMF-221 forward echelon war diary, April 1945, 1; VMF-221 ACA-1 no. 31, 4 April 1945, 1–4; Roberts diary, 49–50.
42. Roberts diary, 50.
43. Moore, *Rain of Steel*, 177; Hammel, *Air War Pacific Chronology*, 616.
44. Prados, *Combined Fleet Decoded*, 711.
45. Roberts diary, 50.
46. Hammel, *Air War Pacific Chronology*, 616.
47. Glendinning, "My Most Terrifying Flight," 132.
48. Glendinning, "My Most Terrifying Flight," 132.
49. Glendinning, "My Most Terrifying Flight," 132.
50. Glendinning, "My Most Terrifying Flight," 132.
51. VMF-221 ACA-1 no. 33, 6 April 1945, 1–5.
52. VMF-221 ACA-1 no. 33, 6 April 1945, 1–5; Gene Cameron, "Combat," in Caswell, *Fighting Falcons*, 135; Roberts diary, 53.
53. Roberts diary, 53; Cameron, "Combat," 135.
54. Johns, "Memories," in Caswell, *Fighting Falcons*, 126.
55. Johns, "Memories," 126.
56. Imel, "My First Meatball," in Caswell, *Fighting Falcons*, 131.
57. Imel, "My First Meatball," 131.
58. Johns, "Memories," 126.
59. VMF-221 ACA-1 no. 34, 6 April 1945, 1–5.
60. Morison, *Victory in the Pacific*, 197.
61. VMF-221 ACA-1 no. 35, 7 April 1945, 1–5; Roberts diary, 55–56.

62. Roberts diary, 57; "CV-17 Action Report, 18 March–11 May 1945," 28–29; Moore, *Rain of Steel*, 203–4, 224, 232; Hammel, *Air War Pacific Chronology*, 618.
63. CV-17 Action Report 14 March–14 May 1945, 28–29; RG 38 NAID 101725137, VMF-451 war diary, April 1945, 4; TG 58.3 Action Report 14 March–1 June 1945, 4.
64. CV-17 Action Report 14 March–14 May 1945, 30–31; Roberts diary, 60; VMF-221 war diary, April 1945, 2.
65. VMF-221 ACA-1 no. 36, 11 April 1945, 4.
66. VMF-221 war diary, April 1945, 2; VMF-221 ACA-1, 11 April 1945 no. 37, 1, 4; TG 58.3 Action Report 14 March–1 June 1945, 5; NHHC, "*Enterprise* (CV-6) 1938–1956," *Dictionary of American Naval Fighting Ships* (10 July 2017).
67. Roberts diary, 61; Moore, *Rain of Steel*, 249; VMF-221 war diary, April 1945, 2–3.
68. VMF-221 ACA-1 no. 38, 12 April 1945, 1–5.
69. Dean Caswell, "Combat," in Caswell, *Fighting Falcons*, 138.
70. VMF-221 ACA-1 no. 39, 12 April 1945, 1–5.
71. Charlie M. Nettles, "Combat over Okinawa," in Caswell, *Fighting Falcons*, 143.
72. VMF-221 ACA-1 no. 39, 12 April 1945, 1–5; Moore, *Rain of Steel*, 134–39.
73. Rielly, *Kamikazes, Corsairs and Picket Ships*, 351.
74. VMF-221 war diary, April 1945, 3; CV-17 Action Report 14 March–14 May 1945, 34–35.
75. VMF-213 muster roll, January 1945; VMF-216 muster roll, October 1944; VMF-217 muster roll, January 1945; VMF-221 muster roll, April 1945; Roberts diary, 63.
76. VMF-221 ACA-1 no. 42, 15 April 1942, 1–5.
77. Moore, *Rain of Steel*, 265; NMUSAF, "Yokosuka MXY7-K1 Ohka."
78. VMF-221 war diary, April 1945, 3; VMF-221 ACA-1, 16 April 1945, no. 43, 1–5.
79. VMF-221 ACA-1, 16 April 1945, no. 43, 4–5.
80. VMF-221 ACA-1, 16 April 1945, no. 43, 4–5.
81. VMF-221 ACA-1, 16 April 1945, no. 43, 4–5.
82. VMF-221 ACA-1, 16 April 1945, no. 44, 4–5.
83. Rielly, *Kamikazes, Corsairs and Picket Ships*, 351–52; Moore, *Rain of Steel*, 279–80.
84. TG 58.3 Action Report 14 March–1 June 1945, 5; Roberts diary, 65–66.
85. VMF-221 war history, April 1945, 4–5.
86. Appleman, *Okinawa*, 248.
87. Frank and Shaw, *Victory and Occupation*, 176–77, 180–83.
88. "TG-58.3 Operations 14 March–1 June 1945," 20, 27–28, 38; CV-17 Action Report, 14 March–14 May 1945, 25–26, 39, 220, pt. VI, sec. B, p. 23.
89. VMF-221 ACA-1, 25 April 1945, no. 51, 1–5; Appleman, *Okinawa*, map, "Attack on Shuri Defenses 25 April–3 May."
90. VMF-221 ACA-1, 26 April 1945, no. 52, 1–5; Roberts diary, 69; Appleman, "Attack on Shuri Defenses 25 April–3 May."
91. VMF-221 ACA-1, 28 April 1945, report no. 54, 1–5.
92. Hammel, *Air War Pacific Chronology*, 634–35.

93. VMF-221 ACA-1, no. 55, 28 April 1945, 1–5.
94. Caswell, "More Combat," in *Fighting Falcons*, 139–40.
95. Caswell, "More Combat,"139–40.
96. VMF-221 ACA-1, no. 55, 1–5.
97. VMF-221 ACA-1, no. 55, 1–5; Roberts diary, 74–75.
98. VMF-221 ACA-1, no. 55, 1–5.
99. Rielly, *Kamikazes, Corsairs and Picket Ships*, 194, 352.
100. VMF-221 ACA-1s, 29–30 April, reports no. 56, 1–5, and no. 57, 1–5.
101. Blaine Imel, "Kamikaze Attack on the *Bunker Hill*," in Caswell, *Fighting Falcons*, 150.
102. Roberts diary, 71–72.
103. VMF-221 ACA-1, no. 58, 3 May 1945, 1–5; CV-17 Action Report 14 March–14 May 1945, 47–48; Moore, *Rain of Steel*, 296–98.
104. Hammel, *Air War Pacific Chronology*, 639–41; Rielly, *Kamikazes, Corsairs and Picket Ships*, 352.
105. Moore, *Rain of Steel*, 304; Frank and Shaw, *Victory and Occupation*, 209–13; VMF-221 ACA-1, no. 59, 4 May 1945, 1–5; CV-17 Action Report 14 March–14 May 1945, 48–49.
106. CV-17 Action Report 14 March–14 May 1945, 49; Roberts diary, 75.
107. CV-17 Action Report 14 March–14 May 1945, 50.
108. VMF-221 ACA-1, 7 May 1945, no. 60, 1–5; Roberts diary, 76.
109. VMF-221 ACA-1, 7 May 1945, no. 61, 1–5; CV-17 Action Report 14 March–14 May 1945, 52–53.

Chapter 15. Attack on USS *Bunker Hill*, 11 May 1945

1. Frank and Shaw, *Victory and Occupation*, 224; Moore, *Rain of Steel*, 512–13; Rielly, *Kamikazes, Corsairs and Picket Ships*, 85, 239.
2. Frank and Shaw, *Victory and Occupation*, 224; CV-17 Action Report 14 March–14 May 1945, 53.
3. CV-17 Action Report 14 March–14 May 1945, VI-B-21; VMF-221 ACA-1 no. 63, 11 May 1945, 1.
4. VMF-221 ACA-1 no. 63, 4.
5. VMF-221 ACA-1 no. 63, 4.
6. VMF-221 ACA-1 no. 63, 4; Ralph O. Glendinning, "Two Kamikazes over the *Bunker Hill*," in Caswell, *Fighting Falcons*, 161.
7. Moore, *Rain of Steel*, 316–20; Rielly, *Kamikazes, Corsairs and Picket Ships*, 248, 353.
8. CV-17 Action Report 18 March–11 May 1945, V-2.
9. Imel, "Kamikaze Attack," 150.
10. Swett, "Homeless," 284; CV-17 Action Report 14 March–14 May 1945, 53.
11. CV-17 Action Report 14 March–14 May 1945, 134–35, 157.
12. CV-17 Action Report 14 March–14 May 1945, 54, 135.
13. CV-17 Action Report 14 March–14 May 1945, 134–38.

14. Donald Balch, "In the Ready Room—Kamikaze!"; and Imel, "Kamikaze Attack," in Caswell, *Fighting Falcons*, 150–52, 155; Lt. Charles Nettles diary, 11 May 1945, reprinted in Caswell, *Kamikaze Madness*, 118–19.
15. Balch, "Ready Room"; and Imel, "Kamikaze Attack."
16. Lt. Dean Caswell, "From His Memoirs," in Caswell, *Kamikaze Madness*, 114–17; CV-17 Action Report 18 March–11 May 1945, V-2.
17. CV-17 Action Report 18 March–11 May 1945, V-2.
18. Caswell, "From His Memoirs," 114–17.
19. Charlie Nettles, "Fire on the *Bunker Hill*," in Caswell, *Fighting Falcons*, 154.
20. Caswell, "From His Memoirs," 114–17.
21. CV-17 Action Report 14 March–14 May 1945, V-2, 3.
22. VMF-221 ACA-1 no. 63, 6; Balch, "Ready Room"; Imel, "Kamikaze Attack."
23. Roberts diary, 77.
24. VMF-221 ACA-1 no. 63, 6; Roberts diary, 77.
25. CV-17 Action Report 14 March–14 May 1945, 261, 263; VMF-221 war diary, May 1945, 3.
26. USMC HD Archives, VMF-221 war diary, May 1945, 2; VMF-221 muster roll, October 1944.
27. Glendinning, "Two Kamikazes," 162.
28. CV-17 Action Report 14 March–14 May 1945, 261, 263; VMF-221 war diary, May 1945, 3.
29. Roberts diary, 82, 84.

Chapter 16. VMF-221's Effectiveness aboard USS *Bunker Hill*

1. CV-17 Action Report 10 February–5 March 1945, 27; CV-17 Action Report 14 March–14 May 1945, 199–200.
2. Dunn, "Ten Days to Kamikaze, Part VII."
3. Caswell, "From My Diary," 114, and "More Combat," 140, in *Fighting Falcons*.
4. VMF-221 1945 war diaries, February, 13, March, 15, April, 14, and May, 9; Moore, *Rain of Steel*, 369.
5. VMF-221 war diaries, February–May 1945; VMF-221 Aircraft Action (ACA-1) Reports, nos. 1–63.
6. TG-58.3 Operations 14 March–1 June 1945, 20.
7. LFASCU, "Special Action Report—Iwo Jima," 4–5.
8. VMF-221 war diaries, February–May 1945; VMF-221 ACA-1 Reports, nos. 1–63.
9. CV-17 Action Report 10 February–5 March 1945, 29; CV-17 Action Report 14 March–14 May 1945, 37, 203–4. The CV-17 action report attributed the loss of Lieutenant Pemble and the two TBFs on 16 February to antiaircraft fire. As Pemble was last seen at high altitude surrounded by enemy fighters, this is unlikely.
10. USSBS, Aircraft Division, *Japanese Aircraft Industry*, table VI-VI, 112–14.

11. USSBS, *The Campaigns of the Pacific War*, 331; Frank and Shaw, *Victory and Occupation*, 365; Spector, *Eagle against the Sun*, 542–43.
12. CV-17 Action Report 10 February–5 March 1945, 43.
13. CAG-84 Action Report 27 May 1945, 2.
14. CV-17 Action Report 14 March–14 May 1945, 226–27.
15. CV-17 Action Report 10 February–5 March 1945, 44; CV-17 Action Report 14 March–14 May 1945, 228.
16. CV-17 Action Report 14 March–14 May 1945, 225; Roberts diary, 76; RG 38 NAID 101703424, CAG-84 action reports, 27 May 1945, 2.
17. TG-58.3 Operations 14 March–1 June 1945, 20, 27–28, 38; CV-17 Action Report 14 March–14 May 1945, 25–26, 39, 220, VI-B-23.
18. CV-17 Action Report 10 February–5 March 1945, 43.
19. TG-58.3 Operations 14 March–1 June 1945, 36–37.
20. TG-58.3 Operations 14 March–1 June 1945, 25–26.
21. CV-17 Action Reports 10 February–5 March 1945 and 14 March–14 May 1945, passim.
22. TG-58.3 Operations 14 March–1 June 1945, 20, 29.
23. TG-58.3 Operations 14 March–1 June 1945, 32, 34–35; CV-17 Action Report 10 February–5 March 1945, 45–46.
24. CV-17 Action Report 14 March–14 May 1945, 165.

Conclusion

1. Millett, *Semper Fidelis*, 361.
2. Berger, Gilday, and Schultz, *Advantage at Sea*, 7.
3. USMC, *Tentative Manual for Expeditionary Advanced Base Operations*, 5-1, 5-2.
4. Berger, Gilday, and Schultz, *Advantage at Sea*, 6.
5. Work, "A Slavish Devotion to Forward Presence"; Zeberlein, "Can-Do Is Not Working."

★BIBLIOGRAPHY★

Archives and Collections

Ancestry.com. Muster Rolls of the U.S. Marine Corps. Retrieved from www.ancestry .com.

Center for Oral and Public History, California State University, Fullerton. El Toro Marine Corps Air Station Oral History Project [El Toro MCAS OHP].

Digital Collections of the National World War II Museum. Oral History Collection. Retrieved from ww2online.org.

Museum of Flight. The American Fighter Aces Association Oral Interviews. "James E. Swett Oral History Interview." Parts 1 and 2. Interview by Eric M. Hammel, circa 1980–90. Audio and transcript retrieved from https://digitalcollections.museumofflight.org/items/show/38146.

Pacific Wrecks online resource. Retrieved from www.pacificwrecks.com.

Records of the National Archives of the United States

Record Group 38. Records of the Office of the Chief of Naval Operations. Entry Group UD 351. World War II Action and Operations Reports. Records in this group are identified by RG 38 and the National Archives Identification number (NAID).

Record Group 127. Records of the U.S. Marine Corps. Records in this group are identified by RG 127, Entry Group, and Box Number.

Entry Group A1 1052. U.S. Marine Corps Aviation Unit War Diaries and Unit Histories, 1941–1949.

Entry Group A1 1053. U.S. Marine Corps Aviation Unit War Diaries and Unit Histories, 1941–1949: Marine Aircraft Wings.

Entry Group A1 1054. U.S. Marine Corps Aviation Unit War Diaries and Unit Histories, 1941–1949: Marine Aircraft Groups.

Entry Group A1 1055. U.S. Marine Corps Aviation Unit War Diaries and Unit Histories, 1941–1949: Shore Commands.

Entry Group A1 237-G [A1]. Correspondence and Reports of Marine Aviation Units.

Record Group 313. Records of Naval Operating Forces, Entry Group 58-3397. Records of Naval Air Station and Naval Operating Base Midway. Retrieved 1 January 2023 from www.midway42.org.

Records of the Archives of the U.S. Marine Corps History Division [USMC HD].

Biography Files

Historical Amphibious Files (HAF)

Marine Corps Medal of Honor Recipients

Oral History Collection (USMC OHC)

Personal Papers Collection (MCPPC)

Who's Who in Marine Corps History

Naval History and Heritage Command (NHHC)

Archives, Histories, Library, Publications, and Photograph Collections. Retrieved from www.history.navy.mil.

Papers of Chester W. Nimitz. Command Summary of Fleet Admiral Chester W. Nimitz, USN 7 December 1941–31 August 1945. Also known as the *Graybook*. Copyright 2011 by American Naval Records Society. Retrieved from http://www.ibiblio.org/anrs/graybook.html.

University of Maryland Special Collections. Collection 0193-MDHC. Gordon W. Prange Papers. Series 7, The Battle of Midway: "Miracle at Midway."

Articles, Books, and Films

Aerology Section. *Aerology and Naval Warfare: The Battle of Midway*, NAVAER 50-40T-1. Washington: Chief of Naval Operations, March 1944.

Air Force Test Center. "September 16, 1944: High Velocity Aircraft Rocket Testing." 16 September 1920. Retrieved from https://www.aftc.af.mil/News/On-This-Day-in-Test-History/Article-Display-Test-History/Article/2315047/september-16-1944-high-velocity-aircraft-rocket-testing/.

Allison, Fred. "The Black Sheep Squadron: A Case Study in U.S. Marine Corps Innovations in Close Air Support." Ph.D. diss. Texas Tech University, 2003. Retrieved from https://ttu-ir.tdl.org/handle/2346/18434?show=full.

———. "Out in Front at Midway." Interview of Capt. John F. Carey, USMC. *Naval History* magazine (June 2004).

AM O1-45HA-1. *Pilot's Handbook of Flight Operating Instructions, Navy Models F4U-1, F4U-1C, F4U-1D, F3A-1, F3A-1D, FG-1, FG-1D.* Washington: Commanding General, Army Air Forces, Chief of the Bureau of Aeronautics, and the Air Council of the United Kingdom, 15 March 1945.

Appleman, Roy Edgar. *Okinawa: The Last Battle. United States Army in World War II. The War in the Pacific* series. Washington: Center of Military History, 2000.

Australian Dictionary of Biography. Retrieved from https://adb.anu.edu.au/biography/.

"Battle of Midway: Army Air Forces." Navy Department Library, 2020. Retrieved from www.history.navy.mil.

Berger, David H. *Commandant's Planning Guidance.* Washington: U.S. Marine Corps, 2018.

Berger, David H., Michael M. Gilday, and Karl L. Schultz. *Advantage at Sea.* Washington: Department of the Navy, December 2020.

Bicheno, Hugh. *Midway.* London: Cassell, 2001.

Blechman, Fred. "F4U Corsair Carrier Qualification." 1997. Retrieved from http://www.justinmuseum.com/famjustin/blechmanbio.html.

Briggs, Fred. "Bail Out." In Dean Caswell, *Fighting Falcons: The Saga of Marine Fighter Squadron 221.* Austin, TX: VMF 221 Foundation, 2004, 111–13.

Brown, Kent B. "Lt. Col. Harold William 'Indian Joe' Bauer—Marine Corps Ace at Guadalcanal." *Acepilots.com*, December 2002, updated July 5, 2011. Retrieved from www.acepilots.com.

———, ed. "War Diary of Harold W. Bauer, December 1, 1941, to October 13, 1942." *Acepilots.com*, 2011 (2002). Retrieved from www.acepilots.com.

Bureau of Aeronautics. Interview of Commander Seldon B. Spangler, USN. 23 April 1943. Retrieved 1 July 2023 from http://www.researcheratlarge.com/Aircraft/1943CdrSpanglerInterview/.

———. *World War II Administrative History.* Volume 20, *Marine Corps Aviation.* Washington: Department of the Navy, 1957.

———. *World War II Administrative History.* Volume 22, *Aviation Personnel, 1939–1945.* Washington: Department of the Navy, n.d.

Burns, Jim. Interview by Peter F. Owen, 6 June 2023. Mr. Burns provided biographical details about his father, Robert R. Burns.

Cameron, Gene. "Combat." In Dean Caswell, *Fighting Falcons: The Saga of Marine Fighter Squadron 221.* Austin, TX: VMF 221 Foundation, 2004, 150.

Carl, Marion, with Barrett Tillman. *Pushing the Envelope: The Career of Fighter Ace and Test Pilot Marion Carl.* First Bluejacket Books edition, Annapolis, MD: Naval Institute Press, 2005. First published in 1994 by Naval Institute Press.

Caswell, Dean. *Fighting Falcons: The Saga of Marine Fighter Squadron 221.* Austin, TX: VMF 221 Foundation, 2004.

———. *Kamikaze Madness and Marine Fighter Pilots: A True Story of a Fighting Ship and Its Marine Fighter Pilots.* Austin, TX: Col. Dean Caswell, USMC (Ret.), 2017.

Claringbould, Michael. *Operation I-Go: Yamamoto's Last Offensive: New Guinea and the Solomons April 1943*. Kent Town, South Australia: Avonmore Books, 2020.

———. *Operation Ro-Go 1943*. Oxford, UK: Osprey Publishing, 2023.

———. *Pacific Adversaries*. Volume 4. Kent Town, South Australia: Avonmore Books, 2021.

"Col. Edward Pugh Awarded Legion of Merit as Leader." *Coronado Eagle and Journal*, 4 November 1943. California Digital Newspaper Collection, University of California Riverside Center for Bibliographical Studies and Research. Retrieved from https://cdnc.ucr.edu.

"Colonel Robert Lee Dickey." *Press Democrat*, 6 September 2005. Retrieved from https://www.legacy.com/us/obituaries/pressdemocrat/name/robert-dickey-obituary?id=15886721.

Commander Aircraft Battle Force. *USF-74, Current Tactical Orders and Doctrine U.S. Fleet Aircraft*. Volume 1, *Carrier Aircraft*. Pearl Harbor, T.H.: United States Pacific Fleet, March 1941.

Commander-in-Chief, United States Fleet. *Battle Experience: Radar Pickets and Methods of Combating Suicide Attacks off Okinawa, March–May 1945*. Washington: Navy Department, 20 July 1945.

"COMO George Albert Seitz." *Find a Grave* (10 April 2009). Retrieved from www.findagrave.com.

Condon, John P. *Corsairs and Flattops*. Annapolis, MD: Naval Institute Press, 1998.

Cox, Jeffrey R. *Dark Waters, Starry Skies: The Guadalcanal–Solomons Campaign March–October 1943*. New York: Osprey Publishing, 2023.

Craven, Wesley Frank, and James Lea Cate, eds. *The Army Air Forces in World War II*. Volume 4, *The Pacific, Guadalcanal to Saipan, August 1942 to July 1944*. 1948. Reprint. Washington: Office of Air Force History, 1983.

———. *The Army Air Forces in World War II*. Volume 5, *The Pacific: Matterhorn to Nagasaki, June 1944 to August 1945*. 1948. Reprint. Washington: Office of Air Force History, 1983.

Cunningham, Alfred A. "Value of Aviation to the Marine Corps." *Marine Corps Gazette* (September 1920).

DeBlanc, Jefferson J. *The Guadalcanal Air War: Col. Jefferson DeBlanc's Story*. Gretna, LA: Pelican Publishing, 2008.

Dreadnaughtz. *Naval Encyclopedia*. Retrieved from https://naval-encyclopedia.com.

Dull, Paul S. *A Battle History of the Imperial Japanese Navy (1941–1945)*. Annapolis, MD: Naval Institute Press, 1978.

Dunn, Richard L. *Exploding Fuel Tanks*. Second edition. Richard L. Dunn, 2011.

———. "Mitsubishi Zero 21—A Question of Speed" (2023). Retrieved from rldunn.com.

———. *South Pacific Air War: The Role of Airpower in the New Guinea and Solomon Island Campaigns, January 1943 to February 1944*. Atglen, PA: Schiffer Publishing, 2024.

———. "Ten Days to Kamikaze. Part VII. Mass Japanese Attacks." 2024. Retrieved from rldunn.com.

Dyer, George C. *The Amphibians Came to Conquer: The Story of Admiral Richmond Kelly Turner.* Volume 1. Washington: Government Printing Office, 1969.

Ellis, Earl H. *Advanced Base Operations in Micronesia (Operation Plan 712).* 1921. Reprinted as FMFRP 12-46. Washington: U.S. Marine Corps, 1992.

Feldt, E. A. "Coastwatching in World War II." U.S. Naval Institute *Proceedings* (September 1961).

Fisher, Stan. *Sustaining the Carrier War: The Deployment of U.S. Naval Air Power to the Pacific.* Annapolis, MD: Naval Institute Press, 2023.

Frank, Benis M., and Henry I. Shaw Jr. *U.S. Marine Corps Operations in World War II.* Volume 5, *Victory and Occupation.* Washington: Headquarters, U.S. Marine Corps, 1968.

Gamble, Bruce. *Black Sheep One: The Life of Gregory Pappy Boyington.* Novato, CA: Presidio, 2000.

Garand, George W., and Truman R. Strobridge. *History of U.S. Marine Corps Operations in World War II.* Volume 4, *Western Pacific Operations.* Washington: Headquarters, U.S. Marine Corps, 1971.

General Headquarters, Far East Area Command, Military Intelligence Section, Allied Translator and Interpreter Section. Japanese Monograph No. 100: "Southeast Area Naval Operations Part III (October 1943–February 1944)."

———. Japanese Monograph No. 122: "Outlines of Southeast Area Naval Air Operations Part III (November 1942–June 1943)," 24 July 1950.

Graff, Cory. "How the Navy Tamed the 'Killer Corsair.'" *Smithsonian* (June 2021). Retrieved from https://www.smithsonianmag.com/air-space-magazine/spoiler-alert-1-180977803/.

Grossnick, Roy A. *United States Naval Aviation, 1910–1995.* Washington: Naval Historical Center, 1997.

———. "The USS *Bunker Hill* and Combat." In Dean Caswell, *Fighting Falcons: The Saga of Marine Fighter Squadron 221.* Austin, TX: VMF 221 Foundation, 2004, 97–98.

Halsey, William F. III. *Admiral Halsey's Story.* New York: McGraw-Hill, 1947.

Hammel, Eric. *Aces against Japan II.* Volume 3, *The American Aces Speak.* Novato, CA: Presidio Press, 1996.

———. *Air War Pacific Chronology: America's Air War against Japan in East Asia and the Pacific, 1941–1945.* Pacifica, CA: Pacifica Press, 1998.

"Harold W. Bauer, USMC." National Medal of Honor Museum. 2022. Retrieved from https://mohmuseum.org/joebauermoh/.

Heinl, Robert D. Jr. *Marines in World War II: Marines at Midway.* Washington: Headquarters, U.S. Marine Corps, 1948.

Hemler, Christopher Kyle. *Delivering Destruction: American Firepower and Amphibious Assault from Tarawa to Iwo Jima.* Annapolis, MD: Naval Institute Press, 2023.

Hirrel, Leo. *Bismarck Archipelago.* Washington: Center of Military History, 1994.

Horan, Mark E. "Midway Combat Reports." *Warbird Forum.* June 2019. Retrieved from https://www.warbirdforum.com/vmf221.htm.

Horan, Mark, Richard Worth, David Williams, and Richard Leonard. "Orders of Battle, Battle of Midway and Aleutians 3–7 June 1942." *Battle of Midway Roundtable.* Retrieved 1 January 2023 from www.midway42.org.

Imel, Blaine. "Kamikaze Attack on the *Bunker Hill.*" In Dean Caswell, *Fighting Falcons: The Saga of Marine Fighter Squadron 221.* Austin, TX: VMF 221 Foundation, 2004, 150.

Jane's Fighting Aircraft of World War II. New York: Crescent Books, 1996.

Johns, George R. A. "Catastrophe on the Flight Deck." In Dean Caswell, *Fighting Falcons: The Saga of Marine Fighter Squadron 221.* Austin, TX: VMF 221 Foundation, 2004, 126–27.

Johnson, Edward C. *Marine Corps Aviation: The Early Years, 1912–1940.* Washington: Headquarters, U.S. Marine Corps, 1977.

Kern, Michael Elliot. "Striking Eagles: Doctrine, Training, and Fighting Squadron Five at War in the Pacific." M.S. thesis, George Washington University, 2011. Retrieved 1 January 2023 from www.proquest.com.

Klase, Al. "Aircraft-to-Carrier Homing: A Secret Weapon of WWII." Retrieved 1 January 2023 from http://www.skywaves.ar88.net/Presentations/YE-ZB%20Presentation.pdf.

Lancaster, Mark. "USS *McKean*: Life and Death in the Darkness." *Low Stone Wall,* 17 November 2016. Retrieved from https://lowstonewall.com/.

Larkins, William T. *U.S. Navy Aircraft 1921–1941. U.S. Marine Corps Aircraft 1914–1959.* New York: Orion Books, 1959, 1961, 1988.

Linn, Don. *F4F Wildcat in Action.* Carrollton, TX: Squadron/Signal Publications, 1988.

Livingood, William C. Individual Pilot Log. Retrieved 1 July 2023 from www.vmf-213.com.

Lundstrom, John. *The First Team: Pacific Naval Air Combat from Pearl Harbor to Midway.* Annapolis, MD: Naval Institute Press, 2013.

Maas, Jim. *F2A Buffalo in Action.* Illustrated by Peter Manley. Carrollton, TX: Squadron/Signal Publications, 1987.

Marine Corps Aviation Association. *Chronolog, 1912–1954.* Paducah, KY: Turner Publishing 1989.

Matt, P. E. "SCR-270/SCR-271 Radar." *Pacific Eagles* (23 February 2019). Retrieved from https://pacificeagles.net/scr-270-scr-271-radar/.

Melson, Charles D. *Condition Red: Marine Defense Battalions in World War II.* Washington: Marine Corps Historical Center, 1996.

———. *Up the Slot: Marines in the Central Solomons.* Washington: Marine Corps Historical Center, 1993.

Miller, Edward S. *War Plan Orange: The U.S. Strategy to Defeat Japan, 1897–1945.* Annapolis, MD: Naval Institute Press, 1991.

Millett, Allan R. *Semper Fidelis: The History of the United States Marine Corps*. New York: Macmillan, 1980.

Moore, Stephen L. *Rain of Steel: Mitscher's Task Force 58, Ugaki's Thunder Gods, and the Kamikaze War off Okinawa*. Annapolis, MD: Naval Institute Press, 2020.

Morison, Samuel Eliot. *History of United States Naval Operations in World War II*. Volume 6, *Breaking the Bismarcks Barrier, 22 July 1942–1 May 1944*. Boston: Little, Brown, 1959.

———. *History of United States Naval Operations in World War II*. Volume 14, *Victory in the Pacific, 1945*. Boston: Little, Brown, 1960.

Morton, Louis. *Strategy and Command: The First Two Years*. Washington: Center of Military History, 1962.

Nalty, Bernard C., and Ralph F. Moody. *A Brief History of U.S. Marine Corps Officer Procurement, 1775–1969*. 1958. Reprint. Washington: Headquarters, U.S. Marine Corps, 1970.

"NATC Pensacola, Florida U.S. Naval Intermediate Flight Training." *E. L. Scharch, USNR AvCad V-5, Naval Aviator AV(N), WWII*. Retrieved 1 January 2023, from www.scharch.org.

National Museum of the United States Air Force. "Civilian Pilot Training Program." Retrieved 3 July 2023 from www.nationalmuseum.af.mil.

———. "Yokosuka MXY7-K1 Ohka." Retrieved 1 November 2023 from www.national museum.af.mil.

National Naval Aviation Museum. "SB2U Vindicator." Retrieved from https://www .history.navy.mil/content/history/museums/nnam/explore/collections/aircraft/s /sb2u-vindicator.html.

Naval Air Operational Training Command. *Fundamental Fixed Gunnery Approaches. Fixed Gunnery and Fighter Tactics* series. Film produced and narrated by James Thach. Los Angeles: Walt Disney Productions, 1943. Digitized by Periscope Films.

Nettles, Charlie M. "Combat over Okinawa." In Dean Caswell, *Fighting Falcons: The Saga of Marine Fighter Squadron 221*. Austin, TX: VMF 221 Foundation, 2004, 143.

Office of the Deputy Chief of Naval Operations (Air). *World War II Administrative History of the Bureau of Aeronautics*. Volume 13, *Aviation Training, 1911–1939*. Washington: Department of the Navy, n.d.

———. *World War II Administrative History of the Bureau of Aeronautics*. Volume 14, *Aviation Training, 1941–1945*. Washington: Department of the Navy, n.d.

Office of Naval Intelligence. *Battle of Midway June 3–6, 1942*. Washington: Government Printing Office, 1943.

———. *Japanese Aircraft Manual*. ONI-249. Washington: Government Printing Office, 25 June 1943.

Olynyk, Frank. *USMC Credits for the Destruction of Enemy Aircraft in Air-to-Air Combat, World War 2*. Aurora, OH: Frank Olynyk, 1982.

"Original U.S. WWII USMC Named Enlisted Fighter Pilot VMF-211 Grouping." *International Military Antiques.* Retrieved 1 July 2023 from https://www.ima-usa.com/products/original-u-s-wwii-usmc-named-enlisted-fighter-pilot-vmf-211-grouping?variant=31537269014597.

Owen, Peter F. "The Marine Corps' Air War over the Pacific." *Naval History* (February 2023).

———. "U.S. Marine Corps Aviation in the Second World War: Its Effectiveness in Support of the Pacific Fleet." Doctoral dissertation, Royal Military College of Canada, 2024. Retrieved from https://espace.rmc.ca/jspui/handle/11264/1663.

Parshall, John B., and Anthony Tully. *Shattered Sword: The Untold Story of the Battle of Midway.* Washington: Potomac Books, 2005.

Pedroncelli, Rich. "The Lone Avenger." *Naval History* (June 2001).

Porter, R. Bruce, with Eric Hammel. *Ace! A Marine Night-Fighter Pilot in World War II.* Pacifica, CA: Pacifica Press, 1985.

Prados, John. *Combined Fleet Decoded: The Secret History of American Intelligence and the Japanese Navy in World War II.* New York: Random House, 1995.

Rielly, Robin L. *Kamikazes, Corsairs and Picket Ships: Okinawa, 1945.* Philadelphia: Casemate Publishers, 2010.

Roberts, Edwin S. Jr. *Tales from World War II.* Compiled by Marta Turner. The Roberts Family, n.d.

———. Unpublished diary. Courtesy of the Roberts family.

Ross, John M. S. "Despatch of No. 52 Radar Unit to Guadalcanal." *Royal New Zealand Air Force.* Wellington, NZ: Historical Publications Branch, 1955. Retrieved from https://nzetc.victoria.ac.nz/tm/scholarly/tei-WH2AirF-c15-3.html.

Run to Honor. *USNA Virtual Memorial Hall.* Retrieved from www.usnamemorialhall.org.

Russell, Ronald W. *No Right to Win: A Continuing Dialogue with Veterans of the Battle of Midway.* Lincoln, NE: iUniverse, 2006.

"The SCR-268 Radar." *Electronics* (September 1945), 100–110.

Shaw, Henry I., Verle E. Ludwig, and Frank O. Hough. *History of U.S. Marine Corps Operations in World War II.* Volume 1, *Pearl Harbor to Guadalcanal.* Washington: Headquarters, U.S. Marine Corps, 1958.

Shaw, Henry I. Jr., and Douglas T. Kane. *History of U.S. Marine Corps Operations in World War II.* Volume 2, *Isolation of Rabaul.* Washington: Headquarters, U.S. Marine Corps, 1958.

Sherrod, Robert. *History of Marine Corps Aviation in World War II.* 1952. Reprint. San Rafael, CA: Presidio Press, 1980.

Smith, Robert. *Triumph in the Philippines.* Washington: Center of Military History, 1993.

Smithsonian Institute National Air and Space Museum. "Rocket, Air-to-Surface, 5-inch, HVAR." Retrieved from https://airandspace.si.edu/collection-objects/rocket-air-to-surface-5-inch-hvar/nasm_A19820116000.

———. "ZB-1 Radio Homing Adapter and Security Cover." Smithsonian Institute, 2012. Retrieved from https://timeandnavigation.si.edu/multimedia-asset/zb-1-radio-homing-adapter-and-security-cover.

Spector, Ronald H. *Eagle against the Sun.* New York: Free Press, 1985.

Swett, James. "Homeless." In Eric Hammel, *Aces against Japan II.* Pacifica, CA: Pacific Press, 1996.

Symonds, Craig L. *The Battle of Midway.* New York: Oxford University Press, 2011.

Tillman, Barrett. *Corsair: The F4U in World War II and Korea.* Annapolis, MD: Naval Institute Press, 2002.

———. *Hellcat: The F6F in World War II.* Annapolis, MD: Naval Institute Press, 2012.

———. *U.S. Marine Corps Fighter Squadrons of World War II.* London: Bloomsbury, 2014.

———. *The Wildcat in World War II.* Annapolis, MD: Naval Institute Press, 2001.

United States Marine Corps. *The Marine Corps Reserve: A History.* Washington: Government Printing Office, 1966.

———. *Tentative Manual for Expeditionary Advanced Base Operations.* Washington: U.S. Marine Corps, 9 May 2023.

United States Naval Academy. *The Lucky Bag, 1938.* Annapolis, MD, 1938.

United States Navy. *Landing Operations Doctrine, 1938 (F.T.P. 167).* Washington: Office of Naval Operations, 1938.

United States Statutes at Large, 1939–41. Volume 54. Washington: Government Printing Office, 1941.

United States Strategic Bombing Survey, Aircraft Division. *The Japanese Aircraft Industry.* Washington: Government Printing Office, May 1947.

United States Strategic Bombing Survey, Naval Analysis Division. *The Allied Campaign against Rabaul.* Washington: U.S. Government Printing Office, 1 September 1946.

———. *The Campaigns of the Pacific War.* Washington: Government Printing Office, 1946.

———. *Interrogations of Japanese Officials.* 2 vols. Washington: Government Printing Office, 1946.

Urwin, Gregory J. *Facing Fearful Odds: The Siege of Wake Island.* Lincoln: University of Nebraska Press, 1997.

"Wildcat." *Naval Aviation News* (December 1971), 20–26.

Winnia, Charles C. *The Diary of a Corsair Pilot in the Solomons, 1943.* Edited and annotated by C. S. Richardson. *Scuttlebutt and Small Chow.* Retrieved 1 January 2023 from https://www.rcgroups.com/forums/showatt.php?attachmentid=1635585.

Work, Robert O. "A Slavish Devotion to Forward Presence Has Nearly Broken the U.S. Navy." U.S. Naval Institute *Proceedings* (December 2021). Retrieved from https://www.usni.org/magazines/proceedings/2021/december/slavish-devotion-forward-presence-has-nearly-broken-us-navy.

Zeberlein, Jeff. "Can-Do Is Not Working." U.S. Naval Institute *Proceedings* 147 (December 2021).

★INDEX★

★ABOUT THE AUTHOR★

PETER F. OWEN served as an infantry officer in the U.S. Marine Corps for more than twenty years. His first book, *To the Limit of Endurance: A Battalion of Marines in the Great War*, received the Marine Corps Heritage Foundation's prestigious General Wallace M. Greene Jr. Award. Dr. Owen majored in history at the U.S. Naval Academy and earned his PhD in war studies from the Royal Military College of Canada. He and his wife live in Fairport, New York.

The Naval Institute Press is the book-publishing arm of the U.S. Naval Institute, a private, nonprofit, membership society for sea service professionals and others who share an interest in naval and maritime affairs. Established in 1873 at the U.S. Naval Academy in Annapolis, Maryland, where its offices remain today, the Naval Institute has members worldwide.

Members of the Naval Institute support the education programs of the society and receive the influential monthly magazine *Proceedings* or the colorful bimonthly magazine *Naval History* and discounts on fine nautical prints and on ship and aircraft photos. They also have access to the transcripts of the Institute's Oral History Program and get discounted admission to any of the Institute-sponsored seminars offered around the country.

The Naval Institute's book-publishing program, begun in 1898 with basic guides to naval practices, has broadened its scope to include books of more general interest. Now the Naval Institute Press publishes about seventy titles each year, ranging from how-to books on boating and navigation to battle histories, biographies, ship and aircraft guides, and novels. Institute members receive significant discounts on the Press' more than eight hundred books in print.

Full-time students are eligible for special half-price membership rates. Life memberships are also available.

For more information about Naval Institute Press books that are currently available, visit www.usni.org/press/books. To learn about joining the U.S. Naval Institute, please write to:

Member Services
U.S. Naval Institute
291 Wood Road
Annapolis, MD 21402-5034
Telephone: (800) 233-8764
Fax: (410) 571-1703
Web address: www.usni.org